Hertfordshire Soldiers of the Great War

Hertfordshire Soldiers of the Great War

Paul Johnson & Dan Hill

FRONTLINE BOOKS

First published in Great Britain in 2020 by
Frontline Books
An imprint of
Pen & Sword Books Ltd
Yorkshire – Philadelphia

ISBN 978 1 47389 393 1

A CIP catalogue record for this book is
available from the British Library.

Printed and bound in the UK by TJ International Ltd,
Padstow, Cornwall.

Pen & Sword Books Limited incorporates the imprints of Atlas,
Archaeology, Aviation, Discovery, Family History, Fiction, History,
Maritime, Military, Military Classics, Politics, Select, Transport,
True Crime, Air World, Frontline Publishing, Leo Cooper, Remember
When, Seaforth Publishing, The Praetorian Press, Wharncliffe
Local History, Wharncliffe Transport, Wharncliffe True Crime
and White Owl.

For a complete list of Pen & Sword titles please contact

PEN & SWORD BOOKS LIMITED
47 Church Street, Barnsley, South Yorkshire, S70 2AS, England
E-mail: enquiries@pen-and-sword.co.uk
Website: www.pen-and-sword.co.uk

Or

PEN AND SWORD BOOKS
1950 Lawrence Rd, Havertown, PA 19083, USA
E-mail: Uspen-and-sword@casematepublishers.com
Website: www.penandswordbooks.com

Contents

Introduction

Although the Great War had its roots set in Europe, it was – throughout its four long years – to eventually engulf most of the world's major powers. An estimated 65 million men were ultimately mobilised across the world, as part of the engaged nations' fighting forces. Civilians too, were expected to sustain their nation's war effort by being involved in supporting the military through both industrial and agricultural production on a scale never before known. Great Britain was a major player in what would be known as the 'War to End all Wars'. Men and women from across the nation were to serve their country on both the home front and overseas. Virtually every town, village and hamlet saw some involvement in the conflict and, consequently, almost every man and woman had a story to tell about their participation, or that of a loved one, friend or neighbour. The *Herts at War* project was originally initiated to uncover the wartime exploits of soldiers from around the county who served during the Great War. Over a period of time, the tales of bravery and heroism, as well as plain, simple, soldiering which emerged, seemed to demand that these stories be preserved for posterity, education, and as an act of remembrance. The purpose of this publication is to reveal a small selection of the stories that have arisen as a result of the project's work within the county, and give the reader an insight into some of the fascinating discoveries concerning the men and women of Hertfordshire who served their country in a time of war; the effects of which still resonate within the population today. Neither the project, nor this publication, could have been produced without the enduring support and contributions of a large number of volunteers. It is they who have helped highlight these stories and, as a consequence of their work, many long-hidden artefacts have been shared with an enthusiastic public, enhancing the exhibitions and displays the project has fashioned since its inception.

Prior to the Great War, many Hertfordshire men had served in local units of the Territorial Force, such as the Hertfordshire Yeomanry, Hertfordshire Regiment, and the Bedfordshire Regiment. These men were part-time soldiers, often referred to as 'Saturday Night Soldiers', coming from all walks of life, training together both at weekends and when attending annual summer camps. Over the succeeding years these ordinary men were thrust into major fighting actions now synonymous with the First World War; Ypres, Loos, The Somme and Passchendaele. There were those, too, who served with the naval and aviation forces across the world, as well as many in vital supporting roles including nursing, volunteer work and becoming conscientious objectors. The latter's refusal to fight in the war often took as much bravery as the soldiers who served in the trenches. Of Course, it has not been possible, within the confines of the publication, to provide the details of every man and woman from the county who served in the military and civilian services during the Great War. However, the authors have ensured they included entries for each element of the armed forces, although this may not be fully reflected in the book title. In conjunction with the Herts at War project a representative collection of stories has been chosen to cover the numerous services and theatres of war, which – it is hoped – will provide the reader with a brief overview of the contribution and sacrifice of Hertfordshire townsfolk.

Throughout the Great War, many of the men and women of Hertfordshire were dispersed across the globe. Whether they were serving with the fighting forces or supporting the war effort, their individual contributions were often proudly reported in the local newspapers of the day. Often their stories lay undiscovered in dusty archives across the county, or in the lofts, basements and garages of both family and friends, many of which, sadly, have been lost to the passage of time.

The war memorials of Hertfordshire contain the names of over 23,000 men and women who gave their lives whilst in the service of their country during the Great War. Whilst this is a small   percentage of the total numbers from across Hertfordshire who saw action in the war, it was these losses that touched all but a few of the communities within the county and it is to their memory that this publication is dedicated.

'Sons of this place, let this of you be said,
That you who live are worthy of your dead.
These gave their lives that you who live may reap
A richer harvest ere you fall asleep.'

(Great Amwell War Memorial – The Reverend T.F. Royds BD)

Principal Towns of Hertfordshire. (© *Paul Johnson & Dan Hill*)

The Structure of the British Armed Forces in the Great War

The British Army

Within this publication you will find regular references relating to the structure of the British Army during the Great War. In an effort to assist you with what is a complex, tiered structure of units and sub-units, the following table provides a very basic overview of the British Army structure at the time, in relation to infantry regiments. The cavalry used different terms but had a similar organisation. Specialist troops, such as the Royal Artillery or Royal Engineers, were grouped into Corps. The structure of these units was not dissimilar to the infantry, but used different terms, such as 'Battery' or 'Troop'.

Command	Description
Army	An army is a formation consisting of two or more Corps. It is commanded by a general or a field marshal. Eleven British armies were formed during the First World War and each army numbered about 150,000 men. More than one army operating together is known as an 'Army Group'.
Corps	A Corps is a tactical formation made up of two or three divisions and usually commanded by a Lieutenant General. Corps are normally identified by Roman numerals.
Division	A division is made up of three infantry brigades and on average numbered around 16,000 men. Divisions are commanded by a Lieutenant General or Major General.
Brigade	A brigade consists of three infantry battalions and numbered between 3,500 and 4,000 men commanded by a Major General or Brigadier.
Battalion	A battalion is between 500 and 1,000 soldiers. It normally consists of a headquarters and three or four companies. A tactical grouping of battalions is called a brigade. Battalions are normally commanded by a Lieutenant-Colonel.
Company	A company is part of a battalion and usually consists of between 150 and 200 men. They are usually lettered A through to D and are commanded by a Major or Captain.

Command	Description
Platoon	A platoon is part of an infantry company and is divided into three or four sections. A British platoon usually consists of 25 to 30 men. Platoons are commanded by a Lieutenant or Second Lieutenant.
Section	A section usually consists of 7 to 12 men, and is part of a platoon. Sections are usually under the command of a non-commissioned officer, often a Corporal or Sergeant.

The Royal Flying Corps

At the outset of the Great War, the structure of the Royal Flying Corps – which was established by Royal Warrant on 13 April 1912 – consisted of the Military Wing, the Naval Wing, the Central Flying School and the Royal Aircraft Factory. Its ranking system mirrored that of the army and the Royal Navy respectively, and its formations were similar to that of the cavalry with aircraft being grouped into squadrons. These elements were combined on 1 April 1918 to form the Royal Air Force.

The Royal Navy

The senior service, the Royal Navy, had a ranking system that was not dissimilar to that of the army. In August 1914 the First Fleet, elements of the Second Fleet and the Home Fleets formed the Grand Fleet. It was initially commanded by Admiral Sir John Jellicoe and he was succeeded by Admiral Sir David Beatty in December 1916. The Grand Fleet was based first at Scapa Flow in the Orkney Islands and later at Rosyth on the Firth of Forth. In April 1919 the Grand Fleet was disbanded, with much of its strength forming a new Atlantic Fleet.

Great War Campaign Medals

The subject of the allocation and entitlement of medals in the Great War period is both complex and extensive. There are a number of recognised publications covering the subject in detail, some of which you will find listed in the bibliography. The following will provide you with an outline of standard British campaign medals issued to members of the armed services in the period 1914 to 1919.

The 1914 Star

Often referred to as the Mons Star and commonly known amongst veterans as 'Pip', this bronze medal was authorised by King George V in April 1917 for those who had served in France or Belgium between 5 August 1914 to midnight on 22 November 1914 inclusive. If you have one of these in your possession, you may also see a small clasp or a small silver rosette with it. The clasp is a narrow horizontal bronze clasp sewn onto the ribbon, bearing the dates '5th AUG.–22nd NOV. 1914' which indicates that the recipient had actually served under enemy fire during that period. Recipients who received the medal with the clasp were also entitled to attach a small silver heraldic rose to the ribbon when just the ribbon was being worn. The reverse of the medal is plain with the recipient's service number, rank, name and unit impressed on it. There were approximately 378,000 of these 1914 Stars issued. Recipients of the 1914 Star were automatically issued with the two other campaign medals, the British War Medal and the Victory Medal.

The 1914–15 Star

This medal is often confused with the 1914 star. The design is exactly the same as the 1914 star, with the exception of the central scrolls. Here you will see the dates 1914–15 inscribed instead of 1914. The two smaller scrolls found on the 1914 Star, 'AUG.' and 'NOV.' are absent in the 1914–15 Star. Somewhat confusingly,

this bronze medal is also known as 'Pip'. It was authorized in 1918 and was issued to a much wider range of recipients. In broad terms, it was awarded to all who served in any theatre of war between 5 August 1914 and 31 December 1915, except those eligible for the 1914 Star. Like the 1914 Star, the 1914–15 Star was awarded in conjunction with the British War Medal and the Victory Medal. The reverse has the recipient's service number, rank, name and unit impressed on it. An estimated 2.4 million of these medals were issued.

The British War Medal

The British War Medal was instigated on 26 July 1919. It was known to veterans as 'Squeak'. The silver medal was awarded to officers and men of the British and Imperial Forces who either entered a theatre of war or entered service overseas between 5 August 1914 and 11 November 1918 inclusive. This was later extended to services in Russia, Siberia and some other areas in 1919 and 1920. The medal has the recipient's service number, rank, name and unit impressed on the rim. A bronze variant of medal was issued mainly to Chinese, Maltese and Indian Labour Corps. Approximately 6.5 million of these medals were issued.

The Allied Victory Medal

This medal was known to veterans as 'Wilfred' and has the recipient's service number, rank, name and unit impressed on the rim. The Allied governments agreed that they should each issue their own bronze victory medal with a similar design, equivalent wording, and identical ribbon. The British version depicts the winged figure of Victory on the front of the medal and on the back the words: 'Great War for Civilisation 1914–1919'. Approximately 5.7 million victory medals were issued.

The Territorial Force War Medal

The Territorial Force War Medal was instituted on 26 April 1920. Only members of the Territorial Force and Territorial Force Nursing Service were eligible for this medal. To receive it, you must have been a member of the Territorial Force on or before 30 September 1914 and had to have served in an operational theatre of war outside the United Kingdom between 5 August 1914 and 11 November 1918. An individual who was eligible to receive the 1914 Star or 1914–15 Star could not receive the Territorial War Medal as well. Approximately 34,000 Territorial Force War Medals were issued.

Mercantile Marine War Medal

Instituted by the Board of Trade to commemorate the war service of the officers and men of the Mercantile Marine. Qualification was one or multiple voyages through a danger zone. Recipients also received the British War Medal and these two medals are the typical issue for the Mercantile Marine. Service solely in the Mercantile Marine does not count for the Victory Medal or the WW1 campaign stars. Service

in coastal trades, such as fishermen, lightships, etc. also qualified for this medal. The recipient's name was impressed around the edge. In total 133,135 Mercantile Marine War Medals were awarded.

The Silver War Badge

The Silver War Badge, often incorrectly called the Silver Wound Badge or Services Rendered Badge, was instigated on 12 September 1916. It was issued to officers and men who were discharged or retired from the military forces as a result of sickness or injury caused by their war service. After April 1918 the eligibility was amended to include civilians serving with the Royal Army Medical Corps, female nurses, staff and aid workers. Each badge has a unique number stamped on the reverse, which can be used to identify

the recipient. It is not related to their Regimental or Service Number. The badge was intended to be worn on the right lapel of a recipient's civilian clothing. It could not be worn on a military uniform. The recipient would also receive a certificate with the badge. There were about 1,150,000 Silver War Badges issued in total for First World War service.

Gallantry Awards

The subject of gallantry awards across the county during the Great War is one that would fill a tome in its own right. Within the confines of this publication we have covered some of the more outstanding awards made to Hertfordshire service personnel. There are a number of awards for conspicuous or gallant acts, usually in the presence of the enemy, whilst serving in the British, Dominion and Colonial armed forces during the Great War, as well as awards issued for distinguished or meritorious service.

The following awards issued throughout the Great War are listed below in order of precedence:

- Victoria Cross (VC)
- Distinguished Service Order (DSO)
- Distinguished Service Cross (DSC)
- Military Cross (MC)
- Distinguished Flying Cross (DFC)
- Air Force Cross (AFC)
- Distinguished Conduct Medal (DCM)
- Conspicuous Gallantry Medal (CGM)
- Distinguished Service Medal (DSM)
- Military Medal (MM)
- Distinguished Flying Medal (DFM)
- Air Force Medal (AFM)
- Meritorious Service Medal (MSM)
- Mentioned in Despatches (MiD)

One only has to view the local newspapers of the period to find numerous entries relating to the award of gallantry medals, the majority of which relate to the Military Medal. Instituted in March 1916, this medal was awarded to non-commissioned officers (NCOs) and men of the British Army for acts of bravery and was later extended to women who showed bravery under fire. There was also a provision for the award of a bar for each further act of bravery; again, the various county newspapers regularly feature such awards.

In excess of 150,000 awards of the Military Medals were made during the Great War and there are very few towns or villages across the county where a soldier from the local community has not been recognised for outstanding bravery. The Hertfordshire Regiment was to see 122 such awards among its ranks, whilst the Bedfordshire Regiment, with its numerous battalions, was to receive 564. Of course, many Hertfordshire men and women were to serve in other regiments and units of the British Army, so the total number of gallantry awards is almost incalculable.

British commanders-in-chief of a theatre of war or campaign were obliged to report their activities and achievements to the War Office in the form of despatches, which were also published in *The London Gazette*. Many reports attached lists of men who were deemed worthy of a mention, though details explaining the precise reason why a particular individual was chosen is uncommon. Some were mentioned on multiple occasions. To be mentioned in despatches can be a condition of receiving certain decorations. Though not a medal, soldiers were entitled to receive a certificate and wear a decoration of a spray of oak leaves in bronze which could be displayed on the Victory Medal.

Numerous Allied and friendly governments issued awards and decorations to men and women serving in the British Armed Services. The French *Croix de Guerre* and *Medaille Militaire* are amongst the more common examples, but there were many more.

The announcement of any award was made in *The London Gazette*, and usually replicated in *The Edinburgh Gazette*. Only honours such as the Victoria Cross and Distinguished Conduct Medal were accompanied by a written citation, explaining the circumstances of the award. Most other awards are only recorded as a listing in either alphabetical or regimental order. Often, but not on every occasion, the recipient had their town or village of residence shown in brackets by the side of their name.

Whilst it is not possible within these pages to identify every Hertfordshire serviceman or woman who was in receipt of an award, it cannot be argued that throughout the Great War the county demonstrated outstanding courage and devotion to duty.

The Death Penny

The immediate next of kin of all who died serving with the British and Empire forces in the First World War were eligible to receive a Next of Kin Memorial Plaque, which would be accompanied by a scroll and a 'King's message'.

The plaque was made from bronze and was popularly known as the 'Dead Man's Penny'. It is also referred to as a 'Death Penny', 'Death Plaque' or 'Widow's Penny'. Because the supply of bronze and paper were problematic at the end of the war, the production of the plaque and scroll did not begin until late in the autumn of 1918. The first plaques began to be produced in December 1918 at the Government's Memorial Plaque Factory in Acton. However, the manufacturing of the plaques at the Acton factory got into difficulty and the production was moved to the Woolwich Arsenal munitions factory in South London. Continuing problems meant that eventually plaques were produced in a number of different locations.

All those who died between 4 August 1914 and 30 April 1919 whilst in military service were entitled to receive a plaque and a scroll. The next of kin of the 306 British and Commonwealth military personnel who were executed following a court martial did not receive a memorial plaque.

Over 1,000,000 plaques and scrolls were sent to next of kin in commemoration of their loved one's service in the Great War. Each plaque has the words *'He died for freedom and honour'* embossed upon it along with the recipient's forenames and surname. Approximately 600 memorial plaques were issued to the next of kin of women who died as a direct consequence of their involvement in the Great War, and in these cases the motto on the plaques was amended to *'She died for freedom and honour.'*

The King's letter accompanying the plaque was written as follows:

> *'Buckingham Palace*
> *I join my grateful people in sending you this memorial of a brave life given for others in the Great War.*
>
> *George R.I.'*

The scroll was sent separately to relatives inside a cardboard tube and – due to the vast numbers being produced – in some cases the scroll and plaque were received by the families some significant time apart.

The scroll reads:

> *'He whom this scroll commemorates was numbered among those who, at the call of King and Country, left all that was dear to them, endured hardness, faced danger, and finally passed out of the sight of men by the path of duty and self-sacrifice, giving up their own lives that others might live in freedom.*
>
> *Let those who come after see to it that his name be not forgotten.'*

The text was to be printed in calligraphic script beneath the Royal Crest followed by the name of the commemorated serviceman giving his rank, name and regiment, this time individually written in calligraphic script.

Families often mounted the bronze plaque in an individually designed frame or mount, whilst others, perhaps unable to accept the death of their loved one, simply placed them in a drawer or cupboard where they may still be found today.

Serving King, Country and County – An Overview of the Hertfordshire Regiment and Yeomanry

The British army had seen little change for several centuries up until 1868, when the Secretary of State for War, Edward Cardwell, a member of Gladstone's Liberal government, began a series of reforms that were designed to provide Britain with a well-organised, professional and well-equipped fighting force. His plans, although not radical, sought to create a regular force supported by an efficient reserve and most importantly, establish shorter terms of service for enlisted men. Up until this time, recruits often found themselves signed up for long terms of service with the army, and harsh discipline – including flogging – was deemed to be the

Edward Cardwell.

norm. Cardwell's plan was to abolish flogging, withdraw British troops from self-governing colonies, cease the sale of officers' commissions and introduce short-term service for recruits. The Cardwell Reforms also saw the introduction of a localisation scheme, whereby the country was divided into 66 Brigade Districts, based on county boundaries and population density.

All line infantry regiments would now consist of two battalions, sharing a depot and an associated recruiting area. One battalion would serve overseas, while the other was stationed at home for training. The militia of that area would usually form a third battalion.

In 1881 another Liberal Secretary of State for War, Hugh Childers, continued the reorganisation with further reforms. The Childers Reforms provided each regiment with two regular battalions and two militia battalions. That same year short service was increased to seven years with the colours and five

Hugh Childers.

with the reserve, of the twelve-year enlistment period that the Cardwell Reforms had previously introduced.

On 1 July 1881, the Childers Reforms came into effect and local militia and rifle volunteer corps were affiliated to new regiments. Accordingly, the 16th Foot became The Bedfordshire Regiment. The regimental district comprised the counties of Bedfordshire and Hertfordshire.

The new formation across the two counties consisted of two regular, two militia and three volunteer battalions.

- 1st Battalion (formerly 1st Battalion, 16th (Bedfordshire) Regiment of Foot.
- 2nd Battalion (formerly 2nd Battalion, 16th (Bedfordshire) Regiment of Foot.
- 3rd (Militia) Battalion (formerly Bedfordshire Light Infantry Militia)
- 4th (Militia) Battalion (formerly Hertfordshire Militia)
- 1st Hertfordshire Rifle Volunteer Corps: designated 1st (Hertfordshire) Volunteer Battalion in 1887
- 2nd Hertfordshire Rifle Volunteer Corps: designated 2nd (Hertfordshire) Volunteer Battalion in 1887
- 1st Bedfordshire Rifle Volunteer Corps: designated 3rd Volunteer Battalion in 1887
- In 1900, the 4th (Huntingdonshire) Volunteer Battalion was raised.

It would, however, be Secretary of State for War, Richard Burton Haldane, who held the post from 1906 to 1912, who would make the most significant reforms to the army, not least being the introduction of the 1907 Territorial and Reserve Forces Act. Haldane's intention was to afford a well-trained reserve for the regular army that was capable of providing individual reinforcements or drafts at short notice as well as an efficient and cost-effective Home Defence organization.

The act would see the militia regiments re-emerge as the Special Reserve, whilst the Yeomanry and volunteers would merge to form a new organisation known as the Territorial Force. This new force was to

Richard Burton Haldane

be re-equipped and based on voluntary service, strongly linked to each county through a County Association. The difference being that this force would have no role in home defence except repelling local raids, but could and would serve abroad in war.

Not unsurprisingly, each of the reformists faced some resistance to their plans, not least from the military. In the case of Richard Haldane, the Yeomanry resisted county control, the militia protested about the possibility of overseas service and so this provision was removed. It can be argued that the concessions Haldane had to make to get the 1907 bill through weakened its purpose as well as the size of the new force. Nevertheless, the seed had been sown and the ground laid for a new force that was soon to play a pivotal role in the conflicts of the twentieth century.

THE HERTFORDSHIRE YEOMANRY

The Hertfordshire Yeomanry, formed in 1794, was a county-based cavalry unit tasked with civil defence at a time of considerable unrest both at home and abroad. It underwent various changes throughout the nineteenth century, including being disbanded and reformed twice before earning its first battle honour in the Boer War of 1899–1902, where it supplied troops to the newly raised Imperial Yeomanry. The men of Hertfordshire took part in many campaigns now synonymous with the Boer conflict such as Ladysmith, Mafeking and operations in the Orange Free State.

The 1/1st Battalion was the fighting arm of the Hertfordshire Yeomanry and comprised of men who had volunteered to serve overseas. The 2/1st remained a 'home service' unit and did so throughout the war.

The 1/1st Hertfordshire Yeomanry was mobilised in August 1914 as part of the Eastern Mounted Brigade. In January 1915 the Yeomanry embarked for service in Egypt where it was eventually absorbed into the Yeomanry Mounted Brigade. The Yeomanry distribution was as follows:

'A' Squadron: Watford
'B' Squadron: Hertford
'C' Squadron: St. Albans
'D' Squadron: High Barnet

As a fighting unit, the Hertfordshire Yeomanry first saw action in the Gallipoli campaign, where they acted as dismounted cavalry throughout the majority of the campaign. They left Abbassia, Egypt on 13 August 1915 with 14 officers, 355 other ranks, 2 horses, 32 mules, 8 wagons and a water cart. After a long, arduous journey they arrived at Suvla Bay on 17 August. Three days later, on 20 August, the battalion was ordered to Lala Baba, where they bivouacked on the beach. The following morning they proceeded to Chocolate Hill and as they advanced over the crest of Lala Baba, the battalion was met with a hailstorm of fire from Turkish artillery. Sadly, the commanding officer, Lieutenant Colonel Samuel Gurney Sheppard DSO, was mortally wounded whilst leading the advance and perished. The battalion returned to Lala Baba the following morning, but found itself back on Chocolate Hill by late afternoon.

Tragedy at Chocolate Hill

On 14 September 1915 Turkish artillery planted several shells into the positions held by the Hertfordshire Yeomanry, resulting in a man being wounded. Sadly, a little time later that day a British artillery shell fell short and struck the Yeomanry

Lieutenant Colonel Samuel Gurney Sheppard DSO.

lines, killing 41-year-old Private Joseph Brand of Broxbourne. He was laid to rest at Salt Lake, where other members of his regiment were also buried. In July 1920 each of the burials in Salt Lake was exhumed and reburied in Green Hill Cemetery.

Egypt & Persia

The battalion left the peninsula on 1 November 1915 aboard the *H.T. Ermine* and returned to Egypt by December 1915. In 1916 the 1/1st Hertfordshire Yeomanry was split into its constituent Squadrons. 'A' Squadron would go on to serve in Palestine as part of the British 54th Division's mounted troops. 'B' Squadron would return to the UK with the 11th Division before later serving again in Egypt and later with their 'A' Squadron comrades in Palestine. 'D' Squadron was employed for much of the war in the Mesopotamia theatre of operations, and spent time with the North Persia Force, in what is now Iraq, as part of the 13th Division Cavalry.

Casualties

The majority of battle casualties suffered by the Hertfordshire Yeomanry occurred during their time at Gallipoli, where the impact of constant artillery fire claimed a number of lives, including their commanding officer. However, it was the effects of dysentery and malaria that were to have the greatest impact upon the men. The unit war diaries record, with ever-increasing monotony, a large number of officers and men reporting sick on a daily basis as a consequence of the

This plaque is located in the War Memorial Chapel at St. Albans Abbey and pays tribute to the men of the Hertfordshire Yeomanry who lost their lives whilst serving with the regiment during the Great War.

effects of life in a harsh environment. This placed an enormous strain on the Battalion resources and impacted on their fighting ability, as it did with many of the Allied units.

The Hertfordshire Yeomanry were able to boast a proud and diverse war record in the Great War, and later went on to serve with distinction in the Second World War. They still have a descendant unit in the British Army today.

THE HERTFORDSHIRE REGIMENT

In 1909, the Hertfordshire Battalion left the Bedfordshire Regiment to become the 1st Battalion, the Hertfordshire Regiment as part of the pre-war Territorial Force. Its ranks were filled with men from across the county who trained mainly at weekends. Once a year each man was required to attend an annual camp and for this, he would be paid an annual bounty.

The distribution of companies and drill stations was as follows:

HQ	Hertford
'A' Company	Hertford; drill stations at Watton, Hatfield and Berkhamsted
'B' Company	St. Albans; drill stations at London Colney and Harpenden
'C' Company	Bishops Stortford; drill stations at Sawbridgeworth, Braughing, Widford, Ware
'D' Company	Watford; drill station at Chorley Wood
'E' Company	Royston; drill stations at Letchworth, Baldock and Ashwell
'F' Company	Hemel Hempstead; drill stations at Great Berkhamsted, Ashridge, Tring and Ivinghoe.
'G' Company	Hitchin; drill stations at Welwyn, Stevenage and Whitwell
'H' Company	Waltham Cross; drill stations at Wormley, Cheshunt and Hoddesdon.

THE GREAT WAR

The regiment served on the Western Front from 6 November 1914 until the Armistice. The men of the battalion sailed from Southampton aboard the SS *City of Chester*, arriving at Le Havre in the early hours of the following morning.

Their first spell in the trenches came in the Observatory Ridge Sector, near Zillebeke in the Ypres Salient. However, by this time they had already suffered a casualty in Private Charles Castle, who had taken his own life whilst the battalion was in transit.

Initially, the battalion was attached to the 4th (Guards) Brigade and, as a result of their tenacity and endurance on the battlefield, they were nicknamed the 'Herts Guards'.

The Regiment was reorganised on a four-company basis, in line with the Guards Brigade, on 19 January 1915.

- A & H became No. 1 Company – Commanded by Major Frank PAGE
- B & F became No. 2 Company – Commanded by Major E Montague JONES
- C & D became No. 3 Company – Commanded by Captain Philip Elton LONGMORE
- E & G became No. 4 Company – Commanded by Captain Aylmer Gustavus CLERK

The names of the company commanders are those who were in situ at the time of the reorganisation. These regularly changed as the war progressed, with a number of NCOs eventually taking up commissions and returning to the unit to command their former colleagues.

The First Victoria Cross

On 27 September 1915, near Cuinchy, the men of the Hertfordshire Regiment were waiting to participate in the Battle of Loos. Amongst its ranks was Corporal Alfred Burt, who was about to perform an act of personal gallantry that would see him bestowed with Britain's highest military gallantry award, the Victoria Cross. The citation for the award states:

For most conspicuous bravery at Cuinchy on 27 September 1915. His company had lined the front trench preparatory to an attack when a large minenwerfer bomb fell into the trench. Corporal Burt, who well knew the destructive power of this class of bomb, might easily have got under cover behind a traverse, but he immediately went forward, put his foot on the fuse, wrenched it out of the bomb and threw it over the parapet, thus rendering the bomb innocuous. His presence of mind and great pluck saved the lives of others in the traverse.

This single act would not only see Alfie Burt awarded the Victoria Cross but would bring with it a series of events that would impact upon him for the rest of his life.

The Somme

The Hertfordshire Regiment served in the area around Cuinchy, Festubert and Le Touret for many months but by the summer of 1916 found themselves in the Somme region, by which time the Battle of the Somme was well underway. In November 1916, they were to find themselves taking part in the last major action in the region, the Battle of the Ancre. Here, they launched a successful attack across the fogbound battlefield, which saw the Germans routed from strongly held positions. Casualties amongst the battalion, although high, were deemed to be acceptable. A large number of men were wounded, some of whom would never see battle again, and some – after prolonged and painful treatment – would lose their lives even after the Armistice had taken place.

Day Of Days – The Battle Of St. Julien

Once the battalion had been brought up to full strength, it went through a period of specialist training in preparation for what was to be known as the Third Battle of Ypres, more commonly known as the Battle of Passchendaele. The story of the Hertfordshire's attack near the village of St. Julien on the morning of 31 July 1917 is perhaps the most significant event in the regiment's history during the Great War.

On this morning, having crossed the Steenbeek River, the battalion assaulted strongly-held German positions on the outskirts of St. Julien. As the attack progressed, all of their officers would become casualties but the battalion continued to move forward under the command of NCOs. It would soon become clear that further progress could not be achieved, and the men of Hertfordshire were forced to withdraw. In a few short hours of battle the Hertfordshire Regiment suffered a 75 per cent casualty rate, with 479 officers and men being reported as either killed, wounded or missing.

Amidst the death and destruction that abounded the battlefield that day, many acts of bravery took place, with almost thirty men being awarded gallantry medals. Yet it would be the story of Private Percy Buck and the actions of a single German soldier, which lay undiscovered for almost 100 years, that would bring a glimpse of humanity from that day of days.

The Spring Offensive

The morning of 21 March 1918 saw the opening of the German Spring Offensive, the 'Kaiserschlacht', or 'Emperor's Battle'. The first part of the offensive, *Operation Michel*, was expected to breach the British front at Arras and then head north to cut off their railway supply lines, allowing the Germans to envelop the British forces and secure their surrender. Following a devastating artillery barrage, the German offensive began across the British Fifth Army front.

The Hertfordshire Regiment initially moved into positions near St. Emilie, after which they spent the following ten days retreating from the ceaseless German onslaught. The battalion fought bravely and doggedly, eventually finding itself in the village of Guignemicourt, where it had an opportunity to lick its wounds. By this time the Hertfordshire Regiment had lost its commanding officer, Lieutenant Colonel Eric Phillips, who had been taken prisoner, and had suffered a high level of casualties.

A Battalion Lost – May 1918

On 11 May 1918, the battalion boarded buses at Orville, and travelled to the village of Fonquevillers, where they dismounted and moved into an old trench system on the east side of the village. At that very moment they were bombarded by a number of German gas shells. The effects were disastrous, with all but one officer and seven men being affected by gas and having to be transported to hospital for treatment. The following morning the officer and his men were also admitted to a Casualty Clearing Station. The Hertfordshire Regiment was, once again, completely devastated.

It was not until 15 May 1918 that the battalion began to reform. On this day, the transport and quartermaster stores moved to Louvencourt, where it was later joined by a draft of 1 officer and 81 other ranks. Then on 22 May 1918 the remainder of the battalion absorbed the remnants of the 6th Battalion, Bedfordshire Regiment; a total of 30 officers and 650 other ranks. These men, blended with the remains of the Hertfordshires, formed the nucleus of a new battalion. It was also the beginnings of a new formation, the Bedfordshire & Hertfordshire Regiment.

Advance To Victory & A Second Victoria Cross

In August 1918, the 1st Battalion Hertfordshire Regiment was located in positions near Bucquoy. As the Germans began to retire from the area, the battalion pushed forward, pursuing the enemy. Major actions at Achiet-le-Grand on 23 August and Havrincourt on 4 September saw a total of 287 officers and men either killed, wounded or missing.

German forces, after a heavy artillery bombardment, attacked the Hertfordshire position near Havrincourt on 18 September 1918. After a hard and gallant fight, the battalion was forced to retire, leaving behind Second Lieutenant Frank Edward Young. For his actions that day, Frank Young was to be posthumously awarded the Victoria Cross and 100 years later his family were to see a memorial laid in his home town of Hitchin, in recognition of his gallant action and award.

The battalion saw action for the last time at Jolimetz on 4 November 1918, after which it retired to the village of Ghissignies, burying its final battle casualties. Demobilisation began almost immediately and on 27 March 1919 the remnants of the battalion left France and headed for home.

Gallantry Awards

Throughout the Great War the regiment would see a large number of gallantry awards bestowed upon its ranks, with two men being awarded the Victoria Cross. Among the officers there would be numerous awards of the Distinguished Service Order and the Military Cross, whilst the other ranks saw nearly thirty men awarded the Distinguished Conduct Medal and over seventy who were to receive the Military Medal. Of these, eight were to earn a Bar to their Military Medal, denoting a second award for gallantry in the field.

Casualties & Pows

Official records show that the casualties for the Hertfordshire Regiment during the Great War were: 41 officers and 797 other ranks who were either killed, died of their wounds or are regarded as missing in action and have no known grave. In addition to this, there were many hundreds of men who were wounded during their service with the regiment, some being wounded on more than one occasion.

Chapter One

1914 – So It Begins

On land, at sea and in the air, the men and women of Hertfordshire served their country, and the county, both at home and abroad. The assassination of the Archduke Franz Ferdinand and his wife Sophie, Duchess of Hohenberg, in Sarajevo on 28 June 1914, was the catalyst for a series of events that would spark a global conflict. Unbeknown to the assassin, Gavrilo Princip, an ethnic Serb from Bosnia, the following weeks would see the Austro-Hungarian government, urged by the Germans, proceed to provoke Serbia into military confrontation. The Serbs, for their part, made considerable efforts to avoid any form of hostility, but their efforts were futile. The Austro-Hungarian government declared war on Serbia on 28 July 1914, confident in the knowledge that they would be fully supported by the Germans in the event that Russia made any sort of military intervention. France and Russia were allies and Britain had cooperated with the two nations since 1904. However, German leaders were ready to risk war because they believed the military balance favoured them.

Following the declaration of war by Austria-Hungary, the Russians began their military preparations, and ordered a general mobilisation on 31 July 1914. Now placed on a war footing, Russia – eager to protect their own interests in the Balkans – expected France to support them. In fear of being surrounded by the might of both Russia and France, Germany put into effect the Schlieffen Plan, which proposed a military assault on France by passing through neutral Belgium, with the capture of Paris as its main objective.

On 3 August 1914 Germany requested permission from the Belgian government to pass through the neutral country, but their request was refused. The following day forty-four divisions of the German Army poured through Belgium in an attempt to attack the French Army which was massed in the northeast of the country, mostly in Lorraine. This act of open aggression caused Great Britain and its Commonwealth territories to declare war against Germany in support of Belgium, with whom Great Britain had a treaty. The first troops of the British Expeditionary Force arrived in France on 14 August to support the French Army. Amongst those early arrivals, mainly soldiers of the regular army, were a significant number of Hertfordshire men, some of whom were to quickly become the county's first casualties in the opening phase of the war.

In the early part of September 1914, the French Army, supported by the British Expeditionary Force, were able to halt the German thrust on the outskirts of Paris during the First Battle of the Marne. The German Army then withdrew north, to a defensive line along the Aisne River. The German invasion of France and Belgium had come excruciatingly close to defeating the French, capturing Paris and ending the First World War before the end of the year. However, the German withdrawal was the first indication that the war was not going to be over quickly as many had thought, and that a long confrontation was to be expected. Hertfordshire newspapers were soon to be filled with letters from serving soldiers, with tales of terror, exhaustion and defeat to tell, all of whom felt that there was a protracted road ahead.

On 12 September, beginning in the Aisne Valley, the opposing forces embarked upon what would be subsequently known as the 'Race to the Sea'. For several weeks, as the Germans and the Allies attempted to pass around the flank of the other, a war of constant movement evolved, resulting in a series of confused battles that brought devastating losses. Eventually the warring factions came to a halt on the shores of the North Sea near the Belgian town of Nieuwpoort. In actions synonymous with this early part of the war, such as La Bassée, Messines and Armentieres, the men of Hertfordshire played their part well, some of whom were never to return home.

The First Battle of Ypres began on 19 October, and continued through to 22 November, with German forces capturing Messines, south of Ypres, on the 1 November 1914. It was during this period that the men of the Hertfordshire Regiment arrived in Flanders. Their efforts helped to stave off the attempted German breakthrough but eventually, exhausted, the two sides proceeded to take up positions behind trenches and defensive works, creating a more or less continuous line of trenches separating the belligerents along the length of what was to become known as The Western Front.

At Sea and In the Air

The ambition to control the world's seas and waterways were a major reason why the Great War spread so quickly. The range and power of the opposing naval fleets and the introduction of new weapons such as mines, torpedoes, and submarines made even the greatest warships vulnerable. The Battle of Coronel, the Battle of the Falkland Islands and other early sea battles soon made it apparent how naval warfare could be used to aid in maintaining control of trade routes.

The first time that the British and German navies clashed in the Great War was at the Battle of Heligoland Bight on 28 August 1914, resulting in a devastating loss for the German High Seas Fleet, with three light cruisers and a destroyer being sunk. Altogether 712 German sailors were killed, many more wounded and 336 taken prisoner. The British, for their part, lost no ships during the battle and the casualties were 35 men killed and 40 wounded. A few weeks later, on 22 September 1914 HMS *Aboukir*, HMS *Hogue* and HMS *Cressy* were all sunk by the German submarine *U-9*, resulting in a significant loss of life, including a number of Hertfordshire sailors. The British hospital ship *Rohilla* was wrecked off Whitby on 30 September and, the following day, HMS *Hermes* was sunk by German submarine off Dover. Again, a number of Hertfordshire men were amongst the lives lost in these tragic events.

The newly invented airplane was to provide each belligerent with a 'bird's eye view' of the battlefield. When the Royal Flying Corps deployed to France in 1914, it had a total strength of 63 aircraft supported by 900 men. The value of this new invention as a reconnaissance tool was proven at the Battle of Mons on 23 August 1914, when the advancing British Army collided with the Germans as they marched towards France. From their vantage point above the opposing armies, a British observation team could see the Germans as they attempted to surround the unsuspecting British army. Alerted, the British high command ordered an immediate retreat into France and, as embarrassing as the withdrawal was for the British, the move saved the army. The airplane's value as an observation platform had been proven but it would be some months before a French pilot would strap a machine gun to the nose of his aircraft to create the first true fighter plane.

The Home Front – 1914

The declaration of war generated a burst of panic food buying amongst the civilian population, who witnessed a sudden hike in food prices. Rumours of food shortages soon began to circulate and in the market town of Hitchin, on the evening of 5 August, a crowd of concerned townsfolk gathered outside the premises of Moss and Sons, a prominent local grocer who had raised their meat prices. After voicing their outrage, the crowd marched to Moss' nearby home to confront him. Soon, the police were reinforced and able to hold the crowd back. Moss was persuaded to address the mob, promising to hold prices to what they had been the previous week. Although the situation had been effectively controlled, a brazen act of vandalism saw the shop windows smashed in the early hours. No one was ever prosecuted for the act. This, of course, was not the only incident during those early months of the war in which the public raised a furious objection against those who sought to financially benefit from the conflict, but it is one of the more prominent occurrences to have taken place in Hertfordshire.

Come on Lad, Join Up!

At the outbreak of war over three-quarters of a million men across Britain were recruited into the army in just eight weeks. Across Hertfordshire a number of recruiting stations appeared and large numbers of local men quickly signed up. Every man had to undergo a series of medical and fitness tests, and a great many were rushed through the process. Recruiting officers regularly turned a blind eye to many of the minimum requirements, allowing underage and unfit men to slip through into the ranks. In order to stem the flow of volunteers, the height limit was raised from 5′ 3″ to 5′ 6″. However, this was subsequently lowered, on more than one occasion, in response to the falling numbers of recruits.

There are varying views about a man's choice of which regiment he served with but, very broadly, if a man enlisted voluntarily prior to January 1916, he would have had a choice as to which unit he initially joined. With the introduction of conscription in January 1916, men were sent where they were needed and had little choice in the matter. After they had been accepted into the army, a man would go through a period of basic training in camps all over the country. Conditions in these camps at this early stage of hostilities were often very basic, and supplies of equipment and uniforms were very limited. In locations such as Berkhamsted, Watford, St. Albans and Hitchin, new recruits were billeted in houses, farms and tented accommodation as their training began in the surrounding fields, parks and meadows of the county.

Many local men joined the Hertfordshire Regiment, part of the Territorial Force. As a pre-war 'Terrier' unit, the men of the Hertfordshire were part-time soldiers coming from all walks of life, training together at weekends and annual summer camps. The divide between the regular army and the men of territorial battalions was all too apparent in the years before the war, with the territorials being looked down upon by the men of the regular army. When war broke out in August 1914, the army was called upon to form the British Expeditionary Force (BEF) along with a small number of territorial units. The 1st Battalion Hertfordshire Regiment was among these units. Over the next few years these ordinary men found themselves involved in fighting in some of the major

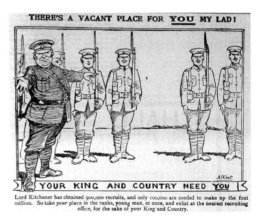

This advert was published in the *Hertfordshire Express* in October 1914.

actions now synonymous with the First World War: Ypres, Loos, the Somme and Passchendaele. Through dedication, professionalism, courage under fire, valuable supporting roles and comradeship whilst fighting with the British Army's elite Guards Brigade, the boys of the Herts earned the respect of the regular army, taking the honorary name of the 'Herts Guards' in the process.

From the very earliest days of the war, the men of Hertfordshire, serving in both combative and non-combative roles, began to arrive on the European continent and by the end of September 1914 the local newspapers were filled with stories of those who had taken part in the early battles, and of those who had fallen. Rolls of Honour were swiftly prepared and published in countless Hertfordshire towns and villages, listing the names of those who had stepped forward to serve their country, as well as those who had made the ultimate sacrifice. By the end of the year, at least one Hertfordshire life had been lost for every day of the conflict.

For the men of the Hertfordshire Regiment, contact with the enemy did not take place until mid-November when they faced the Germans on the outskirts of Ypres, and where a number of casualties were suffered. Their fight with the enemy continued throughout the remainder of the year, with the regiment giving up two precious lives even on Christmas Day 1914. For them, the war was not over by Christmas and there certainly was no question of a truce, a football match or any form of fraternisation. They simply prepared themselves for what the New Year was about to bring.

THE FIRST TO FALL – SECOND LIEUTENANT JOSEPH FREDERICK MEAD

The action at Nimy Bridge on 23 August 1914 is well known in that it was here that the first Victoria Cross awards of the Great War were to be earned. The 4th Battalion, Royal Fusiliers, suffered the loss of 150 officers and men, one of whom was a Hertfordshire man, Second Lieutenant Joseph Frederick Mead.

Joseph was born on 1 February 1892 in Pietermaritzburg, KwaZulu-Natal, South Africa, the son of Frederick Mead of The Moorings, St. Albans, Hertfordshire. He was educated at The Wick, in Hove, and later entered Winchester College. Noted for his fondness of all outdoor sports, he became Head of House and a Commoner Prefect as well as the President of the Boat Club, gaining the gold

Second Lieutenant Joseph Frederick Mead. (Winchester College)

medal for athletics two years in succession. After leaving Winchester College, Joseph entered the Royal Military College at Sandhurst, where he passed as first of his year for the British Army, obtaining a commission in the 4th Battalion, Royal Fusiliers, in February 1912. He played cricket and football for his company, and was a renowned runner. He passed the flying tests at Brooklands in 1913 and was awarded his aviator's certificate. Joseph was due to take a further course in 1914 with a view to joining the Royal Flying Corps Reserve, but the outbreak of war prevented this.

Lieutenant Mead arrived in France on 13 August 1914 when his battalion landed at Le Havre aboard the transport ship *Martaban*. The troops then marched to a rest camp on the outskirts of Le Havre, and it was reported that a great number of men fell out during the march as a result of both the heat and the large number of reservists who were in the battalion at the time, most of whom were not accustomed to the rigours of service life. The battalion spent the next ten days travelling and by 22 August had reached Nimy, just north of Mons, where they were to be involved in one of the first actions of the Great War, the fighting on the Mons-Conde Canal.

It had been a long march to Mons and the men were weary, but they set up a position alongside the canal bank. This offered little protection for the rifle companies, so the night was spent digging and using material found in the surrounding area to make improvised firing positions. 'Y' Company, under the command of Captain Lionel Forbes Ashburner, was set up with its left flank on the Nimy Railway Bridge and the right flank on a swing bridge which had been closed to stop the movement of traffic. In the early hours of 23 August 1914 the approach of a German patrol was heard, and at first light was spotted and fired upon, hitting four of the soldiers and wounding an officer who was taken prisoner. It later emerged that this officer was Lieutenant von Arnim, son of the commander of IV German Army Corps, who had been observing the fusiliers from the Nimy road. Throughout the entire day, the defenders at Nimy were relentlessly attacked by a superior German force, putting up intense resistance in the face of overwhelming odds. The following account of how Joseph Mead met his death was received from an officer of his battalion:

It was on 23 August at Mons. He was in reserve at the railway station with the rest of his company. Captain Ashburner was very hard pressed and sent back for reinforcements. He was defending the bridge over the canal. It was a hopeless position, as the enemy could get within one hundred yards of the bridge and then fire from houses, gardens, etc., and never be seen. Also, I believe five different battalions were recognised in front of this one company. Lieutenant Mead was soon ordered to reinforce the firing line, which he did in the face of a fearful fire.

Directly he got into the trench he was wounded in the head by a bullet. He went to the rear, just a few yards away, to get it dressed, and was quietly whistling all the time. Directly the dressing was finished he went back to the trench, and the second he got there he got a bullet straight through the forehead.

Second Lieutenant Joseph Frederick Mead is buried in St Symphorien Military Cemetery, Belgium, aged 22. He was awarded the 1914 Star, British War Medal and Victory Medal.

Joseph's younger brother, Robert John Mead, who was born on 3 January 1896, also served with the Royal Fusiliers, and was killed in a tragic frontline accident. He too had been educated at The Wick, Hove, and later entered Winchester College, where he was Head of his House in his last year and won Kirby Foils in 1913 and 1914. He had intended to go to Balliol College, Oxford, in October 1914 but on the outbreak of war passed straight from the Winchester Officer Training Corps into the 8th Battalion, Royal Fusiliers and left for France, arriving there at the end of May 1915.

Second Lieutenant
Robert John Mead.
(Winchester College)

Robert was the first officer casualty of the battalion when, on 1 August 1915, he was supervising a digging party at Trench 25, outside of the village of Houplines.

Second Lieutenant Joseph Frederick Mead is buried in St Symphorien Military Cemetery, Belgium, aged 22.

Second Lieutenant Robert John Mead is buried in the Cite Bonjean Military Cemetery, Armentieres, France, aged 19.

Quick Fact

The first other rank from Hertfordshire to become a battle casualty in the Great War was 22-year-old Private Arthur Frank Saunders, the son of Frederick William and Caroline Saunders of Cobden Hill, Radlett, who was reported missing on 24 August 1914 whilst serving with 'A' Squadron, 15th (The King's) Hussars. He has no known grave and his name is recorded on the La Ferte-Sous-Jouarre Memorial, France, which commemorates 3,740 officers and men of the British Expeditionary Force (BEF) who fell at the battles of Mons, Le Cateau, the Marne and the Aisne between the end of August and early October 1914 and who have no known graves. There are known to be seven soldiers from Hertfordshire recorded on its panels. The names of the other six known to be from the county are:

Gunner George Fred Hart – 28th Brigade, Royal Field Artillery – 26/08/1914 aged 21. Son of Charles and Charlotte Elizabeth Hart of Barnet.

Corporal Charles Joseph Darvill – 1st Battalion, Loyal North Lancashire Regiment – 14/09/1914 aged 24. Son of Mr and Mrs J. Darvill of High Barnet.

Sergeant Henry Sutton – 2nd Battalion, King's Royal Rifle Corps – 14/09/1914 aged 28. Son of Elizabeth Sutton of Hemel Hempstead and husband of Edith Sutton of Hucknall, Nottinghamshire.

Private Thomas Law – 1st Battalion, Bedfordshire Regiment – 15/09/1914 aged 32. Brother of Alfred Law of Berkhamsted.

Captain Mortimer Fisher – 1st Battalion, West Yorkshire Regiment (Prince of Wales Own) – 20/09/1914 aged 31. Son of Fred and Clara Fisher of King's Langley and husband of Margaret Fisher of Bexhill-on-Sea, Sussex.

Private Wilfred Noel Franklin – 1st Battalion, South Wales Borderers – 26/09/1914 aged 28. Son of William Franklin of Harpenden.

An unexploded German 'Sausage' bomb, a type of trench mortar, was struck by the pick of one of the working party. One man was killed instantly, Second Lieutenant Mead was mortally wounded and 13 other men were also injured.

Second Lieutenant Robert John Mead died as a result of his injuries at Armentieres on 2 August 1915, and is buried in the Cite Bonjean Military Cemetery, Armentieres, France, aged 19. He was awarded the 1915 Star, British War Medal and Victory Medal.

The names of both brothers are recorded on the St. Albans War Memorial, Hertfordshire.

VICTORIAN WARRIOR – GENERAL SIR HORACE SMITH-DORRIEN

General Sir Horace Smith-Dorrien.

Upon the outbreak of the Great War the eyes of the British public turned expectantly to Britain's small, yet highly professional regular army. It was this army which had gained and held the British Empire during the Victorian period and which had been a global sign of British dominance, alongside the mighty Royal Navy ever since. With so much expected of the greatly outnumbered British Expeditionary Force, the public gaze fell on the major figures who were due to lead the British Army into battle – perhaps none of these commanders were more colourful than Berkhamsted's Horace Smith-Dorrien. Smith-Dorrien was the perfect example of the quintessential British officer of the late Victorian period. Being born at a property known as Haresfoot near Berkhamsted on 26 May 1858, he was twelfth of a rather incredible sixteen children to Colonel Robert Algernon Smith-Dorrien and Mary Ann Drever.

Horace was educated at Harrow School before attending Sandhurst Military Academy, which he entered on 26 February 1876. Horace eventually received a commission into the 95th (Derbyshire) Regiment of Foot. When young Smith-Dorrien first joined the British Army, and for almost two decades afterwards, they were very much still a Victorian force, fighting in the famous red coats of Wellington's era.

Young Horace's first major experience of battle was in none other than the catastrophic destruction of almost the entire 24th Regiment of Foot in the Battle of Isandlwana during the Anglo-Zulu war in 1879.

On 22 January 1879 Smith-Dorrien was serving as a transport officer attached to the Royal Artillery, which was part of No. 3 Column of the British invasion force led by Lieutenant-General Lord Chelmsford as they pushed into Zululand in order to defeat the forces of Zulu King Cetshwayo. That day, a catastrophic blunder made by Lord Chelmsford in detaching a large part of his force to chase down a small detachment of Zulu left around 1,000 British soldiers in defence of an encampment in an exposed position beneath a mountain known as Isandlwana. Unbeknownst to Chelmsford, the main Zulu Army was in fact only a few miles from the camp and once discovered, launched a huge attack with more than 25,000 warriors onto the overextended and unprepared British lines. Over the following two hours, almost the entire British force were overrun and cut down, despite putting up the most gallant of defences against all odds.

One of only five British officers to escape the slaughter was 20-year-old Horace Smith-Dorrien, who was plunged headlong into a river after a 3-mile flight, chased all the way by bands of Zulu Warriors. Only a chance encounter with a riderless horse whose tail he was able to hold on to meant that he would live to fight another day, as the horse pulled him to safety through the Buffalo River.

For the British Army it was a good thing that young Smith-Dorrien survived the day as over the next two decades he rose to prominence in the British Army,

The Battle of Isandlwana.

distinguishing himself during the Boer War at the turn of the century. By 1914 Horace had risen to the rank of general and following the death of a superior he was put in charge of the British Army's II Corps on the Western Front. Despite bitter rivalries and dislike between Smith-Dorrien and his commander-in-chief, Field Marshal French, Smith-Dorrien led his corps with great skill and determination during the Battle of Mons, blunting the German Army's advance at Le Cateau shortly after. Although Smith-Dorrien was clearly an able commander – arguably the BEF's best in 1914 – he was notoriously foul tempered, and throughout the early months of 1915 relations between Smith-Dorrien and French worsened. On 6 May 1915 General Sir Horace Lockwood Smith-Dorrien was sacked from his position as GOC of II Corps. He was informed of this by General Robertson, a

Today, General Sir Horace Smith-Dorrien is buried in the cemetery adjoining St Peter's church in Berkhamsted.

former enlisted man who reportedly said *''Orace, Yer for 'ome.'* Smith-Dorrien's command in 1914–15 would be the last that he held during the Great War. He was eventually posted to East Africa to take charge of British Forces, but was taken ill on the voyage and never held an active command again. Despite being sidelined by 1915, history remembers Smith-Dorrien favourably; a difficult, yet practical and skilful commander who fell afoul of military infighting rather than poor performance.

After the war Smith-Dorrien held the post of Governor of Gibraltar before retiring in 1923. He spent much of his spare time writing his memoirs and was a keen promoter of remembrance for those who fell in the Great War. On 12 August 1930 Smith-Dorrien's vehicle, in which he was a passenger, was involved in a head-on collision with another vehicle at a crossroads near Chippenham in Wiltshire. As a result of the crash, which overturned his vehicle, Smith-Dorrien suffered a fractured skull. He never regained consciousness and died later that morning; he was 72 years of age.

HIGH SEAS AMBUSH – CHAPLAIN EDWARD ROBSON

At the outbreak of war in 1914 most of the world's major navies operated a small number of submarines. They had been in service for a little over a decade and the experience of their employment and designs were largely experimental. With a limited range, minimal armament, low speed and – above all – short underwater endurance, many believed that they posed very little threat to warships. Significant development throughout the First World War was to change these views, but in September 1914 many commanders who had grown up in purely surface navies still held on to such opinions.

Chaplain Edward Robson

On 22 September 1914, a German submarine, *U-9*, commanded by Otto Eduard Weddigen, shocked the world when it ambushed three outdated Royal Navy cruisers manned mainly by reservists whilst on patrol in the North Sea. Otto Weddigen had left Wilhelmshaven on 20 September 1914 with orders to attack British transports landing troops at Ostend on the Belgian coast. Weddigen, aged just 32, was an experienced submariner who had survived a peacetime accident in the submarine *U-3* whereby he and 27 others had escaped through a torpedo tube. The *U-9* was very primitive by later standards, with heavy-oil engines which produced a very visible exhaust plume, and a surface speed of 13.5 knots. The *U-9* was armed with four torpedo tubes (two forward, two aft) and carried reloads for the forward tubes only.

At dawn on 22 September, *U-9* surfaced to find the sea calm with a slow swell. Smoke was seen on the horizon and the *U-9*'s engines were immediately shut down to get rid of their exhaust plume. A quick assessment led Weddigen to order the submarine to submerge as he continued to observe through his periscope. Three vessels were seen on the horizon, HMS *Aboukir*, HMS *Cressy* and HMS *Hogue*. Weddingen steered the submarine towards the British ships using his electric motors, aiming towards the central vessel, HMS *Aboukir*. Undetected, the German submarine closed to within 600 yards of its prey and fired a torpedo

Otto Eduard Weddigen.

towards the enemy's port bow. As the torpedo was still running, Weddigen took the *U-9* down to a depth of 50 feet, then heard 'a dull thud, followed by a shrill-toned crash'. Immediately, there was great rejoicing and cheering amongst the crew of the *U-9*. An officer on watch aboard the *U-9* later wrote: '*In the periscope, a horrifying scene unfolded. We present in the conning tower tried to suppress the terrible impression of drowning men, fighting for their lives in the wreckage, clinging on to capsized lifeboats.*'

The single torpedo was sufficient enough to destroy the aging HMS *Aboukir*. She was hit amidships on the port side; the engine and boiler rooms were flooded and the ship listed to port. Aboard HMS *Pathfinder*, the ship's commander, Captain Drummond, believed that HMS *Aboukir* had been struck by a mine. He ordered HMS *Cressy* and HMS *Hogue* to get closer so that the stricken ship's wounded could be transferred. This move was to prove fatal, as the *U-9*, still unsuspected, observed as HMS *Hogue* and HMS *Cressy* moved ever closer towards the survivors. The submarine, now with its torpedoes reloaded, selected HMS *Hogue* as its next victim. The small craft was stationary and Weddigen fired both bow tubes at the British cruiser. This action altered *U-9*'s balance and her bow broke through the surface, instantly drawing fire from HMS *Hogue*. Weddigen managed to get his craft under the surface again and, as he did so, heard two explosions. HMS *Hogue*, her boats already busy with survivors from the *Aboukir*, suffered a similar fate to her sister ship. Now only HMS *Cressy* remained and she was transmitting distress signals by wireless.

With the *U-9*'s batteries almost depleted, Weddigen continued his attack. Through his periscope he could see the surface strewn with wreckage, bodies, swimmers and overcrowded boats. HMS *Cressy* was now stationary with her boats lowered. Although the submarine's periscope was spotted and the cruiser opened fire, Weddigen pushed on. He brought the *U-9*'s stern tubes to bear and fired both at a range of 1,000 yards. The first torpedo struck HMS *Cressy* but the second missed. The cruiser heeled over, then began to right herself. Some ten minutes later Weddigen fired his last torpedo from the bow tube. HMS *Cressy*, now hit on the port side, rolled over and remained on the surface, bottom up, for a further twenty minutes. Then she too, sunk, her crew's plight all the worse since the boats she had sent off were already crowded with survivors from HMS *Aboukir* and HMS *Houge*.

At least 1,450 sailors were killed in this action; nine of the casualties are known to be men of Hertfordshire. One of these was Chaplain Edward Gleadall Uphill Robson. Born in 1882, he was educated at Malvern College where he excelled at sport. He went up to Clare College, Cambridge in 1901, where he went on to become the captain of the football team in 1904, the year in which he graduated.

Contemporary image of the sinking of HMS *Aboukir* and HMS *Houge*.

He obtained his MA in 1913, and was ordained by the Bishop of St. Albans. He served as curate at the Malvern College Mission, Canning Town and then at Hitchin, Hertfordshire.

Quick Fact

Those Hertfordshire men who are known to have been lost in this action are listed below.

HMS *Hogue*
Leading Stoker William Bishop of Baldock, aged 29.
Stoker 1st Class Jesse Herbert Eason of St. Albans, aged 30.

HMS *Cressy*
Able Seaman John Fairclough of Hitchin, aged 30.
Able Seaman Henry Frank Neary of King's Langley, aged 25.
Ordinary Seaman Albert John Gray of St. Albans, aged 18.

HMS *Aboukir*
Chaplain Edward Gleadall Uphill Robson of Hitchin, aged 32.
Gunner David Page (Royal Marine Artillery) of Hatfield, aged 30.
Stoker 1st Class Henry John Russell of Watford, aged 30.
Stoker 1st Class George Cockman of Hertford, aged 24.

Edward Robson had been the chaplain aboard HMS *Aboukir* for just five weeks and was the first British chaplain to be killed in the Great War. The Reverend Robson, also the first Hitchin man to perish in the sea war, died from possible heart failure and exposure whilst in the water. He had, with many others, survived the sinking of the ship and managed to reach a lifeboat. Heavy seas overturned the small boat several times and he clung desperately to its keel. The medical officer was also clinging to the boat whilst attempting to hold an injured midshipman above the water. Eventually, he saw the chaplain turn blue and go under.

As for Otto Weddigen, he was awarded the Iron Cross First Class, and appointed to command a new submarine, the *U-29*. On 18 March 1915, the *U-29* was rammed by HMS *Dreadnought* in the Pentland Firth. There were no survivors.

BROTHERS IN LIFE, BROTHERS IN DEATH

There can be no greater loss for a parent than that of a child and for numerous Hertfordshire families the pain of such loss would be felt on more than one occasion throughout the Great War. Tragically, in several cases the deaths of their sons would occur on the same day. Current records show that there were 322 sets of brothers across the country who served in the Commonwealth forces that are known to have died on the same day. The following are just some examples of those known to be from Hertfordshire.

The Smeathman Brothers

With three sons serving in the army at the outbreak of the Great War, it is hard to imagine how any parent felt as the tragic events began to unfold in France and Belgium. Julian Missenden Smeathman was the second son of Lovel and Frances Smeathman of Hemel Hempstead. He attended Rugby School in 1902, and passed on to the Royal Military Academy, Woolwich in 1905. After a course of training at Chatham and Newcastle-on-Tyne, he received an appointment at the War Office, and was sent out to South Africa in 1910, where he was stationed at Pretoria.

Julian Smeathman.

On the outbreak of war, Julian returned home to England with his unit, the 55th Field Company, Royal Engineers, part of the 7th Division. On his return he became engaged to Gladys Monica Browne, the youngest daughter of the Reverend Gordon Browne, Vicar of Lympstone, Devon. The couple married on 1 October 1914 and, just a few days later, on 4 October, Julian was ordered to report back to his unit.

Three days later the men of the 55th Field Company found themselves aboard the SS *Cestrian* en route from Southampton to Zeebrugge. The unit, consisting of 6 officers, 159 dismounted NCOs and men and 53 mounted NCOs and men, was swiftly transported to the city of Bruges, where they were billeted in the Cavalry Barracks. The following morning, despite their exhausting journey the previous day, the men marched 22 km to the village of Bredene on the Belgian coast. They spent the next week on the move, quartering in a different location each evening until eventually, on 14 October, they arrived at Ypres, where they were billeted in a local school.

The next day they found themselves on the Voormezeele – Zillebeke Road, where they were engaged in preparing fields of fire and setting up communications. Having now been attached to the 21st Infantry Brigade, the company became responsible for setting up defensive positions in the Ypres Sector, where life was becoming more hazardous. The First Battle of Ypres opened on 21 October, as the German Fourth Army made an advance on the British line. The fighting was intense; with German artillery shelling the British positions on a constant basis, casualties soon began to mount, with the unit war diary now reporting wounded men on most days.

On 24 October, a German shrapnel shell exploded close to where Julian Smeathman was sheltering with his men near Hooge. He was killed and four men were wounded.

His colonel wrote:

His death has been a great blow to us. His Captain had previously told me that he was the best Subaltern he had ever had, and that he could not wish for a better. I, too, had remembered him as a youngster at Chatham, and had marked him then as an officer of much promise.

A brother officer said:

Professionally I had a good deal to do with him, and a better officer in that regiment of distinguished officers it would have been impossible to find.

Cecil Smeathman was just a year younger than his brother and was serving as a Lieutenant with the 1st Battalion, Leicestershire Regiment, part of the 16th Brigade, 6th Division. The battalion left Southampton aboard the Royal Mail

Transport *Braemar Castle* on 8 September, arriving in St. Nazaire on 10 September.

Cecil Smeathman.

It was not until 21 September, when the battalion crossed the River Aisne, that they began to engage with the Germans. Constant shelling by day and sniper fire by night was to soon take a toll on the men of the battalion, as their casualties mounted. The battalion spent a great deal of time over the next few weeks moving locations, but by 20 October 1914 had taken up defensive positions in a small hamlet named Rue Du Bois, near Fleurbaix; a location that would soon become home to the men of the Hertfordshire Regiment.

On 21 October 1914 the battalion was ordered to relieve the West Yorkshire Regiment, who were located in a chemical factory in Rue Du Bois. It was whilst the battalion was in these positions that, on 22 October, the men were very heavily shelled by German artillery. Cecil Smeathman was severely wounded during the bombardment, and died two days later as a consequence of his injuries.

Cecil is buried in the Bailleul Communal Cemetery, Nord, but his brother, who has no known grave, has his name recorded upon the Menin Gate Memorial in Ypres. A window in St Mary's Church, Hemel Hempstead, is dedicated to the brothers, who were both awarded the 1914 Star, British War Medal and the Victory Medal.

Their older brother, Lieutenant Colonel Lovel Francis Smeathman DSO MC, served with the Hertfordshire Regiment and was later the commanding officer of the 9th Battalion, Royal Welsh Fusiliers. He survived the war and lived in the Hemel Hempstead area until his death in 1970.

The Batchelor Brothers

Just a week after the death of the Smeathmans, another pair of Hertfordshire brothers were also to lose their lives. Private Henry William Batchelor and Private Joseph Batchelor were both serving in Belgium with the same regiment, the 2nd Battalion, the Life Guards, part of the 4th Cavalry Brigade of the 1st Cavalry Division. The two brothers had been attached to this unit from their parent regiment, the 3rd Battalion, Dragoon Guards.

Originally born in Kilburn, London, the brothers were the sons of Joseph and Elizabeth Batchelor and moved to Watford with their parents when their father obtained work in the area as a coal porter. Sadly, Joseph senior passed away aged just 38, leaving Elizabeth to raise their five children in a small terraced house in Tucker Street, Watford. Both Henry and Joseph joined the army at an early age and served in various locations across the world with the Dragoon Guards. By 1914 their service had come to an end but they were still part of the Reserve Army and, as such, were mobilised for further service in August 1914. The boys left the shores of the motherland on 5 October 1914 and, unbeknown to them, would not see home again.

On 30 October 1914 their battalion was situated in positions near the Belgian village of Zandvoorde. It was here, the following morning, that 'C' Troop was attacked and overwhelmed by a vastly superior force of German infantry, with only about 10 men escaping.

The Batchelor brothers were amongst those who were reported missing that day and their names are recorded on the Menin Gate memorial, Ypres, Belgium, and also on a plaque in the Bushey Baptist Church. Both men were awarded the 1914 Star, British War Medal and the Victory Medal.

The Cogan Brothers

The Cogan brothers, William, Alfred, Philip and Ernest were all born in the small Wiltshire village of Collingbourne Ducis, the sons of William James and Louisa Anne Cogan. Their father worked as a cowman on local farms, and the developmental changes of farming in the area at the beginning of the twentieth century saw the family move location, eventually settling at East End Farm, Furneaux Pelham, Hertfordshire.

All of the boys joined the army, serving in the Bedfordshire Regiment, with William and Alfred both becoming sergeants in the 1st Battalion. The two brothers arrived in France on 16 August 1914, just twelve days after war had been declared, and saw action at Mons on 23 August, where the battalion was unexpectedly shelled and then attacked by German infantry, in one of the first actions of the Great War. Jointly, they served with the battalion as it fell back in retreat from the advancing enemy, taking part in several major actions including Le Cateau, the First Battle of the Aisne and Battle of La Bassée.

On 6 November 1914 the battalion travelled from Locon to Ypres on a series of buses, and then marched, via Hooge, to trenches in a wood south of the road near Herenthage Chateau. The following morning the Germans broke through the line held by the battalion. Although the enemy were driven back, the battalion suffered significant casualties with 7 officers and 140 other ranks being killed or wounded and a further 7 missing. Amongst those who were missing were Sergeant William Cogan, aged 33, and Sergeant Alfred James Cogan, aged 29. Neither man has a known grave but both their names are recorded on the Le Touret memorial to the missing. They were awarded the 1914 Star, British War Medal and the Victory Medal.

Coincidently, their brother, Philip George Cogan, who was serving with the 2nd Battalion, Bedfordshire Regiment, was one of just seven men who took part in an event that saw an officer of the Bedfordshire Regiment receive the Victoria Cross. On 10 March 1915, British and Indian troops attacked the town of Neuve Chapelle. The 2nd Battalion, Bedfordshire Regiment, was being held in reserve on the northern edge of the town, facing the village of Pietre. The troops were sent into action following the initial assault and advanced across open fields, passing the heavy casualties that had been suffered by the first waves. By late afternoon they had cleared the old German frontlines and settled into new lines for the night in an open field. They spent the next 24 hours in the same location, digging new trenches and awaiting new orders.

On the night of 11 March a company of Royal Scots Fusiliers arrived on the right of the battalion, but they were rushed early in the morning by German infantry and driven from the trench, leaving the Bedfordshires badly exposed.

At about 7.00 am the British counterattacked the enemy in an attempt to regain the lost trench, but the assault was disastrous. Every officer and man was hit, with many of them falling as they left the trenches; the bodies of those who made it into no man's land could be seen lying in a straight line where they fell as a German machine gun took them down with enfilade fire, with only a handful of Bedfords actually making it into the German trenches. Half an hour later word reached battalion HQ of the doomed assault, just as the Scots to their right started suffering badly from British shell fire. The situation was falling into confusion as the Brigadier ordered the trench to be retaken.

Captain Foss, the battalion adjutant, was ordered to go forward to gain an understanding of the situation. It seems that having considered the circumstances, he suggested that one of the newly raised bombing sections should attempt an assault, but neglected to add that he intended to lead them himself. Having taken one such section of bombers from 'D' Company, he led them from the front in a line through the trenches, intending to flank attack the German-held line, and placed himself at the front as the leading bayonet man. Having moved through the 'veritable shambles' that the British trenches had become, overflowing with wounded and dying men as they were, Foss approached the end of the British territory and was faced with open ground between them and the German lines with flooded dykes running across their line of attack. As he describes in his own words:

> *We then launched our attack. The words sound grand; but we felt very 'naked' and 'above ground' in the open field – at least I did. The dyke caused me some amusement – none of the bombers were inclined to get their feet wet and I thoroughly sympathised with them – wet puttees are so cold.*

So, they 'covered' me while I ran and leapt, then I 'covered' them while they ran and leapt. What's more, we all cleared the dyke. This safely negotiated, we threw a few bombs. The bombs, the first I had seen go off in anger, frightened me with their noise and the mess they made of the local Germans. They also stirred the Germans into activity. They got up and crowded round us with their hands up. The bombers thoroughly enjoyed themselves, waving the bombs in their faces, making grimaces and ordering them to hold their hands higher. I had to shout to warn the bombers not to throw any more as they would blow us all up.

Captain Charles Calveley Foss was awarded the Victoria Cross for his part in the Battle of Neuve Chapelle on 12 March 1915. His citation reads:

For most conspicuous bravery … After the enemy had captured a part of one of our trenches, and our counterattack made with one officer and twenty men having failed (all but two of the party being killed or wounded in the attempt), Capt. Foss, on his own initiative, dashed forward with eight men, and under heavy

fire attacked the enemy with bombs, and captured the position, including the fifty-two Germans occupying it. The capture of this position from the enemy was of the greatest importance, and the utmost bravery was displayed in essaying the task with so very few men.

The small group of eight bombers who overcame over fifty German troops with Captain Foss were:

Herenthage Chateau near Ypres, where the Cogan brothers went missing.

- Sergeant William PEGGS Order of St. George 4th Class (Russia) – Died of Wounds on 9 August 1916.
- Private Harold BARNETT
- Private Frederick BROWN
- Private Phillip George COGAN – Killed on 13 March 1915.
- Private William EADE DCM – Accidentally killed on 10 June 1916.
- Private George FRESHWATER MM – Died of Wounds 8 July 1916.
- Private Joseph LOVETT
- Private Stanley Walter SCRIVENER – Killed on 13 March 1915. (St. Albans, Herts.)
- Private Herbert SMITH – Killed on 21 March 1918 (Ashwell, Herts.)

Just a few days later, on 13 March 1915, Phillip, who had arrived in France on 11 November 1914, was killed, along with Private Stanley Scrivener. Records show that a fourth brother, Charles Cogan, was also wounded at Ypres but survived the war.

IN FLANDERS FIELDS – THE FLANDERS STORY

During the Great War, death touched the lives of a large proportion of families in the towns and villages across Great Britain, and Hertfordshire was no exception. Amongst the thousands of casualties that the county suffered is that of the Flanders family, whose lives were filled with a series of tragic events, even before the onset of the Great War. Their story was told through a series of letters and photographs loaned to the *Herts at War* project by family member Nancy Jack. Further research enabled the Flanders story to be told in full, and was later the subject of a presentation made by the project to Anglia Television.

Edward Flanders was a merchant seaman who hailed from King's Lynn, Norfolk. In the summer of 1876 he married Sarah Jane Docking and the couple went on to have eight children: Sarah, Agnes, Emma, Edward, Ellen, Robert, Valentine and Walter. Their mother tended to their needs whilst her husband was away at sea, working mainly on coal carrying coasters. Sadly, things began to go wrong just after the birth of their youngest child. On 3 December 1897, at the age of 43, Sarah died as a consequence of pulmonary heart disease, leaving her husband to determine the future of the children. He was constantly at sea and, in an effort to maintain his family, he had no choice other than to place the children in the care of the local workhouse, the only form of social care available to him. The older children, Sarah, Agnes and Emma were able to avoid the privations of the workhouse but instead found themselves spread across the country. Sarah and Emma worked as domestic servants and Agnes was living with her aunt and

The Flanders family collection as presented to the Herts at War Project. (*All photos supplied by Nancy Jack*)

uncle, John and Cecilia Docking, in King's Lynn. In the summer of 1910 Agnes Flanders married Herbert Large and the couple eventually settled in the new Hertfordshire 'Garden City' of Letchworth. By this time Valentine and Walter had left the workhouse and were living with their sister Ellen in King's Lynn.

On 12 January 1913 tragedy struck the family again when their father, Edward, was amongst the crew of a coastal coaler, SS *Hawkwood*, which was making its way from Glasgow to Hull. The heavily laden ship was caught in a snow squall and is believed to have suffered at least one mechanical breakdown. Eventually, the ship began to list and fearing that it would strike the rocks near Flamborough Head, the crew of 17 men, including Edward Flanders, took to a lifeboat. It seems that the lifeboat became swamped in the heavy seas and the entire crew drowned. In a rather macabre scene, the SS *Hawkwood* turned up several weeks later, afloat but without her entire crew.

Following the death of their father the two youngest boys, Valentine and Walter, went to live with Agnes and her husband at their home in Ridge Road, Letchworth. It was whilst living here that Walter joined the Territorial Army enlisting in the Hertfordshire Regiment just after the outbreak of the Great War. Walter, who was close to his sister Agnes, wrote home as often as possible, keeping her informed of his progress as he trained for war. With such a hectic training schedule, often Walter's reports were little more than brief updates. On 3 October he wrote to her, enclosing a postcard photograph:

Dear Sis,

Orders all changed keeping us for some time yet so let's hear from you soon. No passes to be issued for a while. Don't have a fit when you see this photo, we had just come off a route march so were rather dirty and tired. Goodnight dear sister, love to all. Walter xxx

Walter left the shores of England for service on the Western Front on 6 November 1914. The battalion embarked at Southampton on the merchant vessel SS *City of Chester*, arriving in Le Havre the following day, where they then marched to Rest Camp No. 2. Over the next few days they travelled by both train and bus across France and

Group of soldiers from the Hertfordshire Regiment.

Belgium until they reached the town of Vlamertinghe. After a long and wet journey, they then marched through Ypres until they reached a location known as 'Kilo 3', just on the outskirts of the village of Hooge.

On 12 November the battalion moved about 2 miles along the Ypres-Zonnebeke railway, where they took up positions in a wood, their first time on the frontlines. The battalion experienced severe shelling from German artillery and in the evening they moved back to their bivouacs at Kilo 3. On 14 November they marched to a wood named Nonne Bosschen, where they took over trenches from the men of the Oxfordshire and Buckinghamshire Light Infantry.

Of their eight companies, three were in the trenches and five were in support. On 16 November the battalion was relieved by the 153rd Regiment of the French Army and moved back to their bivouacs at Kilo 3. The following morning the Battalion Headquarters, located at Outpost Farm, was forced to move after it was heavily shelled, killing one man and wounding three others. That evening two companies remained at Kilo 3 whilst the rest of the battalion took over trenches from the 1st Royal Dragoons and the 10th Hussars in Shrewsbury Forest, 1 mile east of Zillebeke. The following morning one man was killed and another reported missing, after their positions were shelled.

On 19 November 1914 Walter Flanders was resting in a dugout with six other members of 'E' Company when it was hit by a German shell. All seven men were buried by the explosion and none survived. Those reported as being killed were:

- Private William Butts (Hitchin)
- Private George Haslear Catlin (Hertingfordbury)
- Private George Edward Ellis (Baldock)
- Private Walter William Flanders (Letchworth)
- Private Joseph William Johnson (Letchworth)
- Private Frank Pulley (Royston)
- Private Henry West (Hertford Heath)

Sadly, none of these men have a known grave but their names are recorded on the Menin Gate memorial in Ypres, Belgium.

Valentine Flanders enlisted into the Bedfordshire Regiment and entered service on the Western Front on 11 August 1915. From letters home to his sister it seems that he initially served with the 2nd Battalion and was wounded on 1 July 1916 during the opening day of the Battle of the Somme. Following his recovery, he was posted to the 6th Battalion and remained with them in France. Like his brother, Val also spent much of his spare time writing to loved ones at home. On Easter Sunday, 1917 Val responded to a letter from his niece:

Dear Little Daphne,
    This is just a wee letter that Uncle Val promised you ever so long ago. I shall put this with Auntie Emma's letter then that will be one each won't it. Thank you

very much for the book of writing paper which as you can see has come in very useful, also for all the nice wafers which I liked very much. Aren't I a lucky chap to have such a nice little girl to send him sweets. Well dear Kid, I have not much time to write as I am just getting ready to run after the Germans. I will write to mam as soon as I can and I hope soon to come home and see you all again, then we shall have a fine time won't we. Well goodbye dear Daphne, give my love to Mum and Dad and Auntie and take heaps of love and kisses from your loving uncle Val.

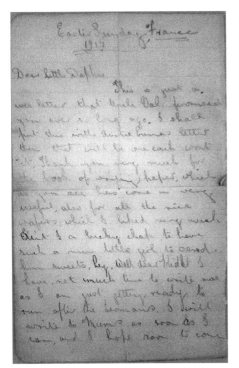

Original letter from Valentine Flanders to his niece.

This would prove to be Valentine's last letter home. On 12 April 1917 he was reported as Missing in Action during the Battle of Arras and subsequently confirmed to have been killed. When Valentine's personal possessions were returned home, his wallet was found to contain a newspaper cutting announcing his brother Walter's death; something

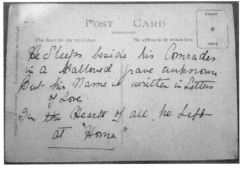

Poem to the Flanders brothers.

he had carried with him for over two years until he, too, fell in action. Like his brother, Valentine has no known grave either, but his name is recorded on the Arras memorial in France.

Amongst the astonishing collection of hundreds of letters and photographs relating to the two brothers that had been kept by Agnes after the war, was a postcard of Valentine with the following on the back, written in her handwriting:

> *'He sleeps beside his comrades in a hallowed grave unknown. But his name is written in letters of love in the hearts of all he left at home.'*

VC & BAR – LIEUTENANT COLONEL ARTHUR MARTIN-LEAKE

Lieutenant Colonel Arthur Martin-Leake VC & Bar was a British double recipient of the Victoria Cross, the highest award for gallantry in the face of the enemy that can be awarded to British and Commonwealth forces. Martin-Leake was the first of only three men in history to be awarded the VC twice.

Lieutenant Colonel Arthur Martin-Leake VC & Bar.

Arthur, the fifth son of Stephen Martin-Leake of Thorpe Hall, Essex, was born at Standon, near Ware, Hertfordshire, and was educated at Westminster School before studying medicine at University College Hospital, qualifying in 1893. He was employed at Hemel Hempstead District Hospital before enlisting in the Imperial Yeomanry to serve in the Boer War in 1899. Martin-Leake first served in the Second Boer War as a trooper in the Imperial Yeomanry. After his year-long service was completed, he stayed on in South Africa as a civil surgeon. He then joined the South African Constabulary and served with the likes of Robert Baden-Powell, whom he did not regard highly. Arthur's first experience of fame came whilst serving in South Africa.

He was 27 years old and a Surgeon Captain in the South African Constabulary attached to No. 5 Field Ambulance on 8 February 1902 when he won his first VC. During the action Martin-Leake approached a severely wounded man and attended to him under heavy fire from about forty Boers less than a hundred yards away. He then went to the assistance of a wounded officer and, whilst trying to place him in a comfortable position, was shot three times but would not give in until he rolled over, thoroughly exhausted. All the men at this point were wounded and while they were lying on the Veldt, Surgeon Captain Martin-

Leake refused water until everyone else had been served. He received the decoration from King Edward VII at St James's Palace on 2 June 1902. Arthur Martin-Leake qualified as a Fellow of the Royal College of Surgeons in 1903 after studying while convalescing from wounds.

Lieutenant Caulfeild – The *Thresher* – Lieutenant Martin-Leake.

Arthur's brother Theodore Edward Martin-Leake, a Lieutenant in the Royal Engineers was drowned in a ballooning accident on 28 May 1907. After taking off in the army balloon *Thresher* from Aldershot on 27 May, it appears the two occupants lost their bearings and crashed into the sea. Theodore's body was discovered in the water at Burton Bradstock, near Bridport, Devon, a week after the body of his companion, Lieutenant William Talbot McClintock Caulfeild, had been discovered in the same vicinity.

Following the death of his brother, Arthur took up an appointment in India as chief medical officer with the Bengal-Nagpur Railway. In 1912 he volunteered to serve with the British Red Cross during the Balkan Wars, attached to the Montenegrin Army, and was present during the Siege of Scutari (1912–13) and at Tarabosh Mountain. He was awarded the Order of the Montenegrin Red Cross.

On the outbreak of the First World War, Martin-Leake returned to service in a rather unorthodox manner; he turned up at the British Embassy in Paris and demanded a commission. As a qualified medical doctor, holding a Victoria Cross no less, his appointment was never in doubt. He was duly commissioned as a Lieutenant with No. 5 Field Ambulance, Royal Army Medical Corps, and began his service on the Western Front.

He earned his second VC aged 40 years, during the period 29 October to 8 November 1914 near Zonnebeke, Belgium whilst serving with the Royal Army Medical Corps, British Army. His award citation reads:

Lieutenant Arthur Martin Leake, Royal Army Medical Corps, who was awarded the Victoria Cross on 13 May, 1902, is granted a Clasp for conspicuous bravery in the present campaign:

'For most conspicuous bravery and devotion to duty throughout the campaign, especially during the period 29 October to 8 November, 1914, near Zonnebeke, in rescuing, whilst exposed to constant fire, a large number of the wounded who were lying close to the enemy's trenches.'

At the time of the announcement there was considerable discussion in Government about what to do with Arthur's award, as nobody had received the VC twice before now. It was eventually decided that a 'bar' was most appropriate. His Victoria Cross is displayed at the Army Medical Services Museum in Aldershot, England. He was promoted to captain in March 1915, major in November the same year, and in April 1917 took command of No. 46 Field Ambulance at the rank of Lieutenant Colonel.

It was whilst in this role that Arthur was part of a unique – although at the time unnoticed – event. On 2 August 1917, soon after the launch of the 3rd Battle of Ypres, he was busy triaging the many wounded coming back from the battlefield at his medical post outside the village of Brandhoek. One of the many men that Arthur saw that day was a fellow doctor, Captain Noel Godfrey Chavasse, VC MC. Noel was most likely unconscious, and in fact, mortally wounded, but Arthur did notice he was wearing the ribbon of the Victoria Cross. What he was not to know was that the dying officer in front of him had just arrived after displaying the most incredible bravery over a three-day period, a feat for which he would become the second man to be awarded the VC & Bar. Noel Chavasse died several hours after this encounter, making this the only time in history that two double VC recipients would meet.

Arthur's other brother, Francis, was a captain aboard the first ship ever to be sunk by a locomotive torpedo fired by a submarine. HMS *Pathfinder* was sunk on 5 September 1914, off St. Abbs Head in the Scottish Borders while on patrol. The submarine, *U-21*, was commanded by Kapitänleutnant Otto Hersing and it appears that, despite the event having been easily visible from shore, it was believed that HMS *Pathfinder* had actually been sunk by a mine. The majority of crew was below deck and had neither the time nor the opportunity to escape, therefore they tragically went down with the ship. There was some confusion at the time over the exact number of crew on board, but research indicates that there were 261 deaths and only 18 survivors, one of whom was Captain Francis Martin-Leake, who stayed with his ship as she went down by the nose but was fortunately picked up and saved.

Arthur Martin-Leake retired from the army after the war and resumed his company employment in India, where he married Winifred Francis Carroll in 1930. A complex, and in some ways rather tragic character, Arthur was a man of many contradictions. Not only did he earn two Victoria Crosses, he did so without even carrying a weapon, resolving only to save lives – yet this was a man who was known as one of the most prolific tiger hunters

Captain Francis Martin-Leake.

in all of India in the 1920s. Sadness was never too far away from Arthur's life. After several unhappy years, Arthur's wife, Winifred, committed suicide, throwing herself under the wheels of the very train on which Arthur was serving as doctor. It is believed he had to deal with the aftermath and certify the death of his own wife.

Arthur stayed in India until his retirement in 1937, when he returned to Hertfordshire to the family home at Marshalls. During the Second World War, Arthur joined the Home Guard and he commanded an ARP post on top of a local pub in High Cross, Herts, just yards from his home.

Arthur Martin-Leake
in his later years.

Lieutenant Colonel Arthur-Martin Leake VC & Bar died aged 79, in his home in Marshalls, High Cross, Hertfordshire. Following cremation at Enfield, Middlesex, Martin-Leake's ashes were buried in St John's Church, High Cross. In a ceremony on Sunday, 26 June 1955, Arthur's cousin, Dr Hugh Martin-Leake, handed over the Victoria Cross and Bar to the Royal Army Medical Corps at their depot in Crookham, near Aldershot. He is commemorated with a plaque and a tree at the National Memorial Arboretum in Alrewas, Staffordshire and a unique 'double VC' paving stone unveiled in 2014 at the Church of St John the Evangelist, just a stone's throw from his home.

A CHRISTMAS TRUCE? – PERCY HUGGINS AND TOM GREGORY

The subject of the Christmas Truce of 1914 is an evocative one. Many leading historians firmly believe that whilst in a small section of the Western Front some form of fraternisation took place, overall the fight for France and Flanders continued, irrespective of any seasonal interruption. Whilst there is no doubt that a truce of sorts did take place in multiple points along the line of trenches formed across this part of Europe, it should also be remembered that this was by no means a universal ceasefire.

Certainly, for the men of the Hertfordshire Regiment, there was no real break in the fighting, with two men of the battalion being killed on Christmas Day. The *Herts at War* project was fortunate enough to be given access to photographs and letters that relate to the tragic event which cost the lives of two Hertfordshire soldiers. The previously untold account came to light after the family of Private Percy Huggins offered up his letters home from the trenches to the project.

Private Percy Huggins. (*Huggins Family*)   Sergeant Tom Gregory. (*Tim Abbott*)

Following receipt of the letters and a study of military records and regimental diaries, the full tragic tale was revealed.

An unofficial diary kept by Lieutenant Bernard Gripper states that on Christmas Eve 1914 the battalion was stationed at Les Lacons Farm and moved into trenches south of Rue Du Bois, near the French village of Festubert, which they took over from the 6th Jats. There were six companies in the trenches with two companies in support. This later changed to five companies in the trenches, with three in support. Each company rotated around in order to take its place in the support trenches, where it remained for 36 hours.

The men of 'D' Company, one of eight companies making up the 1st Battalion, Hertfordshire Regiment, were recruited from the large south Hertfordshire town of Watford. Many of the men had known each other for years, having served as pre-war Territorials and spent summer camps together in the UK. Serving in 'D' Company, commanded by Captain Phillip Elton Longmore, were 36-year-old Lance Sergeant Thomas 'Tom' Gregory and 23-year-old Private Percy Huggins. Tom was an experienced old soldier, and had seen action 15 years earlier in the Boer War as a regular in the Coldstream Guards. He was regarded as a veteran and known throughout the battalion as a crack shot. In contrast, Percy Huggins was a young man from the quiet market town of Ware who made his living as an assistant in his mother's house-furnishing business. Percy's military experience was limited to rifle drill and an annual summer camp with his fellow territorials. There seems little doubt that Percy looked up to his experienced sergeant as a reassuring and steady leader.

The war began for the men of the Hertfordshire Regiment on 5 November 1914 when the battalion set sail from Southampton on the SS *City of Chester*, arriving in Le Havre in the early hours of 6 November. From here, the battalion was put into the line near the Belgian city of Ypres in time to participate in the later stages of the First Battle of Ypres, where the Hertfordshire Regiment suffered their first losses in combat. Young men like Percy finally experienced first-hand what war was really like. For a soldier like Tom Gregory, who had joined the army when Queen Victoria was still on the throne, his job would have been to steady his raw men and set an example, which by all accounts he did admirably.

On 22 November 1914 the regiment, now part of Guards Brigade, left frontline duties for a month's rest in the French town of Meteren, safely behind the lines. In 'D' Company, Private Huggins engaged – like most men – in writing letters home to his loved ones in any spare moment he had. Around 21 December, when Percy was in support near a post known as 'Chocolate Menier Corner', he penned the following letter back home to the local vicar:

Dear Mr & Mrs Daniels,

I feel I must write you a line from the front to let you know how I am getting on since I resolved to do my share in the upholding of Britain's honour. I have had many adventures and experiences since leaving England which, if God spares me, will be listened to with rapt attention at Victoria House. I am glad to be able to tell you that the efforts of our Regt have been appreciated and won for us a good reputation and praise from higher quarters and we are attached to one of the finest Brigades in our army.

We are again ready, having had a good rest, to do our best in whatever position we are placed.

It is our duty and for the protection of our dear ones at home, whose prayers and thoughts are ever for us. I had promised you Sir, that I would commence a home duty at Advent, but God had other work for me to do, I see his Hand in many things.

The lesson I am learning, it shows me how lax I had previously been at prayers and praise. The need of prayers was indeed great, especially one night in the trenches and believe me I prayed as never before, and I asked God to give me strength that I might so live that I do not forget Him in times of peace which I am apt to do. The life here is a hard one and pitfalls are many and I feel that I often slip and do things that were better left undone but each time a lesson is learnt and a special endeavour is made to overcome them and by so doing gain strength.

I trust Mrs Daniels and yourself are both enjoying good health and that the Sunday School is going on successfully. Now must close hoping you will understand this little line.

With very best wishes to you for Xmas and the New Year from yours very sincerely,

Percy Huggins

It was not until the evening of Christmas Eve 1914 that Tom Gregory, Percy Huggins and the rest of their battalion made their way back into frontline trenches around the small French village of Festubert, taking over from the 6th Ghurkha Rifles at a position known as 'Dead Cow Farm'. Upon arriving in the trenches, Major Page Croft, also from Ware and second in command of the battalion, was given a tour of the new trenches by one of the four remaining white officers of the Gurkha Battalion. He remarked of the event: *'the trenches were poor and wide, in this particular sector there was a sap* (small forward trench used as a 'listening post') *running out 150 yards in front of the line to within ten yards of a German sap, and here daily a British officer went up to snap shoot at the enemy with his revolver.'*

These dangerously positioned 'saps' were required to be held by sentries at all times and frequently presented the most dangerous assignment to those troops stationed there.

As the men settled down in the trenches on a bitterly cold night with a frost forming, Private Percy Huggins took a few moments to pen the following letter to his mother, Mrs Agnes Huggins back home in Ware:

My dearest Mum,

Thank you very much indeed for the lovely parcel and letters which arrived safely today. It is good of you all and I can't tell you how grateful I am and how I appreciate all your kindness. I read the letters over and over again. I also received Maude's lovely parcel and a letter from her Auntie and from Mr Harden of Stroud.

The Christmas pudding, we shall dispose of tomorrow if we are here. Am afraid there are no means of boiling or toasting it as French fireplaces, even if we had one, are all of an urn shape and entirely closed in. But you need have no fear for our digestions for they must be like an ostrich's now considering what we have had to eat. So, rest assured dear Mum that although cold the pudding will be appreciated. Thank each one for the gifts which were enclosed for me, and ask them to excuse me if I fail to acknowledge each one, but I am truly very grateful to each one, and thank Sara for her letter which I was very pleased to receive.

Well, Mum dear, we have just had 2 days 'standing fast'. Which means that you must be absolutely ready at any moment for a forced march to the trenches.

The 48 hours have not yet expired, but reports have it that the lines are being held and in parts advances are being made and the probability is we shall not be wanted this time. Yes, dear Mum, I know you all must miss me and no doubt can to some extent realize what my feelings are, for I cannot express them. But I console myself with the thought that I was guided by a High Hand when taking the step which placed me here, where my duty lies, and, believe me Mother, where I am proud to be, and only hope, by the Grace of God, to acquit myself honourably and be permitted to return to all the dear ones in safety.

It seems that Xmas will be spent by us out here, so we will make the best of it and remember you all in thoughts and prayers. I have already asked dear Mum that you will spend as Happy a Xmas as possible and I will do the same. Am glad to think Mr and Mrs Daniells are so interested. I sent them a card a day or two ago and intend writing them but both paper and time are scarce. I had to borrow this piece. Am glad to hear business is going on well and hope Ethel's has started well too and was pleased indeed with her letter. I haven't seen any of the papers that were sent out but things go a long way round before they reach us.

Well, Mother dear, your loving wishes and prayers are treasured in my heart and I long for the day when this terrible conflict will be ended. You consider war a terrible thing but imagination cannot reach far enough, for the horrors of warfare that can be seen on the battlefield are indescribable and I pray that this may be the last war that will ever be. Now must say Goodbye Mum dear and God bless you.

Sometime before dawn on Christmas Day Corporal Clifford Lane of 'H' Company, stationed to the left of the Watford men, reported that the Germans opposite were clearly singing and 'raised up lanterns all along their trenches'. A short while later Lane recalled being visited by an officer from another battalion in the Guards Brigade who instructed the men to open rapid fire toward the enemy, aiming at the lanterns, which they dutifully did. Following this episode, the Germans opposite, apparently quite undisturbed by the enemy fire, brought down their lanterns but continued to sing. Despite this initial 'friendly overtone', it seemed that the truce, which was spreading its way south from the area around 'Plugstreet', would not involve the men of the 4th Guards Brigade. The next hours were quiet and uneventful with the exception of the sound of Christmas carols drifting across no man's land.

Back in the trenches it was the turn of Private Percy Huggins to occupy the British sap poised precariously close to the German line. Leaving his Christmas pudding and gifts from home for later, he made his way up the sap to relieve the sentry on duty. We will never know what occupied Percy's thoughts that bitterly cold morning as he took his turn on watch. Perhaps his thoughts were of home and how his mother, a widow, and seven siblings would be spending their morning opening gifts in front of the fire, or perhaps he was content listening to the German merriment and singing from his position much closer to the enemy line – we will never know.

In the late morning, a solitary shot rang out across no man's land, stilling the chatter and singing that still resonated from the German and British line. An enemy sniper had shot and killed Percy with a single bullet to the head. Reports of the time state that the death of young Huggins that morning enraged the men of 'D' Company, particularly Lance Sergeant Tom Gregory, who approached Captain Longmore, demanding to take Huggins' position in the sap and 'return the favour'. Permission was granted and within minutes Tom and Corporal Hamlet Bloxham of Watford had returned to the site of poor Percy's demise. Scanning the frozen ground along the German line, the old veteran Gregory spotted the sniper and with skill acquired by years of hard campaigning, killed him with a single shot. Sadly, this was not the end of the exchange, as Major Page-Croft wrote, *'shortly afterwards a bullet through the brain sent him to join his young comrade.'* Unbeknownst to Gregory, a second sniper in the German line had spotted him and as he brought his own rifle up to the aim, he was shot, thus raising the death toll in this tragic Christmas exchange to three. Whilst incredible stories of a truce and fraternisation filtered back to the UK in the days following Christmas, Mrs Gregory, Mrs Huggins and an unknown German mother would receive the devastating news that their loved ones would never return. Tom Gregory and Percy Huggins lie today, side by side, in Le Touret Military Cemetery, France.

The painful duty of informing Mrs Agnes Huggins of her son's death fell to Captain Longmore, who wrote, *'we shall always remember your son as a brave and cheerful comrade who was always willing to do anything we asked.'*

The *Watford Illustrated* published the following article in January 1915:

It is with much regret that we have to chronicle the death of a Watford Territorial, L Sergt GREGORY, who was killed in action on Christmas Day… It appears that he was shot through the head whilst taking aim, and died instantly at 12.45 pm. He went through the South African War in the Coldstream Guards, and after serving his time in the Regular Army, joined the Territorials. He was employed at the Watford Post Office, and leaves a widow, and seven children all under eleven years, the youngest infant of only two weeks.

Sergeant Gregory's granddaughter Audrey McLachlan, whose late mother was his eldest daughter, Evelyn, said:

My mother once told me how my grandfather came home on leave in 1914 and he gave her a little girl's tea service. She was running inside with it all excited and she fell over and broke it. She said she never really got over that because that was the last time she saw her father.

The story of Percy and Tom's experiences and tragic demise on Christmas Day 1914 serves to highlight how devastating the impact at home could be. To think that Mrs Huggins and her family enjoyed their Christmas at home, unaware of what had befallen their loved one, only to learn a few days later, really highlights the tragedy of the conflict we know as the Great War.

The graves of Private Percy Huggins and Lance Sergeant Tom Gregory at Le Touret Military Cemetery, France. (Dan Hill)

Chapter Two

1915 – A Year of Adversity

By 1915 the Great War had developed into a truly global event. Germany had begun a campaign of aerial bombing in the form of the aluminium-framed Zeppelins and the wooden framed Schütte-Lanz airships. On 31 May the first aerial bombing of London took place as German raiders killed seven people and injured another thirty-five in the capital, and by September 1915 the first enemy bombs had fallen upon the county from the air.

The Ottomans, who had begun a campaign of forced deportations amongst the Armenian population, launched an unsuccessful attack against the British-controlled Suez Canal, and the French launched their second offensive against German defensive lines in Champagne and were, once again, hampered by the winter weather and lack of heavy artillery. After a month of fighting, the exhausted French broke off the offensive.

In March 1915 British and Indian troops in the Artois region of northern France attacked the Germans around the village of Neuve Chapelle, taking the Germans by complete surprise. The British managed to achieve their final objective but failed to exploit their success and, after three days of fighting, the offensive was suspended.

The Second Battle of Ypres began on 22 April, and was to see the first use of poison gas by the German Army on the Western Front. At the same time, Commonwealth troops landed on the Gallipoli Peninsula in an effort to secure the Dardanelles Strait, following a failed attempt by Allied warships to break through the narrow passage to the Black Sea. Within two weeks, a stalemate developed as the Allies failed to gain any of their objectives and the Ottomans began a series of costly attacks in an attempt to drive out the invaders.

At sea, the U-boats began to tighten their grip on the British mainland. The first German U-boat campaign of the war began with unrestricted attacks against merchant and passenger ships in the waters around the British Isles. On 7 May 1915 a U-boat torpedoed the British passenger liner *Lusitania* off the Irish coast. The ship sank in just 18 minutes, drowning 1,201 people, including 128 Americans.

On 9 May the French attacked a three-mile section of the German front in what would be known as the Second Battle of Artois. Fighting continued for a week with savage encounters on the heights of Notre-Dame-de-Lorette. Ultimately, the success of the French offensive was limited, with the villages of Carency and Ablain-Saint-Nazaire being taken, but Vimy Ridge and thus the control of the surrounding coal basin remained in German hands.

Italy entered the war on 23 May 1915, siding with the Allies by declaring war on Austria-Hungary, with the Italians launching offensives along the 400-mile common border between Austria and Italy. The better-equipped Austrians quickly took advantage of the mountainous terrain to establish strong defensive positions all along the border. The Italians then focused their attacks on the mountain passes at Trentino and the valley of the Isonzo River.

By September, the British had also begun to use poison gas for the first time on the Western Front as they launched an attack against the German 6th Army in the Artois. The Battle of Loos was the British Army's contribution to the major Allied offensive launched simultaneously with the main French offensive in Champagne. The French commander-in-chief, General Joffre, considered that the numerical superiority of his army, however temporary, would be sufficient to bring about the decisive breakthrough. The French Army focused their efforts on the heights of Vimy Ridge, whilst the British were expected to advance into the coal basin below, in the sector of Loos-Hulluch on the Gohelle Plain.

On the 25th, the British advanced and quickly seized their objective, the town of Loos, but then failed to capitalise on the four-mile-wide breach in the German lines. The Germans regrouped and when the British resumed the attack the next day, they were mown down in their hundreds by well-placed German machine gunners. As a result of the failed campaign, British Army Commander John French was sacked and replaced by Douglas Haig. It was during this battle that Corporal Alfred Burt of the Hertfordshire Regiment was to be awarded the Victoria Cross for an action that saved the lives of many of his comrades.

In the Middle East, a British victory occurred at the Battle of Kut Al Amara in Mesopotamia as they defeated the Turks. The victory spurred an ambitious move by the British to venture onward to quickly capture Baghdad. However, that attempt failed and the troops returned to Kut Al Amara and dug in. In the middle of December, the Allies began an orderly withdrawal from the Gallipoli Peninsula in which the Royal Navy successfully evacuated 83,000 survivors by sea as the Turks looked on without firing a shot.

On the Eastern Front, the Germans had used poison gas extensively for the first time against the Russians in January 1915. The fighting on this front was both heavy and bitter, bringing with it an immense level of casualties. In battles such as those at the Masurian Lakes, the Austro-Germans pushed hard against the Russians in an attempt to outflank their positions in central Poland and drive them back beyond the Vistula River. On 21 February the Russian 20th Corps surrendered under the threat of encirclement by the German Army in the Forest of Augustow. Within a few days the German progress eastwards was stopped by an attack from the Russian 12th Army.

By May of 1915 the Germans had taken over command of the Eastern Front and used many of their units to support the increasingly fragmented Austrian formations. By the end of 1915 over two million Russian troops had been lost, over half of them prisoners. The Central Powers of Germany and Austria-Hungary had lost a total of nearly one million, a grim fact of the theatre's impact on the war.

Across Hertfordshire, hundreds of families began to receive War Office telegrams relaying the news that their loved ones had lost their lives, whilst thousands more would bring news of the sick and wounded. For many men and women from the county there would be a bestowal of a vast range of awards, varying from long service to outstanding gallantry, most of which had been achieved in the face of intense adversity.

NEW YEAR'S DISASTER – THE SINKING OF HMS *FORMIDABLE*

At 2.00 am on New Year's Day 1915 two torpedoes fired from the German submarine U-24, captained by Lieutenant Rudolph 'Rudi' Schneider, slammed into HMS *Formidable* some 20 miles off Start Point, Devon. The first torpedo hit the number one boiler port side; a second explosion caused the ship to list heavily to starboard. Huge waves 30 feet high lashed the stricken ship, with strong winds, rain and hail sinking it in less than two hours.

Captain Loxley, his second-in-command Commander Ballard and the signaller stayed at their posts throughout, sending flares and rockets off at regular intervals. There

Chaplain Reverend G Brooke Robinson.

was no panic, the men waiting calmly for the lifeboats to be lowered, but many of the boats were smashed as they were lowered into the water, killing all occupants, or else were swamped and sank. The chaplain, the Reverend George Brooke Robinson, who was formerly Curate of Burton Bradstock, went down with the ship, risking

HMS *Formidable*.

his life by going below to find cigarettes. Suddenly the ship gave a tremendous lurch, the captain shouted, 'Lads, this is the last, all hands for themselves, and may God bless you and guide you to safety.' He then walked to the forebridge, lit a cigarette and, with his terrier Bruce on duty at his side, waited for the end, true to the traditions of the Royal Navy.

One pinnace with 70 men on board was picked up by the trawler *Provident*, 15 miles off Berry Head. A second pinnace took another 71 men. This boat was soon half-filled with water as the men desperately bailed – with boots, caps, even a blanket; anything that came to hand. One seaman sat over a hole in the boat from the time they started away to the time of rescue. The enormous swell was terrifying, but morale was kept up by any means, through humour and singing. The survivors unanimously agreed they owed their lives to Leading Seaman Carroll, coxswain, who continued to cheer and inspire, not allowing them to sink into despair. When dawn broke, the survivors were still out of sight of land. A liner was seen in the distance, and a total of eleven other craft throughout the day. However, the pounding seas and huge waves hid the pinnace from sight. Eventually, night fell, still with relentless gales and no sign of rescue.

Blackout restrictions were in force, but there were two accounts of seamen seeing light coming from the shore. Petty Officer Bing saw a red light seven miles away which could have been the Lyme harbour light, and J. H. Taplin, another survivor, saw a sudden bright light shine out three miles off, which may have been from the Assembly Rooms cinema. The machine had broken down and the operator examining it shone the lamp through the window for a second or two.

The pinnace was first seen in Lyme by Miss Gwen Harding and her parents, walking home along Marine Parade after dining out with friends. She glimpsed the outline of a boat; her mother confirmed her suspicions and the alarm was raised. So began the rescue. Of the 71 men in the pinnace, 48 were brought ashore alive, 6 were dead on arrival on shore, 14 died during the 22 hours the men fought for survival and were buried at sea, and 3 died after landing.

The Pilot Boat Inn became rescue headquarters. Mrs Atkins, the landlady, took many survivors in. Her dog Lassie drew attention to Seaman Cowan, laid on the floor for dead, by licking his face. Many of the townsfolk brought food and blankets. Others took men into their homes to rest and recuperate, while those needing medical aid were sent to hospital. The dead were placed in the entrance to the cinema, a part of the old Assembly Rooms.

Tom Walker, a survivor of the sinking, told his story of survival and felt he would not have lived had it not been for the chaplain's example and assistance. Tom was 18 years of age at the time. He had recently been advanced to Able Seaman and received 'back pay' that included a new gold sovereign. He was keeping this for his mother, in his kit locker between decks. On the night of the sinking Tom was on deck. He remembered it being 'a bright, moonlit night'. The ship was stationary, carrying out the exercise 'pick up survivors'. He heard and felt the shudder of the first torpedo without realising what it was. The second torpedo caused the ship to list to starboard. Then the pipe, *'all hands muster on the quarterdeck.'*

On the quarterdeck he joined the men waiting to go to the boats. Oddly, a few of them were reluctant to leave the ship. Tom shared this feeling; leaving his sovereign behind may have been an influence! He decided to set off for his kit locker. Between decks the illumination was poor; this, coupled with the ship's erratic movements, made the journey slow and tedious. Tom had 'thoughts' about this predicament. He returned to the quarterdeck to find it deserted. The boats had left the ship.

One boat was still quite close; he could not recognise people's faces. Why did they not acknowledge his shouts and waves? They were determinedly pulling away from the ship. He was alone. As if in answer to a prayer, the ship's chaplain arrived on the quarterdeck. A huge feeling of relief ensued. Thankfully the chaplain seemed to know intuitively what to do: Stay on the ship. Wait for their escort to come to them. He was confident that his friend, the First Lieutenant of one of the escort cruisers, would get to them when he discovered that he (the chaplain) was missing. The chaplain had officiated at this officer's wedding; Tom thought they may have been brothers-in-law. The weather continued to deteriorate. The ship was, by now, low in the water, heaving and wallowing in rough seas. The starboard side three parts under water; holding fast on the quarterdeck was precarious. They awaited the moment they dare scramble up to the port guardrails, onto the port side; then, as the ship 'turned turtle', clambered onto the ship's bottom. They rested there for a few minutes then struck out into the sea and held onto a wooden boom that came within range. It was at this time that the ship's propeller struck Tom's left ankle. He felt the blow, not the pain. He hoped that there was still a foot at the end of the leg. They set about securing themselves to the boom as best they could. Large amounts of air from the ship surfaced near them. Their attempts to paddle a safe distance away proved futile; then, as if to please, the ship glided away and disappeared from sight. The large swell running at the time caused the chaplain to lose his grip on the boom and he was not seen again.

Dawn was barely noticeable, visibility was poor, sleep beckoned, moral bottomed. Where, oh where is that escort? Rescue came when Tom had already been in the water for over 14 hours. He was unaware of the escort's arrival and thought he was dreaming. Someone was shouting, *'Formidable … Formidable … Formidable,'* quite close to him. He looked up to see the escort's 'welcome party' looking down on him from the deck. Lines were thrown and Tom had difficulty detaching himself from the boom. He managed to secure himself to a line and was hoisted aboard the escort. On board, Tom was bundled down to the mess deck and rubbed dry on a mess table. The doctor assured him that his left foot was still there and he would soon be in hospital. Later he was taken up and put in a bunk in an officer's cabin. He refused a tot of rum offered to him (having promised his mother that he would never drink). He was left undisturbed until the following day.

This detailed report of the sinking was taken from the *Western Times* on 4th January 1915. Chaplain The Reverend George Brooke Robinson is commemorated on the Chatham Naval Memorial, Kent.

Quick Fact

The following Hertfordshire men are known to have been lost in the sinking of HMS *Formidable*:

Royal Navy
Mechanician John BYGRAVE of Waterford, aged 28.
Ordinary Seaman George GROOM of Little Wymondley, aged 18.
Stoker 1st Class Richard Martin O'DELL of Hitchin, aged 25.

Royal Marine Light Infantry
Captain John Cyril DEED of St. Albans, aged 38.
Private George William COLLINS of St. Albans, aged 36.

A VICTORIA CROSS FOR TRING – PRIVATE EDWARD BARBER VC

The Victoria Cross is the highest and most prestigious award of the British honours system. The origins of the VC, as it is known, can be traced back to 1854, when Britain found itself fighting a major war against Russia. At this time there were no awards available to acknowledge the heroic actions of the ordinary British serviceman. Other European countries already had awards for their armed forces that did not discriminate against class or rank, and so, in 1856 Queen Victoria ordered the War Office to strike a new medal, the Victoria Cross, which was made open to all members of

Private Edward Barber VC.

the British armed forces regardless of rank. The award was to be backdated to 1854 in order to recognise acts of bravery from the Crimean War.

The Naval version originally had a navy blue ribbon, which continued until the end of the Great War when the same purple ribbon was adopted by all services. Of the 1354 awards since 1856, 832 have gone to the Army, 107 to the Navy, 31 to the RAF, 10 to the Royal Marines and 4 to civilians. Bars denoting a second award have been issued on just three occasions. The facility for posthumous awards, made retrospective to 1856, began in 1902 and was confirmed in 1907, while the early practice of forfeitures (eight between 1863 and 1908) was discontinued after the First World War. Each VC is still

Victoria Cross.

made by the same London jewellers, Hancocks & Co, from the bronze of Chinese cannons captured from the Russians at the siege of Sebastopol, large ingots of which are stored at the army's Central Ordnance Depot at Donnington.

A recommendation for the VC is normally issued by an officer at regimental level or equivalent, and has to be supported by three witnesses, although this has been waived on occasion. The recommendation is then passed up the military hierarchy until it reaches the Secretary of State for Defence. The recommendation is then laid before the monarch who approves the award with his or her signature. Victoria Cross awards are always announced in *The London Gazette* with the single exception of the award to the American Unknown Soldier in 1921.

Edward Barber was born on 10 June 1893, the son of William and Sarah Barber of Miswell Lane, Tring. After leaving school, he began his working life as a bricklayer's labourer, enlisting in the army in October 1911. After three years of service Edward was due to be transferred to the army reserve and was considering leaving to join the police. However, the outbreak of the First World War put paid to any career change and Edward, who stood at 6′ 2″ tall and was described as "a man of buoyant spirits and iron will, reckless to a degree, and absolutely without fear" became a member of the 1st Battalion, Grenadier Guards. Edward left the shores of England on 6 October 1914, arriving at Zeebrugge the following day.

Barber earned his VC at the battle of Neuve Chapelle on 12 March 1915, where in a bid to demonstrate British commitment to the Allied cause, the commander-in-chief, Field Marshal Sir John French, ordered General Sir Douglas Haig, the GOC 1st Army to carry out the first independent British attack on the Western Front, an advance on the Aubers Ridge, which ran from the southwest to the northeast, north of La Bassée. This was to take place between 10 and 12 March 1915.

The attack on the morning of 10 March 1915 appeared to be succeeding and the infantry captured Neuve Chapelle itself, but not all the German machine guns had been knocked out by the preliminary bombardment and after three hours the advance stalled. An intense fight took place over the next two days and on 12 March the British made an assault on German lines, with the 1st Battalion, Grenadier Guards supporting the 2nd Battalion, Scots Guards and the 2nd Battalion, Border Regiment to the north of the Yorkshire Regiment. This attack stalled after the 2nd Battalion, Border Regiment suffered heavy losses from machine guns in the Quadrilateral, a German redoubt between Moated Grange Farm and Mauquissart.

However, following an artillery barrage, the Scots Guards and the Border Regiment captured the Quadrilateral, taking 400 prisoners. While the 1st Grenadier Guards became lost in the maze of old communication trenches, a party of their brigade reserve bombers and a company of the 2nd Battalion, Wiltshire Regiment succeeded in weaving their way rapidly through old German trenches in no man's land and overwhelming the enemy in 40 yards of trench, having achieved complete surprise.

Edward Barber had run ahead of his grenade party, throwing bombs at the enemy. Many of them surrendered and by the time the grenade party caught up with Barber, they found him alone, surrounded by surrendered Germans. An extract from *The London Gazette* dated 19 April, 1915, records the following:

> *For most conspicuous bravery on 12 March 1915 at Neuve Chapelle. He ran speedily in front of the grenade company to which he belonged, and threw bombs on the enemy with such effect that a very great number of them at once surrendered. When the grenade party reached Private Barber, they found him quite alone and unsupported, with the enemy surrendering all about him.*

Lance Corporal Wilfred Dolby Fuller and Private Edward Barber particularly distinguished themselves, and were amongst the nine VCs that were awarded for acts of gallantry during the battle.

Edward's body was found by Fuller, who wrote to Edward's cousin explaining, *'while doing his duty he was picked off by a German sniper. The bullet penetrated his brain, death being instantaneous. Your cousin feared nothing and he was the finest man we had, both in wit and courage.'*

Although Wilfred Fuller had found Barber's body, it was never recovered and he was officially reported missing on 14 March. In February 1916 he was officially classified as dead.

The following interview with Mrs Barber for a London newspaper provides a very moving account of Edward.

The announcement we were able to make last week that Private Edward Barber, of the Grenadier Guards, had been awarded the V.C. for conspicuous bravery at Neuve Chapelle was confirmed in Monday's 'London Gazette'.

Edward Barber and his family are well known in the town, and the greatest interest was manifested when it was announced that a Tring man had won the highest military honour that the King has the power to bestow.

Barber's father is employed in the local gas works, and the V.C. himself was a bricklayer's labourer before he joined the army at the age of 18. Curiously enough, both the father and mother are short of stature, while Private Barber is a giant of 6ft. 2½ins.

'Although we are all very proud of Ted,' said his mother, 'I think none of us is a bit surprised that he gained the Victoria Cross. Even as a boy Ted never feared anything or anyone, and would go through with a thing he had decided on, whatever the opposition. He was a rare fighter with his fists, too, and woe betide the boy, whatever his size or age, who offended him or any of his friends in his presence. I do not say that he was not full of mischief, but in school and out of it he was sometimes blamed for things he did not do. He had his schooling at the Church School here, and did quite well.'

Mrs. Barber pointed to a stack of bright-coloured boys' prize books which decorated one side of the small window. The inside covers of the books bore such inscriptions as 'Awarded to Edward Barber for diligence and attendance. Tring Boys' National School, 1903–4,' and 'Awarded to Edward Barber for regularity and conduct. 1905–6.' 'Ted was 21 years of age last June,' his mother continued. It will be remembered that the official statement said that Private Barber 'ran speedily' in front of his grenade company and threw bombs on the enemy.

'Several people have asked us if Ted was fleet of foot," said Mrs. Barber. "He certainly was, and as a little boy he could run like a hare. He was also a fine swimmer. We have heard nothing from him about Neuve Chapelle, or the act which won him the Cross.'

'I knew Ted Barber well,' the local hairdresser told me, 'and he certainly was a rare lad for pluck and mischief. Swimming on Sundays in the reservoir of which Lord Rothschild, as lord of the manor, had the reserved rights, was one of his exploits. But there was nothing bad or mean about Ted. He was just chock-full of mischief.' Private Barber's relatives and friends are much disturbed by two messages from the front about the new V.C. One letter, from an N.C.O., states that Private Barber has been killed by a German sniper's bullet. Another soldier has written from the front to say that the V.C. is among the missing. Official confirmation on both reports, however, is up to the time of writing, lacking.

In addition to the Victoria Cross, Edward Barber was awarded the 1914 Star, British War Medal and Victory Medal. His name is listed on the Le Touret Memorial, France, and on the Tring War Memorial. In 1965 Barber's Walk in Tring was named in his honour and a portrait of Barber hangs in Tring council offices.

PRIVATE EDWARD WARNER VC – A VICTORIA CROSS FOR ST. ALBANS

Private Edward Warner VC.

Another Hertfordshire soldier to be awarded the Victoria Cross was Edward 'Ted' Warner who was born on 18 November 1883 at 36 Cannon Street, St. Albans; the only son of Mark and Charlotte Warner. His father was a platelayer foreman on the railways who was born in Wheathampstead, and his mother, Charlotte (née Barber) was from London.

By 1901 the 17-year-old was working as a straw-hat stiffener and, most likely inspired by the South African War stories that impressed so many young men into joining the army around that time, he enlisted in the Bedfordshire Regiment late in 1903, and was given the regimental number 7602. He served in India before the battalion returned home in 1908. His term in the regulars completed, he became a reservist and was employed by the Deep Well Boring Works for St. Albans Council, as well as the Post Office Telephones Department.

Ted Warner rejoined the 1st Battalion, Bedfordshire Regiment in Ireland as it prepared itself for war service. He landed in France with the battalion on 16 August 1914 amongst the first wave of British troops to arrive on the Western Front. He fought with them at the Battles of Mons, Le Cateau, the Marne, the Aisne, at Givenchy and Ypres before winter set in. After their first winter in the shallow, temporary trenches, the battalion was stationed at the tactically critical mound known as Hill 60, made from the soil removed during the construction of the nearby railway line. In April 1915 it was wrestled from the grasp of the Germans, but because of its commanding view of the surrounding area, the enemy made determined efforts to retake the position.

Ted and his comrades took over the firing trenches on 25 April 1915, which were to the left of Hill 60. After being in the line for six days, they were extremely tired, having had very little sleep or rest. Early on the morning of 1 May 1915 the Germans suddenly attacked with gas shells, in conjunction with a concentrated artillery bombardment. Although the battalion was used to sheltering from German shells by this time, they could do little about the gas and were forced back. Although some German soldiers attacked the battalion positions, many of them were forced back as the gas blew into their own positions.

The Bedfordshires in Trench 46 were driven out, leaving the position completely undefended. However, it would appear that Edward was not happy about events and jumped into the empty trench by himself, keeping the Germans that were attacking from entering and taking control of the trench. Despite the effects of the gas, exhaustion and repeated attempts by the enemy to gain a footing in this small section of the battlefield, the completely isolated Private Warner simply kept on fighting. When he had the chance, he ran back to the battalion and gathered some men to go back with him to carry on defending the trench. He was eventually overcome by the effects of the gas that he had inhaled and he had to be carried back to the First Aid post for treatment.

Ted's friend, Fred Brimm, reported that *'Ted was quite sensible to within half an hour of his death. He knew he was going and only wanted another chance to get at them again. His last words were "They've gone and done for me, the cowards."'*

The citation for Ted's posthumous Victoria Cross, published in *The London Gazette* on 29 June 1915 reads:

> *For most conspicuous bravery near 'Hill 60' on 1 May 1915. After Trench 46 had been vacated by our troops, consequent on a gas attack, Private Warner entered it single-handed in order to prevent the enemy taking possession. Reinforcements were sent to Private Warner, but could not reach him owing to the gas. He then came back and brought up more men, by which time he was completely exhausted, but the trench was held until the enemy's attack ceased. This very gallant soldier died shortly afterwards from the effects of gas poisoning.*

Sadly, Edward's final resting place was lost in the fighting that raged across the ground for a further three years and today he has no known grave. He is remembered on the Menin Gate Memorial to the Missing in Ypres, Belgium and is also listed on the St. Albans War memorial in Hertfordshire. His Victoria Cross is displayed at the Bedfordshire and Hertfordshire Regimental Museum in Wardown Park, Luton, along with his 1914 Star, Victory and British War Medals.

THE BULLARD BROTHERS

Sadly, a family losing more than one son in the Great War was not altogether uncommon. Many families paid a high price, losing more than one loved one over the four-year conflict. One example, brought into a *Herts at War* event, is that of the Bullard family of Therfield, Hertfordshire.

The Bullards were not unusual in having a large family at the turn of the century, James and Lucy Bullard together raised 12 children including seven sons, six of whom would see service in the Great War. The national census of 1911 records the Bullards as living at Dane End, Therfield, Hertfordshire, with each of the sons working as farm labourers, as so many rural families did.

The tranquillity of the rural life was broken in the late summer of 1914, when the possibility of war, which had loomed large over the continent for weeks, finally became a reality. In a wave of national fervour that swept the country over the next few months, millions of men rallied to the colours, enlisting to serve King and Country in the great adventure that was to follow. The Bullard boys were no different; five sons enlisted in the first few months, leaving only the two underage boys at home, doubtless anxiously waiting their chance to join in on their siblings' glorious adventures.

With the passing of time, we now know that the reality of the conflict was very different, although to those early enlisters in 1914, there is no doubt most saw this as an exciting adventure and an opportunity not to be missed. As the rapidly expanding British Army rushed to make up the huge numerical deficit on the Western Front, men like the Bullard brothers were hastily trained and prepared for war. Two of the brothers had had been army reservists prior to the outbreak of war and so proceeded quickly to the front. By mid-1915 five of James' sons were serving abroad, with another training in the UK.

Albert Edward Bullard

Although Albert had only joined the army in May 1915, he was immediately selected, along with his comrades in the 4th Battalion, Worcestershire Regiment, to take part in the infamous Gallipoli Campaign of 1915. He arrived on the peninsula on 3 July 1915, and just a few weeks later, on 8 August 1915, the Worcesters took part in what can only be described as a disastrous attack across the infamous 'Vineyards' in one of three battles for the village of Krithia. The unit war diary highlights the carnage of that day all too clearly:

> *Moved into firing line to assault the Vineyard. 24 officers and 800 other ranks strong. Left details behind (about 50 men) and attacked at 3.50 pm, both flanks cut down by MG fire crossing 300 yards of no man's land. Very few of them made it to Turkish trenches unwounded and those who did were attacked by large numbers of defenders and stood no chance. After 1 hour, just 30 men led by a Sgt were holding on in trenches. 12 survivors returned. Casualties 16 officers 752 other ranks.*

The casualties sustained by the 4th Worcesters that day were amongst the very highest of the Great War. Somewhere in this engagement Albert Bullard, married to Elizabeth Bullard and father of three young children, was killed, his body never to be found.

The Vineyards of Krithia as they can be seen today.

Back home in Therfield, James and Lucy Bullard were told their son was missing in action, and would have no doubt waited anxiously for news. Sadly when it did come, it was reporting Albert's death. His name is recorded on the Helles Memorial, Turkey, and he was awarded the 1915 Star, British War Medal and Victory Medal.

The following year, 1916, is today known for one of the most tumultuous events in which the British Army was involved, the 'Somme Campaign'; a series of battles on the Western Front that, over several months, would take a heavy toll on many families across Hertfordshire, including the bereaved Bullard family. As the British and French Armies made a joint effort in a large-scale offensive planned to begin in July 1916, brothers James, Sidney and William Ralph were all serving in different battalions of the Bedfordshire Regiment. It is fair to say that the British Offensive did not start well, with 19,240 men killed in the first day alone, making it the bloodiest day in the history of the British Army.

William Ralph Bullard

The next news received from the front came in the form of a letter sent to Lucy Bullard by a man in the Bedfordshire Regiment who was serving with William Ralph Bullard. It said:

William Ralph Bullard.

> *It is with deep regret that I have to tell you that poor old Bill has been killed. He was killed on the 8th (Saturday) by a shell. Bill was hit and buried by the trench falling in. They got him out and took him to the dressing station but he died soon after reaching there. Poor old Bill was greatly respected by everyone who knew him and I have lost as good a pal as any man ever had.*

The loss of Bill was compounded later that month by the news that both James, the oldest son, and his brother Walter were wounded on the same day whilst serving with the Bedfordshire Regiment on 27 July. Walter was wounded in the arm and James very badly in the arm, abdomen, back, leg and neck.

Sydney Bullard

Private Sidney Bullard.

Within days, another of the dreaded telegrams would arrive at the family home in Dane End, informing the grief-stricken parents that their only other son serving in France was missing in action. Private Sydney Bullard of the 1st Battalion, Bedfordshire Regiment was last seen when his unit took part in a night reconnaissance of German lines on 27 July. He was, on that day, serving with his older brother James, and whilst James was very severely wounded, his brother Sidney was reported missing in action. He would remain missing for many years.

For the boys' parents back home, the torment of having loved ones 'missing' should not be underestimated. At the end of September 1916 James and Lucy Bullard now had two sons killed, two wounded – one very severely – and another missing in action. Their youngest son Frank, also known as Benjamin, was only 17 years old and still in training in the UK.

Of the two sons wounded, James was so badly hit that he was sent home and released from military service, his surviving military record reporting 'gunshot wound (GSW) left thigh, foot, back, left arm, right finger'. James was assessed as having 50 per cent disability upon discharge from the army.

The other wounded brother, Walter, who had been hit by shellfire in the left arm, eventually recovered in time to be posted back out to France in October 1916.

Private James Bullard.

It was here that in April 1917 Walter, back with his comrades in the 4th Battalion, Bedfordshire Regiment, took part in the Battle of Arras. On the evening of 15 April 1917 the 4th Bedfordshires undertook a night reconnaissance mission near the small French village of Gavrelle, preparatory to a planned assault a few days later. In what descended into a chaos, 55 men were killed or wounded, and when the remainder of the patrol made it back to friendly lines, Walter Thomas Bullard was nowhere to be seen. Yet again, the Bullard family faced the horror of uncertainty for some months, before finally receiving the feared news that Walter, too, had been killed in action that day.

By mid-1917 Albert, Walter and William were reported as killed, Sydney was missing in action (later officially reported as killed), James was discharged from the army seriously wounded and the youngest son, Frank, was just finishing his training with the Rifle Brigade. It perhaps should come as no surprise that Lucy Bullard was somewhat fearful for the fate of her youngest boy, her 'Benjamin', who was not yet 18 but due for service at the front nevertheless.

Private Walter Thomas Bullard.

Clearly in a very anxious state, she contacted the War Office to highlight her family's sacrifice in the desperate hope that her boy would be spared the carnage of the Western Front. The local paper, the *Royston Crowe*, published an article in 1917, highlighting the plight of the family.

Sadly for Mrs Bullard, there would be no last minute reprieve, the army stating that the need for extra manpower was too great. It is impossible today to understand the grief that this response must have caused, and the anxiety she suffered as her son sailed off to war in 1918.

Mrs Doreen Oakman, daughter of Frank, still retains a treasured letter written by her father from France on 17 March 1918 to his sister, which states:

Dear sister,

Just a line in answer to your letter which I received today hoping it will find you in the best of health as it leaves me at present. I had a letter from mother the other day, she said she had a bad hand but the others were all alright. Is there a chap in Royston named Shepherd got the VC because I saw his name in the Sunday pictorial and it said his home was at Royston, I didn't know if it was the one near us. Have you heard from Mabel or Milly lately? Remember me to Win when you write to her again. I don't think I have any more to say this time so I must close with love.

From your loving brother Frank.'

The bottom right corner of the same letter contains an added note in a different hand which states:

'I have been wounded, I am now at CCS (Casualty Clearing Station).'

Presumably this additional note would have caused quite some alarm to those at home.

Morlancourt No.1 British Cemetery on the Somme. The last resting place of Private William Ralph Bullard.

Rifleman Frank Bullard photographed in 1917 just prior to leaving for war.

The following week an article appeared in the *Royston Crow* newspaper in April 1918 relating to the sixth son of Mr and Mrs Bullard of Therfield, Hertfordshire.

Frank's daughter later recalled her father talking about his wounds: *'He was lying in hospital in Glasgow and remembered seeing his mother appear from around the curtain and seeing the sadness in her face. He decided then and there that she would not lose another son and that he would live, despite his life-threatening wounds.'*

Thankfully Frank did recover, and several months after the war had come to an end was able to return home to Therfield to support his parents in what was quite one of the heaviest prices paid by any family in the Great War.

In a moving example of fortunes in war, the family of Samuel Bullard, the brother of James Senior, also had seven sons, each one fighting in the Great War. All seven of his sons returned; a stark contrast to the price paid by their closest kin.

Of the four sons lost to Mr and Mrs Bullard, three have no known grave, remembered only on Memorials to the Missing. Only William Ralph is buried in a known location, lying today in Morlancourt British Cemetery in the Somme.

THE ALDENHAM MYSTERY – PRIVATE WILLIAM DAVID SMITH

William David Smith was born in Kimpton, Hertfordshire, in 1883 as the eldest son of David and Eliza Smith. The family lived at Kimpton Bottom, where David worked on the farm, and Eliza managed the family, which also included: Rose Mary (born in 1885), Bertram John (born in 1887), Edith Ellen (born in 1888) and Anne (born in 1890).

A family photo brought into a *Herts at War* event depicts a young William wearing a Royal Engineers uniform, most likely taken at the turn of the century, when he would have been serving for 7 years in the army, followed by a further 5 years in the reserve.

His younger brother, Bertram John Smith, served in the 4th Battalion, Bedfordshire Regiment for a short period of time. He joined the regiment at St. Albans on 31 October 1906 with the regimental number 5727. At the time Bertram was living at Marble Ark, Radlett, Hertfordshire, and was working as a general labourer for a local company named Goodchild & Jefferies. He was discharged the same year.

William, working as a general labourer for a sewer contractor, married Alice Rowson in the autumn of 1908, and by 1911 the couple were living at No. 3 The Flats, Radlett, Hertfordshire, with their 2-year-old daughter, Edith Ellen, and their son, Herbert William, who was just 1 year old. Another daughter, Dorothy, was born in 1913.

Private William David Smith.

Unfortunately, a service record for William has not survived, but there are quite a number of facts that are known with regard to his service in the army. He served with the 2nd Battalion, Middlesex Regiment, who were part of the 23rd Brigade of the 8th Division, and was given the regimental number S/7422. The prefix 'S' was issued to men who served with the special reserve or extra reserve, and was most likely given to William on the basis that he had served with the Royal Engineers prior to the First World War. It is interesting to note that his experience in sewer work would have made William a possible candidate for service with the Royal Engineers tunnelling companies. The document produced by the Graves Registration Unit, following his death, initially stated that he was a member of the 173rd Tunnelling Company, who were attached to the same corps as the 8th Division,

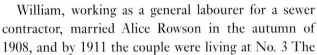

Graves Registration Document for William David Smith showing the amendments made to his unit.

but this has been amended and indicates that William was, in fact, serving with Middlesex Regiment when he was killed.

Throughout January 1915 the battalion received a series of reinforcements, one of whom was William Smith, who arrived in France on 4 January. This is established by his medal index card, which confirms the date of his arrival on the Western Front, and the fact that he was entitled to three campaign medals, the 1915 Star, the British War Medal and the Victory Medal, each of which would have had his name, rank, regimental number and regiment inscribed upon them.

Medal Index Card for William David Smith.

The unit war diary shows that one officer and 34 other ranks joined the battalion on 19 January 1915. Given that most infantrymen would be held at a base depot for about two weeks before being posted to their battalion, it is reasonable to assume that William was amongst this contingent. At the time he joined the battalion, it was located at Pont Richon, and the following day the troops marched into frontline trenches at Rue du Bacquerot, taking over positions that were held by the West Yorkshire Regiment. William would have spent those cold winter months rotating in and out of the frontline trenches, where he would have witnessed many of his comrades being killed and wounded. In the period between 19 January and 10 March 1915 the battalion suffered 39 men killed, and very many more being wounded. On top of this, William would have also seen a great number of men leaving the battalion as a consequence of sickness, promotion or other personnel changes.

The Battle of Neuve Chappelle

The Battle of Neuve Chapelle was the first major attack launched by the British Army in 1915, following its emergence from the rigours of winter warfare in the trenches. The village of Neuve Chapelle lies on the road between Bethune, Fleurbaix and Armentieres, near its junction with the Estaires – La Bassée road. The frontlines ran parallel with the Bethune–Armentieres road, a little way to the east of the village. The ground here is flat and cut by many small drainage ditches.

At 11.00 pm on the night of 9 March the 2nd Middlesex marched out of Estaires, with 'D' Company leading, and headed for the trenches west of Neuve Chapelle, from which the attack was to take place.

The night was wet, with light snow, which later turned to damp mist. On arriving at Rue du Bacquerot the battalion halted and a hot meal was served

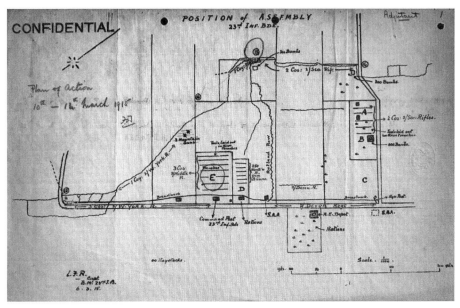

Point 'E' is where William and the men of the 2nd Middlesex waited to take part in the attack.

to the men whilst the officers congregated in a small house nearby. The march was resumed across country to a line of shallow trenches in an apple orchard near the Rue Tilleloy, where three companies were ordered to lie down, whilst the company detailed to make the initial attack crept forward to the assembly trenches known as Point 15.

The following morning, at about 4.30 am, Lieutenant Colonel Hayes reported to 23rd Brigade Headquarters that his battalion was ready and in its assembly positions. All companies on a four-platoon frontage, one company at Point 15 and three at Point 'E'. Two companies of the 2nd Scottish Rifles were on the right of the 2nd Middlesex, and one company of West Yorkshires on the left. By 5.30 am, the Brigade Diary records that all movement had ceased and *'there has apparently been no hitch. Enemy very quiet and appear to have no inkling of our preparations.'*

Just after dawn broke, about 5.30 am, a German aeroplane, flying low, passed from north to south over the British lines. It was uncertain if the observer had seen the closely packed trenches, which were shallow and very crowded. Time crept on, and as the hour of attack approached, the enemy gave no sign that they expected an attack. In order to give the enemy no clue to the impending battle, the guns had been ordered to continue the usual process of firing upon the German trenches until 7.30 am. At that hour, however, a general bombardment of the enemy's positions, bringing heavy artillery fire down on their wire entanglements, especially in front of Point 15, was set to begin.

At 7.30 am the thunderous sound of a single large calibre gun broke upon the ears of the lines of waiting troops. This was *Granny*, a huge 15-inch howitzer, firing the signal for the artillery bombardment to open. *Granny* was situated in an apple orchard in Labourse, south of the La Bassée Canal. Immediately there was an ear-splitting roar, shaking the ground and deafening the troops as they stood ready in the frontline trenches to go 'over the top', or lay on the ground in their support or reserve positions. For half an hour, the waiting troops watched the inferno across no man's land; a wall of dust and smoke – 50 to 100 feet high – had shot up from the German trenches as the shells fell thick and fast upon the enemy's barbed wire and frontline. It seemed impossible that any living thing could emerge from the wreckage created by that awful tornado of smoke and shrapnel.

Timber and sandbags, clods of dirt, heads, arms, legs and mangled bodies were flung about in horrible confusion. The upper half of a German officer, with the cap thrust down over the distorted face, fell in the frontline British trenches. Only with great difficulty could the British officers restrain their men and persuade them to keep their heads down until that dreadful half hour ended. Fascinated, even though the shells from British guns engaged in wire cutting passed barely a few feet above them, they could hardly turn their eyes from the frightful things happening across no man's land, where the Germans were being driven stark raving mad from artillery fire like they had never before experienced.

The 2nd Middlesex, with the Scottish Rifles on their right and one company of 2nd West Yorkshires on their left, watched and waited for the hour of attack. At 8.05 am whistles sounded all along the British line and at the same time, shells began to burst further ahead as the guns had lengthened their range to the village itself. As if on parade, the troops forming the frontline rose to their feet and dashed out into no man's land towards the German trenches. A sheet of flame flashed from behind the enemy's wire and a murderous machine gun fire from Points 21 and 76 swept the ranks of the advancing men. Along the front of the Indian Corps, the 25th Brigade and 'B' Company of the Scottish Rifles, the terrible wire entanglement had been mostly cut by the British guns. But in front of 'A' Company of the Scotsmen, and the sector allotted to the 2nd Middlesex, the enemy's wire was practically uncut.

'*The frontline advanced,*' said Sergeant Daws of the 2nd Battalion, watching the advance from the third line, '*and as they leave their trenches we shout, "Go on the Middlesex! Go on the Die-Hards!"*' They were met by terrible machine gun fire. '*Of the first wave of Middlesex men few reached the German wire, but these tore in vain at the thick entanglements until their hands were torn and bleeding and their uniforms in rags.*' The second line was then ordered forward and as the men, led by their officers, sprang over the top into no man's land, the sight which met them was appalling; a long lane of dead and dying, lying about in horrible confusion, marked the advance of the first wave right up to the German wire, where a few frantic survivors could still be seen tearing madly at the entanglements. The second line met the same fate as the first, only a few gallant men reaching the German wire, from behind which the enemy's machine guns and rifles were spitting out death.

An order ran down the third line: Get ready! Advance! *'We ran as fast as the spongy ground would allow us,'* said Sergeant Daws, continuing his story, *'and reached an old trench of ours which was full of Devons.* (The 2nd Devonshire Regiment was on the right of the 3rd Company of 2nd Middlesex at Point 'E'.) *We then ran up the trench, and here I saw poor Lieutenant MacFarlane, the tallest and most popular officer of ours, killed. He led the bomb-throwers and made too good a target.'* Apparently up to this time the third line had remained in the old frontline, but soon these men also received orders to go forward. *'A whistle sounds, and over the parapet we go. Go on Die-Hards! ... The sight which met our eyes almost staggered us, our poor first and second lines lying in all positions. Then we saw red. We reached the barbed wire, trampled on it, cut and hacked it, the barbs cutting us in all places. We were beaten back.'*

Although three attempts had been made in the face of a murderous fire, the attack had failed. The preliminary bombardment had failed to cut the barbed wire in front of the left sector of trenches from which the attack was made. A further bombardment was necessary, and Colonel Hayes was fortunate in getting a message back, asking for additional artillery bombardment.

At 11.45 am the guns again plastered the enemy's wire entanglements and forward trenches. This was followed by another attempt by the Middlesex to secure the German trenches. This time they were successful and managed to secure the German trenches. Bombing parties immediately moved along the trench in the direction of Point 60. At the crossroads, just before reaching Point 60, a party of Germans who had been sniping the men of the Middlesex, indicated that they intended to surrender. But on seeing that the foremost party of Middlesex bombers numbered only one officer and six men, the Germans ducked down in the trench again and reopened fire. Without hesitation, the Middlesex bombers pushed on, pelting the enemy with bombs, eventually driving the Germans out into the open, where they were caught by machine gun fire and shot down. The Middlesex men pressed forward to their objective, a large orchard north of the village (Point 6), where serious resistance was anticipate, but the Devons had already secured the position. With the Devonshire men and the remnants of the 2nd Middlesex, Point 6 was consolidated. They then helped the Royal Engineers to put the place in a state of defence. The time was now about 5.00 pm.

The whole of Neuve Chapelle had fallen, but at what cost? There were 8 officers killed and 8 wounded, one of whom died of his wounds three days later;

70 other ranks killed, 299 wounded and 89 missing were the losses amongst the other ranks of the 2nd Middlesex. 'A', 'B' and 'C' Companies were almost entirely wiped out.

A Quiet Period?

On 14 March 1915, William and the men of his battalion were relieved by the 13th London Regiment and marched back to billets at Rouge Croix. They remained here for a few days whilst reinforcing drafts were brought in to replace the men who had become casualties. A few days later, whilst addressing the 2nd Battalion, Sir John French said: *'I am proud of you. No regiment has upheld its traditions better than you, and I know that if called upon to repeat what you have done, you would not hesitate.'*

On 19 March, following a few days of rest, the battalion again entered the trenches. This time they were relieving the men of the West Yorkshire Regiment on the Rue Tilleloy. During this short stay in the trenches the battalion was to see another 6 men killed, and 10 wounded, mostly as a consequence of shellfire from German artillery. They left the trenches on 21 March 1915, and moved back to Pont Du Hem, after which they moved back to Fleurbaix. With the exception of three days between 29 and 31 March, where they again occupied trenches, the battalion spent its time in the reserve area.

Battle of Aubers Ridge

Throughout April 1915 the battalion again spent its time moving in and out of frontline positions in the Fleurbaix – Neuve Chappelle area. They remained out of frontline positions for the first few days of May 1915, but then returned to the trenches in preparation for the Battle of Aubers Ridge.

This slight rise in the ground, barely 20 feet higher than the surrounding area, provided an observation advantage. The German lines in the immediate vicinity were very lightly defended.

The British attack was to be launched by General Sir Douglas Haig's First Army. It was intended to send in two attacks, to the north and south of Neuve Chapelle, with the hope that the two attacking forces could meet up behind the German frontlines. Haig had requested extra artillery to increase the strength of the 40-minute bombardment planned for the morning of 9 May, but all available artillery reserves had been sucked into the fighting at the second battle of Ypres, still raging just to the north.

The Germans had greatly strengthened their lines around Neuve Chapelle after they had been overrun during the recent battle, and the British artillery bombardment was simply not heavy enough to destroy the new German lines. The Battle of Aubers Ridge fits the popular image of a First World War battle better than most. The British troops went over the top early on the morning of 9 May and were cut down by German machine gun fire. The survivors, pinned down in no man's land, could make no significant progress, and early on 10 May Douglas Haig ended the offensive. The British suffered 11,000 casualties in one day of fighting on a narrow front. William Smith was to be one of those who survived the offensive, and lived to fight another day. The month of May had seen a further 109 men of the battalion become casualties on this part of the Western Front.

Killed by Shellfire?

The battalion spent June 1915 rotating in and out of frontline positions at Vangerie, this time suffering very few casualties. The unit war diary for July 1915 simply indicates that the battalion was in a location near Croix Blanche, and it is here that William was most likely killed by shellfire. The diary indicates that only three men were wounded in the period between 7 and 13 July. This gives rise to the question: was he in fact serving with the battalion at the time, or had he indeed been detached to the Royal Engineers?

Private William David Smith is buried in Grave III.C.3. at the Rue-Du-Bois Military Cemetery, Fleurbaix, France. His name is recorded in the Roll of Honour in Aldenham Parish Church, and on the Aldenham War memorial.

The grave of Private William David Smith at Rue-Du-Bois Military Cemetery, Fleurbaix, France.

Croix Blance, southwest of Fleurbaix, where William Smith was killed by shellfire.

OVER THE TOP – ALFRED ALEXANDER BURT VC

Alfred Alexander Burt was born on 3 March 1895 and was a resident of Port Vale in Hertford. He was a gas fitter for the Hertford Gas Company before the war and joined the Hertfordshire Regiment as a part-time Territorial Force soldier in 1911.

Corporal Alfred Burt VC.

Private Burt was mobilised with the battalion on 4 August 1914 and following initial training in Romford and Bury St. Edmunds, he went to the Western Front with the battalion on 6 November 1914. He served with the Hertfordshire Regiment throughout their first uncomfortable winter in the trenches, surviving the constant patrolling and raiding, as well as his involvement in the Battle of Festubert in May 1915. It was during the Battle of Loos in September 1915 that Alfred Burt, by then a Corporal, won the Victoria Cross.

On 27 September 1915 the battalion was lined up in their trenches waiting to go 'over the top' near the famous Cuinchy Brickstacks, close to the La Bassée Canal. Their role was to continue the general advance as part of the third day of the battle of Loos, making an advance following the release of chlorine gas onto German positions opposite. As the men of No. 2 Company waited expectantly for the order to advance, a German trench mortar barrage hit them and an incredibly powerful *minenwerfer* shell landed in their midst. It did not explode immediately so without thought, Alfred ran to it, held it firm with one foot, pulled the fuse out and threw it over the parapet before it could explode amongst his comrades. It was estimated that his selfless actions saved the lives of twenty or more of his comrades.

He was admitted to No. 19 Field Ambulance with myalgia on 11 November 1915, which then developed into influenza, so he was transferred to No. 11 Stationary Hospital at Rouen. Alfie was posted to No. 1 Infantry Base Depot on 30 November and did not return to his regiment until 23 January 1916. He was evacuated to England, having been gassed, on 2 February 1916, being placed on the strength of the administrative centre in Hertford. His VC was presented to Alfie by King George V at Buckingham Palace on 4 March 1916 and he was discharged on 31 March, being no longer fit for service.

Alfie married Jane Elizabeth West on 23 December 1916 at Hertford. His wife's younger brother, Private William Horace West, a native of Hertford serving with the 8th Battalion, Bedfordshire Regiment, had died of wounds two days earlier. The sad news arrived as they left the church. William is buried in Bethune Town Cemetery, France.

Alfred and Jane went on to have two children, Jenny May Burt (1917) and Alfred Victor Charles Burt (1920). Alfie returned to fitting for the Hertford Gas Company and was a member of the VC Guard at the interment of the Unknown Warrior on 11 November 1920. He rejoined the 1st Hertfordshire Regiment as a Private on 12 April 1922 and was appointed unpaid Lance Corporal on 29 July, but was discharged at his own request on 26 August 1925 when he moved to Chesham and became landlord of the New Inn.

Just before the Second World War Alfie returned to gas fitting and during the war worked for Arthur Lyon in Chesham, producing searchlights and generators. Poor health stopped any thoughts of him serving during the Second World War, although he was an ARP Warden for a time. He was amongst the Victoria Cross holders who attended the end of Second World War Victory Day Celebration Reception held at the Dorchester Hotel in London on 8 June 1946. The years took their toll and he was disabled from the early 1950s and was wheelchair bound by 1956, although he managed to attend the 100th anniversary of the inception of the Victoria Cross. Alfie died of lung cancer at Tindal General Hospital, Chesham on 9 June 1962, aged 67, and was cremated at West Hertfordshire Crematorium, Watford.

In addition to his VC, he was awarded the 1914 Star with 'Mons' clasp, British War Medal 1914–20, Victory Medal 1914–19, George VI Coronation Medal 1937 and Elizabeth II Coronation Medal 1953. The medals were gifted to the Bedfordshire and Hertfordshire Regimental Museum by his daughter in 1979 and are held at the Regimental Museum in Hertford. In commemoration, a street was named after him in Chesham to mark the bravery of this Hertfordshire-born soldier.

Alfred Burt VC in his later years.

CAPTAIN FERGUS BOWES-LYON

The outbreak of the First World War was declared on the 14th birthday of Lady Elizabeth Bowes-Lyon (later Queen Elizabeth The Queen Mother). Her birthday celebrations were most likely low-key as a result of the declaration of war. Out of her eight surviving siblings, three were serving officers in the army. Patrick, the oldest of the brothers who was titled Lord Glamis, was a major in the 1/5th Battalion, the Black Watch. Fergus was also an officer in the same regiment, and Michael was a Second Lieutenant in the Royal Scots. A fourth brother, John –

known as Jock – was a stockbroker but was to eventually join his older brother in the 1/5th Black Watch.

Patrick, Michael and John went to France with their regiments in November and December 1914. Fergus, however, had been held back in order to help train the 8th Battalion Black Watch – one of Kitchener's New Army battalions. This battalion, part of the 9th (Scottish) Division, arrived in France on 10 May 1915.

Meanwhile, the two brothers in the 1/5th Battalion had found themselves involved in the preparations for a major offensive. Their battalion was part of the 8th Division and was to be engaged in the Battle of Aubers Ridge which commenced on 9 May. It is, however, not certain how much of the fighting Jock was involved in. It would appear that just prior to the battle, Jock shot himself in the finger. This may have been entirely accidental of course, but such injuries were often considered to be highly suspicious as possible 'self-inflicted wounds'.

The Battle of Aubers Ridge was a failure for the British Army but later in the year a much larger offensive was to take place, in which Fergus was involved. The Battle of Loos was, by a significant margin, the biggest battle the British Expeditionary Force was involved in during 1915. The 9th (Scottish) Division, with Fergus's 8th Black Watch, was to attack the position known as the Hohenzollern Redoubt, a warren of trenches that surrounded the mining complex of Fosse 8. Although the troops who attacked on 25 September were initially able to penetrate the Hohenzollern Redoubt, German resistance was fierce and over the following days, only a small part of the redoubt remained in British hands. It was on the third day of the Battle, 27 September, that Fergus Bowes-Lyon was killed.

As with other families up and down the country, the shock of the death of a family member must have been severe. This tragedy was magnified after the war by the fact that Fergus's grave was lost and his name was added to the thousands of others commemorated on the Loos Memorial to the Missing, which surrounds Dud Corner Cemetery at Loos.

His grandson wrote to the War Graves Commission in November 2011 after having visited Quarry Cemetery, Vermelles. He produced contemporary evidence that his grandfather had been buried in the quarry and that a grave marker with his name on it was still in place at the end of the war. The Commission's grave registration documents were found to record his burial in the cemetery in 1920, but these documents were superseded by the final grave registration forms, dating from 1925, which do not include Captain Bowes-Lyon's name.

Captain Fergus Bowes-Lyon.

Under these circumstances, the Commission has agreed that the evidence for Captain Bowes-Lyon being buried in the cemetery is sufficient to allow the erection of a named headstone within the cemetery. The special memorial headstone to Captain Bowes-Lyon is inscribed, *'Buried near this spot.'* as there is no certainty about the precise location of his remains within the cemetery. The majority of the headstones in Quarry Cemetery, Vermelles are, in fact, of this type, as the cemetery remained on the frontline after 1915 and suffered extensive shell damage before the end of the war. This made precise grave identification extremely problematic. The headstone was installed in the cemetery in 2012.

On 26 April 1923, Lady Elizabeth Bowes-Lyon married Prince Albert, the Duke of York – the future King George VI – at Westminster Abbey. Before the ceremony, Elizabeth – destined to be the future Queen – laid her bouquet on the Tomb of the Unknown Warrior. This action set a tradition which has been followed by other Royal brides ever since. Whether the action by Elizabeth Bowes-Lyon was spontaneous or pre-planned is not known, but it is without doubt that it was prompted by the memory of her elder brother.

CORPORAL REGINALD EVANS – THE SIXPENNY DCM

The Distinguished Conduct Medal was instituted by Queen Victoria on 4 December 1854 during the Crimean War as a means of recognition of acts of gallantry in action performed by warrant officers, non-commissioned officers and men. The decoration was the second highest award for gallantry in action for all ranks below commissioned officers, after the Victoria Cross. Recipients were entitled to add the letters 'DCM' after their name. Based on concerns that the overwhelming demand for medals would lessen the prestige of those Distinguished Conduct Medals already issued, the Military Medal was instituted as an alternative to the DCM from March 1916. Although the DCM remained available, the Military Medal was more commonly awarded from this date and the DCM reserved for exceptional acts of bravery. Conferment of the award was announced in *The London Gazette* accompanied by a citation.

The story of Hertfordshire soldier Corporal Reginald 'Jack' Evans DCM is one of bravery and tenacity, both on and off the battlefield. He was born in 1888 and by the time he enlisted in the Hertfordshire Regiment on 29 April 1913, he was living in Broad Street, Hemel Hempstead, where he worked as a brush maker for the Kent Brush Company. In his original enlistment papers Jack is described as being a fit 25-year-old who stood at 5′ 6″ in height. He was given the regimental number 2170. He was posted to France on 5 November 1914, and set in motion a chain of events that would see him

Lance Corporal 'Jack' Evans prior to his award of the DCM and promotion to Corporal.

promoted to the rank of Sergeant, earn one of Britain's highest gallantry awards and suffer a devastating injury that impacted on the remainder of his life.

On 22 September 1915, whilst the Hertfordshire Regiment was located near the Brickworks at Cuinchy, Reg Evans was awarded one of the Battalion's first Distinguished Conduct Medal. His citation reads:

For conspicuous gallantry and ability at Cuinchy on 22 September 1915, when he went out in bright moonlight 150 yards to see how far the wire had been cut by artillery fire. He made an exhaustive examination of it, remained out an hour and a half, and returned with a report which was most valuable. He knew that our machine guns were ordered to open fire at 10.00 pm, but in order to complete his reconnaissance thoroughly, he did not return till 10.30 pm. He has frequently volunteered for and carried out useful patrol work of this nature.

In fact, Jack had made his way, in total darkness, to within 50 yards of the German positions and gleaned detailed information about the condition of the enemy wire, their trenches and their troop strengths.

A few days later, on 25 September, the men of No. 3 and No. 4 Company were in support of the 1st King's Liverpool Regiment as they attacked several of the German positions known as Brickstack 'A'. Prior to the attack, the British unleashed a deadly gas attack which, despite warnings from the officer commanding the Royal Engineers that the wind conditions were not favourable, suddenly blew back across the British lines. Now facing a serious setback, the men of the King's Regiment left the safety of the trenches to undertake the attack. Immediately, devastating German machine gun fire poured into the men of the King's Regiment, almost completely annihilating them. The supporting

Hertfordshire men were forced back by the withering fire, suffering a total of 16 casualties, one of whom was Corporal Jack Evans. It was not long before he recovered from his injuries and was back with his company, having found himself promoted to the rank of lance sergeant.

It was on 14 February 1916 that Hertfordshires were on the frontline near Festubert. On this day they suffered just one single casualty: Sergeant Jack Evans. He was grievously wounded in the face and jaw by a devastating blast injury from a shell. He was quickly passed along the evacuation chain through No. 5 Field Ambulance and No. 33 Casualty Clearing Station at Bethune. On his arrival at No. 10 Stationary Hospital in St. Omer, his problems heightened. Apart from his facial injuries, he had also now developed scarlet fever and his prospects were not good. He was moved to No. 7 General Hospital in St. Omer and then to No. 14 Stationary Hospital at Wimereux on the French coast. Eventually, he was transported back to Blighty on the hospital ship *St Andrew*. Jack spent many months in hospital, where he underwent twelve operations. Eventually, he was to be treated with pioneering surgical treatment performed by Captain Harold Gillies at Britain's first plastic surgery unit, which had been formed at the Cambridge Hospital, Aldershot. Despite a remarkable recovery, he was not deemed fit enough to return to France, and was attached to the 11th Bedfordshire Regiment. Under Army Council Instructions in January 1917, in which the Territorial Force troops were issued with six-digit regimental numbers, Reg was allocated a new regimental number: 265319.

On 19 August 1918 he was compulsorily transferred to the 13th Battalion, East Surrey Regiment. A few weeks later, on 9 September, he was again transferred, only this time to the 11th Battalion, Royal Sussex Regiment, after which he volunteered for service with the Northern Russian Expeditionary Force. His regimental number again changed to 207623, and he prepared himself for service in Russia.

The 11th Battalion had absorbed the remnants of the 12th and 13th Battalions when it was withdrawn from France, and reformed at Mytchett Camp, Farnborough, where it was commanded by Lieutenant Colonel Albion Ernest Andrews OBE. On 17 September 1918, after re-equipping and training, the battalion, with a total of 34 officers and 943 other ranks, entrained at Aldershot and travelled to Leith in Scotland. Here, the following day the troops embarked on HMT *Leicestershire*, but did not set

Jack Evans as he progressed through the groundbreaking process of facial reconstruction.

sail until 20 September, with the ship taking six days to reach the Russian port of Murmansk.

It was not until 28 September that the battalion disembarked, and 'B' and 'C' Companies were sent by train to Kola. The remainder of the battalion re-embarked on the SS *Cameron* and sailed to Petchenga. As there was no accommodation available, the troops had to spend the night on the top deck, where it was wet and cold and proved a most uncomfortable voyage. They disembarked at Petchenga on 29 September and were billeted in the town. Between 4 October 1918 and 28 February 1919 the battalion carried out guard duties and provided working parties for the Royal Engineers. They also carried out small arms training, drill and exercises, including skiing classes. Jack was admitted to hospital on 7 January 1919, having suffered an injury to his left knee, and was not released until 10 February, when the daytime temperature was described as being –13 °F (–25 °C).

On 5 March 1919, the Mobile Company, consisting of 6 officers and 164 other ranks, moved to Kola on reindeer sledges, accompanied by the commanding officer. On 9 March, Battalion headquarters and details comprising 3 officers and 122 other ranks embarked on SS *Zoshimar* and sailed to Murmansk, through floating ice, arriving on 10 March and then moving by rail to join the Mobile Company at Kola.

The Mobile Company moved to Kandalaksha on 29 March 1919, where from 1 April it was – as described in the war diary – *'taking precautions against disturbances with the Finns'*. From 30 April until 30 June, work was carried out on improving the camp. By 25 July, Jack was ready for a spot of home leave, and embarked on the SS *Cornishman* back to the UK. He returned to Russia aboard the SS *Kursk* on 28 August, having spent almost a year in the region. This was to be the last time he saw the country, for he was sent back to the UK on 8 October 1919 aboard the SS *Toboa* to be demobilised.

His service came to an end on 14 December 1919, after 6 years and 235 days with the colours. His troubles, however, were not over. In 1920 Jack, now living back at Broad Street, Hemel Hempstead, was forced to hand back a £20 gratuity given to

Jack Evans after the completion of facial reconstruction.

Jack Evans whilst serving with the Home Guard during the Second World War.

him for the award of his Distinguished Conduct Medal. This was to enable him to increase his war pension by a miserly sixpence (2.5p) a day.

Reginald married Evelyn Minnie Walker in 1924 and the couple had three children. They settled in his wife's home village of Armitage, Staffordshire, where he took great pride in working for the good of the village, particularly amongst the ex-servicemen, who knew him as their friend. Whilst acting as secretary of the British Legion Joint Benevolent Committee, he fought for benefits for disabled ex-servicemen where cases had seemed hopeless, but he eventually won them.

At the outbreak of the Second World War Jack, who was already a member of the local Observer Corps, joined the Local Defence Volunteers, eventually becoming a Lieutenant in the Home Guard. However, ill health dogged his later years, forcing him to retire from the Home Guard in 1942. On 11 February 1943, at his home in Farladys, Armitage, Reginald Evans DCM passed away, aged 55 years. His funeral was attended by many ex-servicemen, and his coffin was carried by those who had been awarded both the Distinguished Conduct Medal and the Military Medal.

Chapter Three

1916 – The Big Push

In February 1916, following seventeen months of fighting, the German colony of Cameroon, West Africa fell to the French and British. This left only one German colony remaining in Africa, known as German East Africa. There, 10,000 troops, skilfully commanded by General Paul von Lettow-Vorbeck, proved to be an elusive but deadly target as they were pursued by a British-led force ten times larger.

On the Western Front, the German Fifth Army attacked the French Second Army north of the historic city of Verdun. The Germans, under Chief of the General Staff Erich von Falkenhayn, sought to 'bleed' the French Army to death. The German offensive soon stalled as the French rushed in massive reinforcements and strengthened their defences. A new French commander, Henri Petain, was determined to save Verdun. An early spring thaw turned the entire battlefield into mud, hampering offensive manoeuvres. By March the Germans had renewed their offensive, targeting two strategic hills northwest of Verdun that formed the main French position. By the end of the month, the heavily defended hills were only partially in German hands.

In April a U-boat sunk the passenger ferry *Sussex* in the English Channel. The attack marked the beginning of a new U-boat campaign around the British Isles. In the Middle East, the five-month siege at Kut Al Amara in Mesopotamia ended as 13,000 British and Indian soldiers on the verge of starvation surrendered to the Turks. The largest-ever surrender by the British Army came after four failed attempts by British relief troops to break through to the surrounded garrison.

In Britain, universal conscription took effect on 25 May 1916, bringing the era of the all-volunteer British Army to an end, and requiring all eligible men between the ages of 19 and 40 to report – excluding men working in agriculture, mining or the railroads. The County of Hertfordshire was to see an increase in the number of appeals against conscription, with many land owners and small businesses facing financial ruin if key employees were forced into the armed services.

31 May 1916 saw the main German and British naval fleets clash in the Battle of Jutland in the North Sea, as both sides tried – but failed – to score a decisive victory. Despite considerable efforts by the Germans, the British Navy retained its dominance of the North Sea and the naval blockade of Germany remained intact for the remainder of the war.

In June, the Germans at Verdun tried to continue their offensive success along the Meuse River, using poisonous phosgene gas at the start of the attack. Targeting Fort Vaux and the fortification at Thiaumont, both objectives were taken as the French suffered heavy casualties. The Germans now pushed onward toward a ridge that overlooked Verdun and edged toward the Meuse bridges. The entire nation of France now rallied behind their troops in the defence of Verdun as French generals vowed it would not be taken.

On the Eastern Front four Russian Armies, under their innovative new commander, General Alexei Brusilov, began a general offensive in the southwest along a 300-mile front. Thinly stretched Austro-Hungarian troops defending this portion of the Front were taken by surprise. In an effort to support the front, the Germans pulled four divisions from Verdun and sent them east. By the end of the summer, the Germans had sent twenty divisions eastwards and merged the Austro-Hungarian troops into the Germany Army.

Battle of the Somme

In December 1915 Allied commanders met to discuss strategies for the upcoming year and agreed to launch a joint French and British attack in the region of the River Somme in the summer of 1916. In February 1916 the German Fifth Army, under the leadership of General Erich von Falkenhayn, attacked French forces at Verdun. In an effort to relieve the pressure on the French, their commander, General Joffre, called for an assault by British and Commonwealth forces in the Somme region. Preparations for what was to be known as the 'Big Push' took several months to put into place and it was apparent to all that there was going to be an attack. The British were faced with German defences that had been carefully laid out over many months. The enormity of the planning for the battle is difficult to gauge. The task involved preparing men, arms, ammunition and supplies for what was to be a major offensive on well-defended positions along a 43-km front north of the River Somme to relieve the pressure on French forces.

The Allies began a week-long artillery bombardment of German defensive positions on 24 June 1916. Over 1.5 million shells were fired along a 15-mile front to pulverize the German trench system and to blow apart the rows of barbed wire that were protecting them. The British commander, Douglas Haig, believed this would allow an unhindered infantry advance and a rapid breakthrough of the German Front on the first day of battle. Many Hertfordshire men served with both the artillery units and the assaulting infantry.

On 1 July 1916 the British infantry attacked in broad daylight, advancing in organised waves, only to be systematically mown down. The British Army suffered its worst single-day death toll in its history, as over 19,240 soldiers were killed on the first day alone. The thirteen divisions involved in the attacks encountered many defenses that were still intact despite the bombardment designed to knock them out.

The Somme offensive quickly became a battle of attrition as British and French troops made marginal gains against the Germans but repeatedly failed to break through the entire front.

On 13 July the British launched an attack against German positions along a 3.5-mile portion of the Somme Front. After advancing nearly 1,000 yards, the advance was halted as the Germans regrouped their defences. Two days later, the British once again penetrated the German line and advanced to High Wood, but were then pushed back.

The first-ever appearance of tanks on a battlefield occurred on 15 September 1916 as British troops renewed the offensive and attacked German positions along a 5-mile front, advancing some 2,000 yards. The British infantry advanced, and individual tanks provided support by blasting and rolling over the German barbed wire, piercing the frontline defence, and then rolling along the length of the trench, raking the German soldiers with machine gun fire. By the end of September heavy rain had turned the entire battlefield to mud, preventing effective manoeuvres.

British troops staged a surprise attack on 13 November in what was known as the Battle of the Ancre, and captured the towns of Beaumont Hamel and Beaucourt at the northern end of the Somme Front. The Hertfordshire Regiment was heavily involved in this assault and whilst it suffered some casualties, they were able to achieve their objectives, with some of the regiment's contingent being awarded gallantry medals for their efforts. A few days later, the Battle of the Somme came to an end following the first snowfall in the region. By now, the Germans had been pushed back just a few miles along a 15-mile front, but the major breakthrough the Allies had planned never occurred. Both sides had suffered over 600,000 casualties during the five-month battle.

There are very few towns, villages or hamlets across Hertfordshire that were not touched by the fighting that took place throughout 1916, both on land and at sea. Over the course of the Somme battle, as British forces took a strip of territory just 6 miles (10 km) deep by 20 miles (32 km) in

Poster advertising the film *Battle of the Somme*, seen by over 20 million people in the UK.

length, the combatants would suffer over a million casualties. At home, the names of the dead and wounded filled the pages of local newspapers as the enormity of the campaign became apparent. For the first time, too, British cinema audiences were brought face to face with the horrors of the Great War with the release of an official documentary film, *The Battle of the Somme*. Filmed by cinematographers Geoffrey Malins and John McDowell, it was the first feature-length film to record soldiers in action, taking the audience from the build-up and early days of the battle through to the concluding images of the dead, wounded and the devastation. Although the film was seen by 20 million people across the country, it still could not prepare them for what the following year would bring.

THE GARDEN CITY MOURNS – JACK & WALTER SATTERTHWAITE

The story of the Satterthwaite brothers and their wartime experiences first came to light in June 2014, when Walter's grandson, Brian, donated a collection of medals, photographs and wartime documents forgotten for almost 100 years to Letchworth's *First Garden City Collection*, a major partner of the *Herts at War* project. The collection and the family story are incredibly poignant, and stand out as one that tells of the terrible legacy of war, even claiming a victim decades after the events took place. The ordeal that the Satterthwaites endured at the time and the impact of the Great War so many years after the event, serve to highlight the legacy of the conflict and the people who served in it.

When the Great War broke out in 1914, Letchworth Garden City was a young town, founded on socialist principles and renowned nationally as a free-thinking utopia. Consequently, the Garden City movement drew people from all around the country including families like the Satterthwaites of Finchley, Middlesex. Of working-class background, the Satterthwaite family with their two oldest sons, John (known as Jack) and Walter, moved to Letchworth in the late 1900s to work in the town's emerging printing industry. During their time in Letchworth, both brothers joined the local Territorial Unit, the Hertfordshire Regiment. At the time, this would have meant that they spent their weekends and summer holidays training for a war that most did not even consider as a possibility. Jack, the eldest son, was soon found to be a highly capable soldier and rose to the rank of Sergeant, becoming Platoon Sergeant to some of the men from Letchworth. When war was declared in the late summer of 1914, men rushed to enlist from all over the country, although for ready-assembled units such as the Hertfordshire Regiment, the wait was significantly less.

The Hertfordshire Regiment was called on to follow the regular army out to the Western Front to meet the threat of the numerically superior German Army, who were invading the low countries via Belgium. Sergeant Jack Satterthwaite, without his underage brother Walter, left the train station at Letchworth Garden City in October 1914 to head off to war. He arrived in France with the original contingent of the Hertfordshire Regiment on 6 November 1914. As Platoon Sergeant and de facto representative for the men from Letchworth, Jack regularly wrote home, his letters appearing in *The Citizen* newspaper on a regular basis.

Walter Satterthwaite re-enlisted in the army on 15 November 1915 and eventually fought with the Hertfordshire Regiment in

SERGT SATTERTHWAITE WRITES.

HOME-SICK FOR THE SKITTLES.

The following letter, dated Dec. 10th, has been received by Mr. W. G. Furmston, of the Skittles Inn, from Sergt. J. Satterthwaite, of Letchworth, who is at the Front with the 1st Herts Territorials:—

"I have been asked by the Letchworth boys to drop you a line, as they would like to be remembered to you, and hope you are going on all right. I daresay you have read of our experiences, and I am sorry to say losses, but some of the statements in the papers are not all gospel. Still, we were busy for a week or so, and we have done very well. We are now at a rest camp which was much needed, as a large number of us were suffering with bad feet, chiefly frost-bitten, but are now all right. We do not know when or where we are going to next, but would not mind if it was to the Skittles for a game of billiards!"

A letter from Sergeant Jack Satterthwaite printed in the local newspaper.

France under the protective eye of his elder sibling. Sadly, the reunion between the two brothers would be short-lived, as on 17 April 1916 the newly promoted Company Quartermaster Sergeant Satterthwaite was struck by shellfire and badly wounded in multiple locations. Jack was taken back through the casualty evacuation chain, receiving treatment the whole time until he reached a Casualty Clearing Station near the village of St Venant in France. Sadly, here Jack succumbed to his wounds on 22 April 1916, aged 25.

After his death, the following obituary appeared in *The Citizen*, highlighting the esteem in which Jack was held by all in the community.

Letchworth people will learn with deep regret and sorrow that Sergeant Jack Satterthwaite of the 1st Hertfordshire Regiment died of wounds last Saturday. The sergeant was probably the best known of our Territorials, having been a Territorial for a long time before the war, and having been in France since his regiment went out there in the autumn of 1914. He has been on home leave three times since the war began; the first time after a short spell in the trenches. Some months ago, his period of service in the Territorials having expired and he having also served the extra year the country can demand in time of war, in a spirit of patriotism and feelings of loyalty to his Letchworth comrades in the trenches, Sergeant Satterthwaite signed on again for foreign service. In recognition of this, the authorities granted him a month's furlough, which he spent in Letchworth.

Only three weeks ago, he was home again from the trenches on seven days' leave and, on that occasion, we had many chats with him. He was in fine health and spoke modestly of the part he was playing in the war. The sergeant had returned to the trenches only a week after his leave when he was shot in the body on the 17th inst. The sergeant underwent an operation and on Tuesday his parents, Mr & Mrs James Satterthwaite, who live at 6 North Avenue, received a letter from the chaplain at the hospital saying that the sergeant was still dangerously ill and his condition had become worse.

His condition continued to fail and on Thursday his parents received a letter from the kindly chaplain intimating that their gallant son had passed away. Sergeant Satterthwaite was one of the brightest young fellows in Letchworth. He possessed a fine physique and was of a sunny, genial and sociable nature. He was very widely known and greatly liked by all. We have frequently heard his comrades in the regiment speak in the highest terms of the great care he took of his men and the anxiety to see after their comfort rather than their own. When he went back to the trenches three weeks ago he took back 500 cigarettes for the boys, although he had quite as much as he could well carry without them. But as Mr Beddows had the cigarettes ready (they were the gift of the customers) he wished to take them back with him so that the Letchworth lads could get at them at the earliest possible moment. Sergeant Satterthwaite was formerly employed at Messrs W.H Smith & Sons Bookbinding Company, afterwards in connection with Letchworth Model Dairy in Station Road and later at the Garden City Press. He was very well known at the Skittles Inn where he used to resort for a game of billiards. It seems incredible that we are never again going to see one who had become so familiar to us. Several of his letters from the front have appeared in the Citizen *and he was always glad to tell us anything he could when he was on leave. We are sure the citizens of Letchworth will join us in extending their sincerest and deepest sympathy to the sergeant's bereaved parents and their family. Theirs is a terrible loss. Mr & Mrs Satterthwaite's only other surviving son Walter is also in the army.*

Today CQMS Jack Satterthwaite lies in St Venant Military Cemetery in northern France. After the war, Jack's parents were asked if they would like to add an inscription to the base of his headstone. They chose:

Though far away we mourn him still. Peace perfect peace.

Despite the loss of his brother, the war was not over for Walter Satterthwaite, who was transferred to the 6th Battalion, Berkshire Regiment after their devastating losses at the Somme in late 1916. Walter himself was wounded in 1916, suffered a broken ankle in 1917, earned a coveted Military Medal for bravery in the field in recognition of his service, promoted to the rank of Sergeant and was once again badly wounded in the closing stages of the war, leaving his right leg immobile for life.

After recuperation in the United Kingdom, Walter was honourably discharged in 1919. Despite his debilitating injuries, he adapted back into civilian life well and worked full-time for over thirty years, rarely missing a day's work. To aid his mobility, he was given a specially adapted motorised bicycle that allowed him to travel freely and also made him a well-known figure in the local area. In an interesting aside Walter's wife, Alice, was of German descent and the Satterthwaite brothers had cousins serving in the German Army during the Great War, a fact that makes their dedication and devotion to duty all the more commendable.

The grave of Sergeant Jack Satterthwaite at St Venant Military Cemetery.

Tragically, even over forty years later, the impact of the Great War would still affect the lives of the Satterthwaites. With increasing pain from his wartime wound, Walter was taken to hospital for an operation to amputate the limb and sadly died the following day as a result; one of the last casualties of a war that was fought from 1914–1918 but which took its toll for many years to come.

Walter's grandson, Brian, said of his family: '*My grandfather never spoke about the war and although we knew that Jack had died in the Great War, we have never known any detail about what he did. I wanted the collection to go to somewhere where it could do some good and help others learn about the Great War.*'

UNRECOGNISED BRAVERY – PRIVATE DOUGLAS EATON ENTICKNAP

On the outskirts of the Belgian town of Ypres can be found a British cemetery named Essex Farm. The neatly maintained graves within it are lovingly preserved by the Commonwealth War Graves Commission. The location is well known, as it's the last resting place of one of the youngest Tommies to have been killed in the Great War; Private Valentine Joseph Strudwick, who was just 15 years old. It is also believed that this is the location where war poet John McRae penned *In Flanders Fields*, the well-known war poem. If you have the opportunity to visit this location, you will also find the grave of some Hertfordshire soldiers including that of Private Douglas Enticknap, the son of Alfred and Ellen Enticknap, of London Colney.

A short article appeared in the *Hertfordshire Express*, in which it was stated:

Grave of Private Douglas Eaton Enticknap at Essex Farm, Ypres.

> *Private Douglas Enticknap, of the machine gun section, Bedfordshire Regiment, had been recommended for the Distinguished Conduct Medal for gallant conduct near Ypres on 19 April 1916. On the night in question the Germans attacked the British trenches, but Private Enticknap, single-handed, held them up until the brigade rushed the enemy out with heavy losses. When the attack was delivered, Private Enticknap was working his gun with two more soldiers, but both his companions were killed by a shell. About 100 Germans were found dead in front of the trench where this gallant soldier was stationed.*

Douglas was born in Pagham, a parish of Bognor Regis, and his family later moved to Cheshunt, Hertfordshire, where he attended the local school along with his brother Alf. In 1904 the family moved location again, this time settling in London Colney. His story is indicative of so many young men who enlisted in the armed forces at the outbreak of the Great War, and whose army service records did not survive, being destroyed in an air raid on London in 1940.

He arrived in France on 24 September 1915 and joined the 8th Battalion, Bedfordshire Regiment, serving on the Western Front throughout the latter part of 1915 and early 1916, during which time the battalion was heavily engaged in action with the enemy.

On 16 April 1916 the battalion moved into trenches in a location known as Willows, on the outskirts of Ypres, where they relieved the 10th Rifle Brigade. On the night of 19–20 April, after a severe artillery bombardment, German infantry attacked the position and gained a footing in trenches in the area where the battalion was located. It was here that Douglas held up the enemy attack, for which he was later recommended for the Distinguished Conduct Medal.

The battalion remained in the same location for the next few weeks, and it was here that Douglas was killed on 30 May 1916, aged just 19, his award having never been confirmed.

'THE MANIAC' – LIEUTENANT COLONEL MEREDITH MAGNIAC

Perhaps the single best-known action on 1 July 1916 is the iconic attack of the 1st Battalion Lancashire Fusiliers who attacked out of the 'Sunken Lane' at Beaumont Hamel towards German positions at 7.30 am on the opening day of the battle of the Somme. What is far less known is that the man to lead that attack was Meredith Magniac, a professional soldier who hailed from Hitchin.

Lieutenant Colonel Meredith Magniac.

Meredith Magniac was born in Hitchin in 1880, the son of Major General Francis Magniac, former commander of the Madras Light Cavalry. Meredith was educated at Clifton College and later attended Eton where he excelled in cricket, all the time destined to follow in his father's military footsteps. Meredith was gazetted into the Lancashire Fusiliers on 2 August 1899 and held various posts, including that of Instructor of Musketry. Meredith was promoted to Captain in 1904 and subsequently passed into the Staff College at Quetta from which he graduated in 1912. Soon after the outbreak of war, he relinquished a staff appointment as brigade major in Ireland, and went to Gallipoli as a Captain on the staff of General Sir Julian Byng.

Magniac first found fame with the 1st Battalion Lancashire Fusiliers in April 1915 when his battalion was part of the leading wave of the 29th Division's assault on the Gallipoli Peninsular. Magniac, affectionately known as 'The Maniac', was in fact one of the individuals put forward for the rather unusual 'ballot' for the famous 'six before breakfast' episode. This was to award six Victoria Crosses to members of the battalion who had performed particularly well during the landings. Whilst Magniac, then a Captain, was not one of the six drawn, his reputation as a fearless leader and a conscientious and brave officer was cemented in Gallipoli.

Magniac was involved in both evacuations at the end of the Gallipoli Campaign, being mentioned in despatches three times for his bravery and leadership during the most trying of times. In March 1916 he arrived in France in command of his battalion to join the war on the Western Front. In a rare spell of home leave in the spring of 1916 he married Winifred Sayers, the daughter of a well-known cricketer.

On 1 July 1916, Magniac, who had already seen considerable fighting and experienced considerable loss, was to preside over one of the most infamous actions on the opening day of the Battle of the Somme. On that day, several hundred men of 1st Lancashire Fusiliers were to attack from a sunken lane in no man's land toward German positions outside the village of Beaumont Hamel, with the remainder attacking from an

Men of the Lancashire Fusiliers in the Sunken Lane, at Beaumont-Hamel on 1 July 1916.

area known as White City, several hundred yards to the rear. Also in the sunken lane that dawn was cinematographer Geoffey Malins, who recorded men of the Lancashire Fusiliers in the minutes before the attack, a piece of footage that is perhaps the single most iconic of the entire Great War. On the evening before the attack, Magniac and his men, along with machine gunners and trench mortar men, had occupied the sunken lane and considerably shortened the distance they were to cross at 7.30 the next morning.

Unfortunately, one of the major mines that had been dug in advance of that attack, in this case under the Hawthorn Redoubt, was blown at 7.20 am, a full ten minutes before the attack was to start. This had the undesirable effect of alerting every German within a large radius of the impending attack and

consequently, when the Lancashire Fusiliers advanced, they did so into a hail of machine gun and rifle fire from their front and flank. In just a few minutes, almost 90 per cent of the battalion became casualties; killed, wounded or prisoner. Magniac, who was reported to have acted incredibly courageously that morning, was somehow left unwounded and would continue to lead his battalion through the remainder of the year. For his leadership on 1 July, Lieutenant Colonel Magniac was awarded the Distinguished Service Order.

Meredith's war came to an end in April 1917 when during the battle of Arras he was killed by shellfire outside the village of Monchy-Le-Preux. After his death, a fellow officer wrote:

The grave of Lieutenant Colonel Meredith Magniac at the Beaurains Road Cemetery, Arras.

He was, of course, in the frontline with his men. I do not think there was an officer in the division who did not admire and respect the colonel, and not an officer or man in the battalion who did not love him. He was the finest soldier I ever met, a strong man, a born leader, and a very gallant gentleman.

Just three days after Meredith's death, his younger brother Erskine Magniac, himself a colonel in the Indian Army, was to fall in action, killed by a sniper in Mesopotamia.

A MOTHER'S LOVE – PRIVATE EDWARD ERNEST AMBROSE

Perhaps one of the single most powerful collection of Great War artefacts to come to light as a result of the *Herts at War* project has been the possessions of Private Ernest Edward Ambrose of Wallington near Baldock.

In 2014 the project was contacted by relatives of 'Ted' who had discovered a suitcase in the loft of their family home which they believed contained items relating to the First World War. Upon inspection, the suitcase turned out to contain the entire wartime possessions of Ted Ambrose, returned to his mother after his death on the Somme in 1916 and locked away, unseen since the early 1920s. The story of sorrow and grief that this time capsule revealed is an incredibly powerful one, told here in full for the first time.

Ted Ambrose was born into a working-class family in the rural village of Wallington near Baldock in 1898. Ted's parents were simple, hard-working and fervently religious farmers and had been for generations. In the early 1900s it looked certain that Ted, their firstborn, was to follow in his father's footsteps.

All the family plans changed in 1914 when the Great War erupted across Europe, drawing to the colours hundreds of thousands of young volunteers such as 17-year-old Ted, who joined up with a neighbouring county battalion of the Bedfordshire Regiment. As a member of a 'Kitchener' Battalion, Ted embarked immediately upon training to become a soldier, learning his new trade at Ampthill Park along with several thousand other volunteers. By the time 1916 arrived, the war was well underway and the reality of the dangers of the Western

The home of Private Edward Ernest Ambrose.

Front was known to all. Ted received news of his imminent departure in March of that year and made his farewells to his parents and his girlfriend Gladys, giving a brooch to her as a gift. From his father, he received a letter, which he would carry with him throughout his time on the Western Front. The letter, thoroughly considered and beautifully written, reads as follows:

Dear Son,

Just a few lines to you trusting they will find you quite well and in the best of health. No doubt you will think it strange to get a letter from dad but I thought I must just write you a few lines before you sail away from home.

I remind you that you are quite young so therefore you must try and take great care of yourself and don't forget to ask your heavenly father to help you. We will all pray to God for you and for your safe return home again when the war is ended and trust in him that it may soon be finished with and lasting peace so that we all live happily again.

Take great care of this letter and read it sometimes and then you won't forget to do what I have asked of you. Let us know as often as you can how you are getting along and if there is anything that you want if we can. I think this is all, so with all our best love from one and all to you and heaps of kisses, Your loving dad.

With the advice of his father safely kept, Ted left for war, landing in France in April 1916 to play his part in the great adventure to come.

Ted's early experiences in the field were fraught with bad luck and misfortune. On his first turn in the frontlines, Ted was dazed by a nearby shell explosion which perforated his eardrums and led to a spell in hospital to recover. Within a short time, Ted returned to the frontlines, only to be invalided out once more. He wrote home to his parents on 3 March 1916.

Dear M & F, just a line to say I am sorry to tell you that I am in the hospital and what should you think, with German measles. That won't be very pleasing to you. Well I hope you won't worry because I am going on quite well, well I received a little parcel on Friday with the pocket case and I went into hospital on Saturday. I am not sending you the new address as we are not settled here, will send you the new address as soon as possible and will write and let you know as often as I can how I am getting on, now must close. From your loving son Ted.

Around the same time Ted also wrote home to his sweetheart Gladys, informing her of his illness, to which she immediately replied, light-heartedly reprimanding him as he *'must have been cuddling German girls!'*

By mid-June he was once more 'in the line', this time further south in preparation for the upcoming British summer campaign in the Somme region. On 24 June Gladys wrote to him:

My dear boy, just a few lines in answer to your most loving letter which I got quite safe this morning. Glad to hear you are quite well and that you think your luck has changed. Did you know Sam Clark of Sandon when you were at Ampthill has been out in France and got killed on 19 May, he was only out there a fortnight. Well dear I am enclosing a small packet of cigarettes which I hope you will like. Perhaps you will get them if I send them like this rather than one big packet. Ain't we having some rotten weather again? There are no more soldiers to come yet but they are going to try to get some as it has made the trade so bad for the town. No more news so will close with best love and kisses from your only loving girl Gladys xxxxx.

On 1 July 1916 the British and French Armies launched the largest offensive of the war to that date, with mixed consequences. In the north, British forces fared exceedingly badly, with a staggering 57,000 men killed, wounded or captured on the first day alone. The French, further to the south along with some British units, fared much better, having considerable success in areas. For Ted and the men of the 6th Bedfordshires, their role this day was one of support. Although they were not involved in the attack on 1 July, they doubtless knew that their time would come.

Gladys, the sweetheart of Ted Ambrose.

On 6 July 1916 Ted once more wrote home to his mother, interestingly deciding not to mention anything of the incredible battle going on around him. His thoughts at this time seem to have been of home. He was not to know that this would be his last letter.

My Dear M & F,

I now take the pleasure in answering your nice letter that I got yesterday as I ought to have answered you before. I sent you a card to say I am quite well and hope you are all the same and to say I had your letter. Well I enjoyed your cake very much as I just finished it yesterday, I made this one last longer and I enjoyed it, it was very nice. Well how is aunty Nellie and grandmother? Did they come and see you? I wish I was there so as I could see them once again as it seems a very long time since I came out here. It seems like twelve months but actually it is about six. Well I am thinking about the time when we get back, we shan't know what to do with ourselves. Well I can't think of much to say this time so I will end my letter, sending you all the best of love and kisses. I remain your loving son Ted. Xxxxxx.

On the morning of 9 July 1916 near the village of La Boiselle, whilst holding the frontlines, the men of the 6th Bedfordshires were struck by a terrific artillery bombardment, which in a little over an hour caused close to 100 casualties; numbered amongst them was Private Ted Ambrose, who had been seriously wounded in the leg and head.

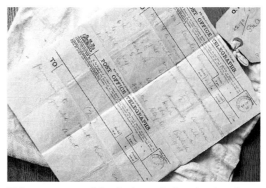

Telegram sent to Mrs Ambrose informing her that her son was 'dangerously ill'.

In the days that followed, Ted was brought back via several hospitals until he reached the French coast and a major British Army medical facility at Etaples. Here Ted underwent several operations in an attempt to stabilise his condition and save his life. A chaplain also contacted Ted's anxious mother, who had already received news of his wound and was desperately awaiting further information and a response to her request to travel to France and see her firstborn child.

The response, written by a chaplain at the hospital read: *'Regret to inform you, Private E E Ambrose, 6th Beds, dangerously ill, G.S.W (gunshot wound) to head. Regret permission to visit cannot be granted.'* This refusal must have come as a severe blow to Harriett Ambrose and seems particularly harsh in the circumstances, although on closer examination of the document, the reason becomes clear.

Ted's mother, Harriett Ambrose.

The telegram was time-stamped upon receipt in the UK just an hour before Ted finally succumbed to his wounds. 18-year-old Ted Ambrose died on 13 July 1916 and was buried with full military honours in Etaples Military Cemetery, France.

Following Ted's death, his possessions were returned to his grief-stricken mother, who placed them in a case, unable to look at such sad memories. They remained unopened in the family loft for over 90 years. When discovered in 2014, the case – a time capsule of one young man's life in the Great War – brought the story of Ted Ambrose back to life so that we can remember him, and so many like him, once more.

THE CANON GLOSSOP MEMORIALS – TWO SOLDIERS FROM ST. ALBANS

St. Albans is steeped in history and by 1914 was a prosperous cathedral city with a varied economy. The population of the borough at the time was just over 24,000 and this was soon vastly increased by an influx of military personnel, as the city and the surrounding areas – with their road and rail links to the capital – became home to elements of the rapidly expanding armed forces.

Following the Armistice, a number of memorials and monuments were erected across the city, outlining its casualties in the conflict. The city war memorial, located in St Peter's Street, lists the names of 640 men who died. Ten unique street plaques, listing 110 names of those men who lived and worked in the vicinity, were also erected. These plaques are a permanent reminder of the tragic impact of world events on the ordinary people of Hertfordshire.

Canon George Henry Pownall Glossop, who served the Abbey for over forty years, and who himself lost two sons in the war, promoted the plan for the plaques. The City Council still officially refers to these plaques as 'The Canon Glossop Memorials', although many other people were actively involved in their creation. The City Council has been awarded a Grade II listing for the preservation of these poignant memorials. Records show that the Abbey curate, the Reverend Harry Evans, made street collections to fund the scheme and it is claimed that when he visited the grieving families of the parish, he suggested the idea of the plaques as a form of comfort. The following are just two of the stories from those plaques.

Cannon George Henry Pownall Glossop, whose sons, Ernest and Bertram, were killed in the Great War, promoted the plan for the St. Albans memorial plaques.

The Ridgmont Road Plaque – Private Alfred George Hatten

One of the memorial plaques is fixed to the wall of Antony Gibbs House in Ridgmont Road and contains the names of ten former employees of the Vyse & Son straw hat factory. The original building was demolished but the memorial was retained. Amongst the names that can be seen on this particular plaque is that of Alfred George Hatten, the youngest son of William Francis and Emily Jane Hatten, the family home being at 66 Ramsbury Road, St. Albans. William worked as a railway gatekeeper in St. Albans, whilst his wife raised a total of eight children, four boys and four girls – although records indicate that there was a ninth child, Richard, a twin to their second son, Arthur.

Plaques fixed to the wall of Antony Gibbs House in Ridgmont Road, St. Albans bearing the name of Alfred Hatten.

Alfred Hatten was born in March 1895, and after finishing his education, worked at the Vyse & Son factory with his older sister, Ellen, being employed as a straw blocker's assistant. Alfred was the last of the four boys to join up, enlisting in the Bedfordshire Regiment and being posted to the 6th Battalion with the regimental number 10579.

He arrived in France on 30 July 1915 and was to be employed on one of the most dangerous jobs for an infantryman, that of battalion scout, a role that was essentially the eyes and ears of the infantry. Each company contained at least one non-commissioned officer and six privates who were selected and trained as scouts. Each man had to

Private Alfred Hatten. (*Paul Johnson*)

demonstrate that they had a good level of intelligence, good eyesight and good powers of observation, but most of all could be self-reliant. They were trained how to reconnoitre an enemy or an area of country; how to judge distance with accuracy, how to recognise and estimate enemy numbers and how to then rapidly transmit the information by written report, semaphore and verbal message. Scouts were taught to discriminate between what was of importance and what was not, and to be absolutely accurate in their statements. Their primary duty was to see and report without being seen and they were trained to move unobserved, take advantage of cover, and use folds in the ground for concealment.

On 13 July 1916 the 6th Battalion, Bedfordshire Regiment moved into positions on the Tara-Usna Line, between Albert and La Boiselle. Two days later, on 15 July, they took part in the Battle of Bazentin. This involved an attack on the village of Pozieres by 112th Brigade – at that time part of the 34th Division – from trenches south of Contalmaison.

Albert Hatten can be seen third from the left in the back row of this photograph of the scouts from the 6th Battalion, Bedfordshire Regiment. (*Paul Johnson*)

A report from the 112th Infantry Brigade states that on 15 July 1916 the village of Pozieres was reported to only be lightly held by the enemy. The brigade was set to attack the village from the south at 9.20 am, in conjunction with the 25th Division and the 1st Division. The objective of the brigade in the first instance was the German trenches between the Contalmaison–Pozieres and the Bailiff Wood – Pozieres Roads. The 8th East Lancashire Regiment was set to carry out the attack, with the 6th Bedfordshire Regiment in support.

The battalion began to move forward when it was held up by hostile machine guns and established itself about 100 yards from the cimitiere and dug in. The casualties suffered during the attack were: 3 officers killed, 32 other ranks killed and 25 missing. There were a further 9 officers and 174 other ranks wounded.

Alfred Hatten was amongst those who were killed that day and is buried in the Pozieres British Cemetery on the Somme. His name is recorded on the St. Albans City War Memorial as well as the Ridgmont Road street plaque.

Research has established that Alfred was, in fact, from a soldiering background, with his three older brothers having served in the army long before the outbreak of the Great War.

Alfred's eldest brother, William Francis Hatten (Jnr.), was born on 9 August 1887 and after leaving school, he worked for a short time as a printer's assistant. Just two weeks after his 17th birthday, on 23 August 1904, William left home to join the army. Claiming he was 18, he became a Private in the 6th Battalion, Middlesex Regiment and was issued with the regimental number 3442. Following the completion of his service in 1911, William returned to St. Albans, where he settled

William Francis Hatten Jnr.

back into his old job with a local printer. With the outbreak of the Great War, he rejoined the army as a reservist and entered service with his old regiment, this time as a Sergeant in 'B' Company of the 2nd Middlesex Regiment, with the regimental number L/9892.

He arrived in France on 11 August 1914, just a few days after the outbreak of the war, as part of the 1st Battalion, who came under command of 19th Infantry Brigade on 22 August 1914 and was in action the following day in defence of the Mons-Conde canal. William was amongst the many British troops who took part in the Retreat from Mons and his battalion later saw action at Le Cateau and at Néry.

Arthur Horace Hatten.

On 17 February 1915 William's name appeared in *The London Gazette* as being mentioned in despatches. Just a few months later, on 5 June 1915, he was admitted to hospital, via No. 16 Ambulance Train, after being wounded by shellfire in his right leg during a German artillery bombardment on a location known as Artillery Mansions, a row of ruined houses near the village of Rue Du Bois, France.

William, having survived many actions of the Great War, was awarded the 1914 Star, British War Medal and Victory Medal. This Old Contemptible passed away on 12 November 1969, aged 82.

Arthur Horace Hatten was born on 19 June 1889. Like his older brother William, he joined the army as a boy soldier, enlisting in the 2nd Battalion, Middlesex Regiment on 14 December 1908. At the outbreak of the Great War the battalion was stationed in Malta and his battalion was recalled from the island fortress for service on the Western Front, initially returning to Hursley Park, where they became part of the 23rd Brigade, 8th Division. Within a short space of time, the battalion left England, landing at Le Havre on 7 November 1914 and moving rapidly inland to help stem the German advance.

Arthur, whose regimental number was L/12409, was serving with 'C' Company. There being no service record for him, it is difficult to say with any certainty exactly where he served during this period but the battalion was involved in significant actions at Neuve Chapelle, Aubers Ridge and Bois Grenier throughout the spring and summer of 1915. At some point he was severely wounded, resulting in his discharge from the army on 29 December 1915 as a consequence of his injuries. Arthur married Alice Annie Osman on 18 July 1916 at the St Pancras Parish Chapel, London. Tragedy struck the young couple when their first son, Leonard, died in his infancy on 13 September 1917. Exactly a year later, on 13 September 1918, their daughter, Marjorie, was born. On 17 July 1923, the eve of their seventh wedding anniversary, Annie gave birth to a son, Alfred John, named after Arthur's brother who had perished in the Great War. The couple lived in the St. Albans area, where Arthur ran his own building company. Alice passed away on 26 November 1978 aged 86, and Arthur lived to the age of 93, passing away on 12 January 1982.

For his services in the Great War, Arthur was awarded a Silver War Badge, numbered 111335, as well as the 1914 Star, British War Medal and Victory Medal.

Sergeant Albert George Hatten – Hertfordshire Yeomanry.

The third brother, Albert George, was born on 28 July 1891. He attended Priory Park School in St. Albans and following the completion of his education, took up employment as an accounts clerk with the Midland Railway Company in February 1908. Like many other young men at this time, Albert joined the Territorial Army, becoming a member of the Hertfordshire Yeomanry, with the regimental number 1236.

With the outbreak of the Great War, the 1/1st Battalion, Hertfordshire Yeomanry, came under the command of the Eastern Mounted Brigade. Albert was quickly mobilised and after giving up his employment, on 10 September 1914 sailed for Egypt, arriving on the North African coast on 5 November.

It was on 19 January 1915 that the battalion joined the Yeomanry Mounted Brigade. This was originally an independent command. It moved in August 1915 to Gallipoli as dismounted troops, and was placed under the command of the 2nd Mounted Division, being retitled as the 5th Mounted Brigade.

In December 1915 the battalion withdrew from Gallipoli and returned to Egypt, where in March 1916 it was split up. Albert was serving with 'A' Squadron, which along with the Regimental Headquarters, joined the 54th (East Anglian) Division. In January 1917 there was a reorganisation of regimental numbers and Albert was given number 105029. At this time Albert – now a Sergeant – had been considered as a potential

Lieutenant Albert George Hatten – Royal Air Force.

officer. He applied for entry to an officer cadet unit in March 1917, requesting a temporary commission in the British Army.

It would be a full year before Albert would begin his journey to a commission. On 10 April 1918 he left the army and joined the Royal Air Force. Although he underwent his pilot training and was commissioned as a Lieutenant, the Great War was to draw to a close before he could become an active combat pilot. Albert was entitled to the 1915 Star, British War Medal and the Victory Medal.

He passed away on 23 February 1975 aged 84, his home still being at 66 Ramsbury Road, St. Albans.

The Albert Street Plaque – Private Robert Holder

Robert Holder was the son of Robert and Jane Holder of Albert Street, St. Albans, Hertfordshire. His father was a local bricklayer and Robert was one of six children. He had four sisters; Jane, Sarah, Ellen and Fanny, and a brother, George. Robert was christened on 14 April 1889 in St. Albans and attended school in the area. On 6 August 1910 Robert married Florence Ethel Deacon in Frogmore, Hertfordshire. At this time, he was employed as a carman, a job that involved the delivery and collections of goods and parcels, and the couple had a home at 39 Albert Street, St. Albans.

Albert Street Memorial, St. Albans, bearing the name of Robert Holder.

A service record for Robert has not survived but other records indicate that he joined the 9th (Service) Battalion, Essex Regiment in the Arras area at the end of August 1916 when 170 other ranks were drafted in to replace those who had been lost during fighting on the Somme in July. The battalion, which had been formed at Warley in August 1914, came under the command of 35th Brigade, 12th (Eastern) Division.

In September 1916 his battalion was in reserve in the Arras area and was engaged in training and preparation work, after which they were bussed to Le Souich, some twenty miles northwest of Albert, for drill and bomb

Private Robert Holder (Seated).

throwing training. On 29 September 1916 they were taken by French transport to a location within two miles of Albert. After debussing, they marched a distance of about five miles to a tented camp at Bécordel-Bécourt. The ground had been hard-fought over during the summer and was the location of a large artillery depot. Many troops bivouacked here as they made their way up the lines. The village lies in a valley, and so was protected from the lines near Fricourt to the east by the contours of the land.

Because of this, it was also an area used by the medical facilities of the army. The battalion was located here on 1 October in preparation for moving to Montauban, four miles northwest, the following day. They arrived in Montauban and camped in some old trenches and hastily built shelters. The weather was very bad and the troops suffered 'great discomfort'. As such, each man was given an issue of rum to help cheer them up. The following day all men were put to work on the construction of shelters, using both sandbags and corrugated iron. These were covered in canvas and the war diary indicates that 'good shelters' were built. Although some attack training was carried over the following days, the weather was very bad and the state of the ground made training virtually impossible.

The Battle of Arras, which began on Easter Monday, 9 April 1917, may be considered as one of the successes of the war. The number of troops involved was about the same as that on the first day of the Somme (14 divisions) but these men would be attacking with a far superior weight of artillery to back them up. 200,000 soldiers were strung out on a line 3 km deep, along a front of 32 km to the east of Arras. The British artillery had been doing remarkable work in keeping German gunners' heads down, and for the moment the Royal Flying Corps were keeping the skies above the British lines clear from prying eyes. British commanders had worried that such a concentration of troops would not go unnoticed by the enemy or that a haphazard bombardment would cause severe casualties and disrupt the timing of the show. Above all though, the local German command was convinced that no attack would be delivered over Easter weekend. Their intelligence pointed to an Allied attack but as they were already aware of General Nivelle's attack on the Chemin des Dames, they thought the British were not yet ready.

The task of VI Corps was to attack the area between the village of Tilloy les Mofflaines on the main Cambrai Road and the Scarpe River on their left. The 12th Division had been sheltered throughout the build-up to the battle deep in the caves and tunnels under Arras. Their casualties whilst manning the frontline had been negligible and the soldiers were fit and well rested. The division would advance on the left of the 3rd Division with the Arras–Cambrai Road on their right. The division opted for a leap frog form of attack with the 36th and 37th Brigades taking the attack as far as the Hindenburg Line and then allowing the

35th Brigade to pass through and sweep across the valley. To the north of Tilloy les Mofflaines is a ridge which runs northwards towards the village of Feuchy. This was known to the British as Observation Ridge for the obvious reason that the Germans had a fine view of everything taking place on the British side of no man's land. The Germans, however, were taking risks. As they had such an excellent field of observation, they had decided to leave their artillery clustered behind the ridge in what was known as Battery Valley. If the ridge fell, the artillery would be lost with it.

At 5.30 am the 12th Division launched their attack. Despite a few spirited efforts of resistance, most of the German frontline positions were taken relatively easily. Some positions held out and their determination to fight it out would have a knock-on effect during the battle. The 35th Brigade, who had only moved up out of the Arras tunnels at 7.30 am, were now preparing themselves for their advance to the brown line, named the Wancourt-Feuchy Line. At 11.00 am the 7th Norfolk Regiment was told to force the issue along the Cambrai Road and had little in the way of opposition as they did so, up until they arrived in front of Feuchy Chapel, where the very same strongpoint that was managing to hold up the 3rd Division now put the Norfolks to ground as well. On their left, 9th Essex and 5th Royal Berkshire Regiments started their traverse of Battery Valley. The scene was almost Napoleonic with some batteries of guns abandoned, others trying to limber up and get away and others whose crews were intending to stay and fight it out. The cannons lowered their muzzles and started firing point blank into the ranks of the advancing British. Times had changed though and the attackers were no longer in deep formation and their own weapons were far more accurate. Batteries started to fall and by the end of the day, the Essex had captured nine guns and the Berkshires had not only captured twenty-two, but had succeeded in turning some around and shelling their former owners. Importantly, the 9th Essex had also swung to their right and captured Feuchy Chapel.

On 1 August 1917 the battalion relieved the 11th Middlesex Regiment on the frontline. The unit war diary describes the night and the following two days as 'unusually quiet'. At about 6.00 pm on 3 August 1917 the battalion war diary contains the following details:

12th (Eastern) Division Monument sits on the rise of the hill as you come out of Arras.

At that hour the enemy opened heavy fire on the left sub-sector of the brigade front occupied by the 7th Battalion Norfolk Regiment. The bombardment also fell on the support trench of our left company, and the trench was practically obliterated. Firing was intense till about 12.30 am and during that time the enemy attacked and secured an entry into the frontline between Pick Avenue and Vine Avenue. The right company of the Norfolks fell back on our left company, but later in the proceeding 2/Lieutenant E. R. Capper of this battalion led bombing parties first of our battalion and later of 7th Norfolk Regiment and succeeded in driving the enemy back to within 15 yards south of the junction of Pick Avenue and the frontline. The 7th Norfolks also attacked and by 10.00 am on the 3rd the original line held by that unit was again in their sole occupation. Our casualties were slight and were mostly caused by artillery.

On 4 August 1917 the battalion was relieved by the 5th Royal Berkshire Regiment and moved back to the location named the brown line. Between this date and 12 August, the men spent their time refitting, cleaning and training in preparation for returning to the frontline. Working parties were provided for the continuing repair of trenches and shelters, as well as working on the building of new ones.

On 12 August 1917 the battalion moved to fresh positions in the Wancourt-Feuchy Line, just north of Sword Lane, a trench on the outskirts of Monchy-le-Preux. Here they continued their training in the art of attack and prepared to move back into the frontline.

Major Edwin Baskerville Hickox MC.

It was whilst training was taking place in the Sword Lane area that eight men were injured by the accidental explosion of a grenade, three of whom died on the day as a result of their injuries, and one who died on 18 August. These were:

- Major Edwin Baskerville HICKOX
- Lieutenant Frederick Elliott BRASTED – Died of Wounds on 18 August 1917
- 34937 Private Charles Henry LAWRENCE
- 40527 Private Robert HOLDER

All four men were taken to No. 8 Casualty Clearing Station at Agnez-Les-Duisans, where they died as a result of their injuries. The position was previously held by No. 19 Casualty Clearing Station, which differs from the entry made in the National Roll of the Great War. They are all buried next to each other at Duisans British Cemetery, Etrun, France, and they were all aged 28.

Robert Holder's name is recorded on both the Albert Street War Memorial and the Town War Memorial in St. Albans, Hertfordshire.

FROM EAST AFRICA TO THE SOMME – DR. ALEC BAMFORD MC, VD, MA, PhD.

Alec Bamford.

A small collection of photographs and medals were brought into the *Herts at War* exhibition in Letchworth in 2015. The owner was the grandson of Alec Bamford, to whom the medals were awarded. He asked the project team if they could establish anything about his military career. The following is a consequence of in-depth research into his service.

Alec Joscelyne Bamford was born in Shanghai, China on 9 April 1885, the son of the Reverend Alfred John Bamford and Mary Bamford (née Heward). In 1881 his father's first wife, Helena Joscelyne, died and it was whilst in the performance of his work in Hong Kong that he met his second wife, Mary, hence their son's middle name. The family eventually returned from the Far East to England, where they settled in the newly established Garden City of Letchworth, Hertfordshire.

Alec was educated at Malvern College and Emmanuel College, Cambridge, during which time he spent three years serving with the Cambridge University Rifle Volunteers. After graduating in 1907, he left the shores of England on 29 October 1908 aboard the liner *Nubia* in order to take up a post at the Colombo Observatory in Ceylon. By 1913 he had become its superintendent and was responsible for many improvements in the work of the Observatory, among which was the initiation of a programme of pilot balloon observations and of a radio time service for the benefit of shipping. Additionally, Alec investigated the possibility of forecasting flood data for the Kelani River, using the rainfall figures reported daily in the Kelani Valley. Eventually, he devised a method of obtaining the forecasts, which was adopted officially for flood warnings. He generated many investigations, chiefly on the meteorology of Ceylon, and published his results in scientific journals in both Ceylon and Europe. Apart from his Observatory duties, he acted as a professor and lecturer in physics at the University College of Colombo.

Aside from his civilian career, he served in the local volunteer force, the Ceylon Planters Rifle Corps, where he achieved the rank of Colour Sergeant. He took leave from the C.P.R.C. to enable him to accept a commission in the British Army, and at the time of his application requested an appointment to the Motor Machine Gun Service.

East Africa

Sir John Willoughby, who had become infamous some years previously for his involvement in the Jameson Raids of 1895 into the South African Transvaal, was commissioned in 1915 by the War Office to raise a force to fight the Germans in East Africa. Willoughby privately funded a new armoured unit, which he named No. 1 (Willoughby's) Armoured Motor Battery. The War Office, who had agreed to Willoughby's naming under some pressure, assigned it the official army designation of No. 322 Company, Army Service Corps.

Members of the 1st Armoured Motor Brigade.

Willoughby acted as the commanding officer, and the small unit was equipped with four Leyland armoured cars, four Leyland 3-ton lorries, one workshop lorry, four light lorries, three Leyland passenger cars, eighteen Douglas motorcycles and a contingent of 120 men.

One of the unit's officers was Alec Bamford. The unit left Devonport on 7 February 1916 aboard the Troopship HMT *Huntsgreen*, a German ship originally named *Derflinger* which had been captured by the British at Port Said and used in the Mediterranean, serving at Gallipoli. The ship arrived at Kilindini, British East Africa, on 16 March 1916.

Early in 1914 Colonel Paul von Lettow-Vorbeck had been appointed commander in chief in German East Africa. He commanded a small force of German nationals and African soldiers, known as 'askaris', who were loyal, well disciplined, well trained and well paid. Colonel von Lettow-Vorbeck realised that German East Africa would only be a sideshow with little support from Berlin, so his policy was to try and avoid confrontation, keeping ahead of the Allied Forces by leading them into the remote and disease-ridden country, where sickness and malnutrition would kill and tie down many Allied troops, keeping them away from the Western Front and other battle areas. This policy succeeded in that it maintained a campaign without placing too much of a demand on Germany for additional resources. Military action in the region killed and maimed far fewer troops and porters than were lost to disease and malnutrition.

German East Africa was to become a battleground that was imposed on the local population, who were largely unaware of this remote quarrel between the Europeans. However, it was a strategic failure in the sense that it never diverted much in the way of British men and material from the Western Front itself.

The terrain and climate of East Africa made this campaign particularly difficult for British troops, and a very different

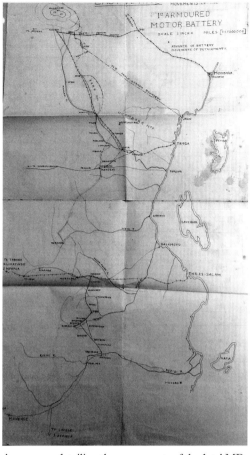

A rare map detailing the movements of the 1st AMB.

experience to that of the Western Front. The deadly tsetse fly prevented the use of draft animals or mounted infantry. Motor cars and lorries were often found to be practically useless owing to the lack of roads and the heavy rainfall. Local porters were regarded as the best available means of transporting supplies and ammunition along the supply lines of communication, which were sometimes up to 300 miles long.

Hundreds of thousands of porters were employed and requisitioned by both sides. Their absence removed a vital part of the village work force, resulting in crops not being sown or harvested. The villagers' yields and herds were further depleted by the Germans who lived off the country and operated a scorched earth policy. The Allies, too, had to sometimes live off the land, their food supplies were further depleted by the Germans leaving behind civilians, the sick and the wounded, trusting that the Allies would look after them.

Unlike the actions seen on the Western Front, the encounters with the enemy in East Africa consisted of brief engagements in thick bush, where short bursts of rifle or machine gun fire brought the matter to a swift conclusion. Whilst sniping by the askari troops was one of the most significant irritants to the Allied troops, it was disease that generated the larger proportion of casualties, and the 1st AMB diaries indicate – with monotonous regularity – the number of men taken sick during their time in East Africa.

On Saturday, 24 June 1916 the unit came under fire from some askari snipers, who were quickly driven off. However, they had managed to damage the radiator of one of the armoured cars, but this was soon repaired by removing some of the tubes and filling the holes with green wood, which swelled when it became wet and prevented the water from escaping; a further example of the 'mend and make do' type of war that was undertaken in the African bush. On Monday, 7 August 1916 Lieutenant Alec Bamford led a party of four cyclists to accompany the 29th Punjabis on a reconnaissance patrol to Ruhungu. They found the road had been blocked by felled trees and thick bush, which made it impossible for any motor vehicles to pass. A large rock nearby had been prepared as a sniping position, with a good view along the rough road; another instance of how war was waged in the theatre. The unit war diary also reports that in the six months after leaving England, three-quarters of the personnel were hospitalised as a consequence of sickness.

Whilst there were no real military objectives as the distances involved were vast and the forces involved quite small, it was the terrain and the weather that had the most impact on movement. The heavy armoured cars of the 1st AMB struggled in the non-existent roads of the East African terrain and vehicles constantly broke down, despite the fact that many had been specifically adapted to deal with the poor ground conditions. Eventually, the unit was disbanded and the vehicles were moved to Egypt, where the army attempted to take over the component, as it was technically part of the Army Service Corps. John Willoughby resigned in protest and the vehicles were forwarded to Mesopotamia, where their armour was removed and they were converted into anti-aircraft lorries.

Alec Bamford again boarded the HMT *Huntsgreen*, this time at Darussalam on 18 May 1917, bound for Egypt. During the journey he found he had been awarded the Military Cross in the 1917 Birthday Honours list, which celebrated the official birthday of King George V, and were published in *The London Gazette* on 4 June. Arriving at Alexandria on 11 June 1917, he was initially attached to the Intelligence Branch of the General Staff of the 1st Echelon. With his meteorological expertise, Alec was posted to a Royal Engineers Survey Company on 17 September 1917, where he was engaged in sound ranging and survey work. He remained with them until 1 April 1918, when he was posted to the staff of the

Military Governor in Jerusalem. He left the Suez region on 10 May 1918 aboard a troopship, arriving in England in June. Following his return to the UK, he lived in his parent's home for a short while, at 4 Hillshot, Letchworth, Hertfordshire.

The Somme

By the time Alec returned to England, the Allied forces on the Western Front were preparing for the Battle of Amiens, one of a series of offensives that were to become known as the 'Last 100 Days'. Alec had a role to play as an officer of the Machine Gun Corps and arrived in France on 27 July 1918, initially being stationed at the Machine Gun Corps base depot in Camiers.

On 24 August 1918 Alec was posted to the 38th Battalion, Machine Gun Corps, part of the 38th (Welsh) Division, joining them the following day at Forceville, with a draft of 30 other ranks. The battalion had been seriously mauled the previous day during actions at Contalmaison and La Boiselle, and total casualties had been high.

Alec quickly found himself involved in the Second Battle of Bapaume, which took place between 31 August and 3 September 1918. During this time, the battalion again suffered a large number of casualties, and Alec would have seen a very different type of war during this brief period than the one he had witnessed in East Africa.

It was on 14 September 1918, when the battalion was located in positions at Etricourt, that Alec was wounded by a gas shell. He was initially evacuated to No. 130 Field Ambulance and following preliminary treatment, was moved to No. 3 Canadian Casualty Clearing Station. By 18 September he had been evacuated to the 2nd British Red Cross Hospital at Rouen. He was invalided home to the UK on 20 September 1918, after which he spent some time recovering from the effects of his injury. By this time the Armistice had taken place and Alec eventually relinquished his commission on 11 July 1919.

Post War

Alec married Margaret Campbell in 1919 and the couple later had two children: Margaret, born in Letchworth in 1921, who travelled with them in 1924 when Alec returned to Colombo to take up his role as the Observatory Supervisor, and John Alexander Campbell Bamford, who was born on 27 March 1926.

Like his father, John was educated at Emmanuel College, Cambridge, where he graduated in 1948. He worked at Guy's Hospital, London, qualifying with the Conjoint diploma in 1950 and graduating the following year. He proceeded to MA in 1952 and became a doctor in obstetrics and gynaecology a year later.

After serving as house physician at Guy's Hospital, he took up practice in Australia in 1952. He was one of the very early members of the Royal Australian College of General Practitioners, and had a great interest in research and medical education. Sadly, he died on 29 November 1970 at the age of 44.

After Alec Bamford returned to England, he was engaged in teaching for a number of years. During the Second World War he accepted a post in the Meteorological Office and was posted to the Marine

Military Cross, British War Medal, Victory Medal and Colonial Auxiliary Forces Long Service Medal belonging to Alec Bamford. (*All items and photos were provided to the* Herts at War *project by the Bamford family*)

Branch, which had been evacuated to Stonehouse, Gloucestershire. His work here involved the principal wartime activity of the branch, the production of meteorological atlases covering all oceans of the world. Throughout the Second World War, Alec Bamford served with the Home Guard. He retired from the Meteorological Office in 1946 and moved to Ferring, Sussex. His wife, Margaret, passed away on 16 July 1954 and Alec lived alone until he passed away after a brief illness on 19 November 1957, aged 73.

Chapter Four

1917 – Mud & Devastation

Following the devastating losses suffered on the Somme battlefields and in the maritime Battle of Jutland during 1916, it was hoped that 1917 would bring victory to the Allies. However, early in February the Germans resumed unrestricted submarine warfare around the British Isles with the goal of knocking Britain out of the war. By cutting off all their imports, the German Navy planned to starve the British people into submission. By the end of April that year, U-boats had sunk more than 500 merchant ships and had all the hallmarks of becoming a success. In response to the U-boat attacks, Allied merchant ships began to sail in convoys, escorted by warships. Although the convoys were harder to find and attack, the U-boats still posed a terrifying threat. By the end of 1917, 3,170 Allied and neutral ships, totalling nearly six million tons, had been sunk. But the new convoy tactics, when combined with limited air support near the coasts, and an increase in Allied war vessels, allowed the all-important logistical lifeline to continue across the Atlantic and sustain the Allied war effort.

By the middle of the month, the Germans along the central portion of the Western Front began a strategic withdrawal to the Hindenburg Line, shortening the overall front by 25 miles and eliminating an unneeded bulge. Their intention was to fortify the ground they had held since 1914, and the Allies were fully aware of the economic and political effects that would result from a lingering continuance of war. The enemy, however, continued to inflict heavy casualties upon the Allied forces and the Hertfordshire newspapers were filled with reports of German trench raids, terrific artillery bombardments and the names of local men who had been killed, wounded or taken prisoner.

In the Middle East, the newly reinforced and replenished British troops captured Kut Al Amara in Mesopotamia from the outnumbered Turks and continued their advance to capture Baghdad, Ramadi and Tikrit. By the beginning of March, a mass protest by Russian civilians in St. Petersburg erupted into a revolution, and within days Russian soldiers had mutinied and joined the uprising. The 300-year-old Romanov dynasty was brought to an abrupt end with the abdication of Tsar Nicholas II, and Great Britain, France, Italy and the United States all rushed to recognise the new government in the hope that Russia would stay in the war and maintain the Eastern Front.

In April, US President Woodrow Wilson declared war on Germany, bringing American troops into the conflict. The British army, supported by Canadian and Australian troops, made rapid advances north of the Hindenburg Line at Arras and Vimy. The news of devastating losses again began to filter across the county, as well as tales of heroic deeds which brought the bestowal of gallantry awards such as the Military Medal and Distinguished Conduct Medal to the men of Hertfordshire.

The French Fifth and Sixth Armies attacked along a 25-mile front south of the Hindenburg Line and the new French commander-in-chief, Robert Nivelle, introduced a creeping barrage tactic, in which troops advanced in stages, closely behind successive waves of artillery fire. However, his plan was poorly coordinated and the troops fell far behind. The Germans, benefiting from good intelligence and aerial reconnaissance, soon became aware of the French plan, and Nivelle's offensive collapsed within days with over 100,000 casualties. Nivelle was relieved of his command and replaced by General Henri Petain, who had to deal with a French Army that was showing signs of mutiny. The mutinous atmosphere in the French Army erupted into open insubordination as soldiers refused orders to advance. More than half of the French divisions on the Western Front experienced some degree of disruption by disgruntled soldiers, angry over the unending battles of attrition and appalling living conditions in the muddy, rat and lice-infested trenches. Petain cracked down on the mutiny by ordering mass arrests followed by several firing squad executions that served as a warning. He then suspended all French offensives and visited the troops to personally promise an improvement of the whole situation. With the French Army in disarray, the main burden on the Western Front now fell squarely upon the British Army.

On 7 June a tremendous series of underground explosions on the German-held Messines Ridge south of Ypres, a 250-foot-high point which had given the Germans a commanding defensive position, announced the commencement of a fresh Allied assault. British, Australian and Canadian tunnellers had worked for a year to dig mines and place 600 tons of explosives under the German defences. The British stormed the ridge, forcing the surviving Germans to withdraw to a new defensive position further eastward.

Following on from its successes at Messines, the British attempted once more to break through the German lines, this time by attacking positions east of Ypres, Belgium, in what is now known as the Third Battle of Ypres. On 31 July 1917 the British attacked the vastly improved German defences on the outskirts of the Belgian town. It was on this day that the men of the Hertfordshire Regiment were to experience their most devastating losses of the Great War. The Hertfordshires, attacking the village of St. Julien, were to see 100 per cent of their officers and 75 per cent of other ranks become casualties. Although the British Fifth Army succeeded in securing forward trench positions, further progress was halted by heavy artillery barrages from the German Fourth Army and heavy rainfall in the area. This was the period in which the county suffered its highest level of battle casualties, with virtually every town and village receiving distressing news of the loss and injury to its menfolk.

The British resumed their attack at Ypres on 10 August, focusing on German artillery positions around Gheluvelt. The attack produced a few gains as the Germans effectively bombarded the attackers and then successfully counterattacked the Allied troops. Six days later the British tried again with similar results. The entire Ypres offensive then ground to a halt and Douglas Haig pondered his strategy. On 20 September a revised British approach began at Ypres, designed to wear down the Germans. It featured a series of intensive, narrowly-focused artillery and troop attacks with limited objectives to be launched every six days. The first such attack, along the Menin Road towards Gheluvelt, produced a gain of about 1,000 yards with 22,000 British and Australian casualties. Subsequent attacks yielded similar results. The Ypres offensive culminated around the village of Passchendaele on 10 October, as Australian and New Zealand troops died by the thousands while attempting to press forward across a battlefield of liquid mud, advancing just 100 yards. Steady October rains created a slippery quagmire in which wounded soldiers routinely drowned in mud-filled shell craters.

A rout of the Italian Army began on 24 October as thirty-five German and Austrian divisions crossed the Isonzo River at Caporetto and then rapidly pushed forty-one Italian divisions sixty miles southward. By now, the Italians had been worn down from years of costly but inconclusive battles along the Isonzo and in the Trentino, amid a perceived lack of Allied support. Nearly 300,000 Italians surrendered as the Austro-Germans advanced, while some 400,000 deserted. The Austro-Germans halted at the Piave River north of Venice, only as a consequence of supply lines becoming stretched to the limit.

On 26 October a second attempt was made to capture the village of Passchendaele using Canadian troops but failed. Four days later the Allies attacked again, gaining ground as the Germans began pulling out. The village of Passchendaele was eventually captured by Canadian troops on 6 November, bringing the Third Battle of Ypres to an end with no significant gains amid 500,000 casualties experienced by all sides.

At the end of October, in the Middle East, the British led by General Edmund Allenby began an attack against Turkish defensive lines stretching between Gaza and Beersheba in southern Palestine. The initial attack surprised the Turks and they pulled troops away from Gaza, which the British attacked secondly. The Turks then retreated northward toward Jerusalem with the Allies in pursuit.

Aiding the Allies were a group of Arab fighters led by T. E. Lawrence, an Arab-speaking English archaeologist, later known as Lawrence of Arabia. He was instrumental in encouraging Arab opposition against the Turks and in disrupting their railroad and communication system.

In Russia, Bolsheviks led by Vladimir Lenin and Leon Trotsky overthrew the Provisional Government in what came to be known as the October Revolution. They established a non-democratic Soviet Government based on Marxism, and Lenin announced that Soviet Russia would immediately end its involvement in the war and renounce all existing treaties with the Allies.

The German High Command, led by Erich Ludendorff, gathered at Mons, Belgium, on 11 November to map out a strategy for 1918. Ludendorff bluntly stated that he was willing to accept a million German casualties in a daring plan to achieve victory in early 1918, before the American Army arrived in force. The objective was to drive a wedge between the British and French armies on the Western Front via a series of all-out offensives using intensive storm troop tactics. Once this succeeded, the plan was firstly to decimate the British Army and knock Britain out of the war, and then to decimate the French Army, and thus secure final victory.

On 20 November 1917 the first-ever mass attack by tanks occurred as the British Third Army rolled 381 tanks accompanied by six infantry divisions in a coordinated attack of German trenches near Cambrai, an important rail centre. The attack centred on a 6-mile-wide portion of the front and by the end of the first day appeared to be a spectacular success with 5 miles gained and two Germans divisions wrecked. This news was celebrated by the ringing of church bells in England, for the first time since 1914. However, similar to past offensives, the Allies failed to exploit the gains and following the arrival of heavy German reinforcements and an effective counterattack, the Germans took back most of the ground they lost.

Jerusalem was captured on 9 December by the British, thus ending four centuries of control by the Ottoman (Turkish) Empire. Finally, in mid-December, Soviet Russia signed an armistice with Germany. With Russia's departure from the Eastern Front, forty-four German divisions became available to be redeployed to the Western Front in time for Ludendorff's Spring Offensive.

By the end of the year, the county of Hertfordshire had seen its menfolk serving in every theatre of war across the globe, many of whom were not to return to their homes. For others, there would be a long road of recovery and for some, a lifetime of physical pain and mental torture. Still, the people of the county remained hopeful that the new year would bring a final victory, and see the boys come home.

BOY SOLDIERS – ROWLAND NEWLING & WILLIAM STOTEN

The emotive subject of 'boy soldiers' is something that has been debated by many eminent historians over the decades. The recruitment of young men under the age of 18 has been practised by the British armed forces for centuries and the rank of 'Boy' was commonplace for those between 12 and 16 years of age, particularly in the Royal Navy and Merchant Marine. At the time of the Great War, the minimum age for a Territorial Army recruit was 17, whilst a Regular Army recruit had to be 18. Anyone required to serve overseas had to be a minimum of 19 years of age. With this in mind, it should also be remembered that for every 'underage' soldier serving in the British Army during the Great War, there were a comparable number of 'overage' men who, by rights, should not have been on the fighting front, yet were also to serve abroad.

Nevertheless, the story of 'boys' is an incredibly powerful one and one that we feel deserves a mention here. For its part, the British government laid claim to the fact it was not actively recruiting underage soldiers; it was simply the case that there were a number of applications from men who had lied about their age and were, in fact not suitable for military service. Hertfordshire, like most other British counties, had its fair share of applications from teenagers, and official records demonstrate that more than 30 servicemen from the county, under the age of 18, were to lose their lives in the Great War. Whilst we look more closely at the stories of Rowland Newling and William Stoten, the following are the details of just a few of the Hertfordshire 'boys'.

- Boy 1st Class John Borkwood Symes of Lord Street, Hoddesdon, was the first to die when he was killed aboard HMS *Hawke* on 15 October 1914, aged 16. His name is recorded on the Portsmouth Naval Memorial.
- Private Frederick John William Jarvis of 'The Mount,' London Road, Rickmansworth, died of his wounds on 26 April 1915 whilst serving with the 2nd Battalion, East Surrey Regiment. He was aged 17 and is buried in the Hazebrouck Communal Cemetery, France.
- Private William Bird of High Cross, Aldenham, was reported as Missing in Action on 18 January 1916 whilst serving with the 9th Battalion, Rifle Brigade. He has no known grave and is remembered on the Menin Gate Memorial, Ypres, Belgium. He was 16 years old.
- Ordinary Seaman George Edward Pinnock of The Gardens, Little Gaddesden, Berkhamsted, and Boy Servant Frederick Charles Webb of Hill Farm Cottage, Cuffley; both perished aboard HMS *Black Prince* when the ship was sunk on 31 May 1916 during the Battle of Jutland. Pinnock was 17 years old and Webb

was just 16. Their names are recorded on the Chatham and Portsmouth Naval Memorials respectively.

- Private John Frederick Johnson of Willow Lane, Watford, serving with the 6th Battalion, Bedfordshire Regiment, was reported as Missing in Action in 7 August 1916. He has no known grave and his name is recorded on the Thiepval Memorial, Somme, France. He was aged just 17.

- The last known Hertfordshire teenage battle casualty is Private Albert Long of Bowling Road, Ware, who was killed in action on 8 April 1918 whilst serving with the 1/5th Battalion, Yorkshire Regiment. He was 17 years old and is buried in the Croix-Du-Bac British Cemetery, Steenwerck, France.

One of the most poignant losses is that of Apprentice Richard Owen, who was reported as lost at sea aboard the merchant ship *Highbury* on 31 May 1917. The merchant sailor was 15 years old. The steam cargo ship, completed in 1912 by Bartram & Sons for Britain Steamship Co. Ltd, was posted missing and is believed to have been sunk on 14 June 1917 by German submarine *U-82* at a position 100 nautical miles west/southwest of Bishop Rock. She was travelling from Antofagasta to Birkenhead with a cargo of nitrate. On this basis, it is presumed that Richard may have been washed overboard prior to the ship being sunk.

Private Rowland Newling aged 16. This photograph was taken just a few weeks before he was killed.

The market town of Royston was to see the loss of two of its teenagers, both of whom were serving in the Hertfordshire Regiment when they were killed.

Rowland Newling was the youngest son of James and Louisa Newling of The Warren, Royston. The 1911 Census confirms that he was an 11-year-old schoolboy and was just 15 years old when he joined the Hertfordshire Regiment on 15 June 1915. His older brothers were all serving in the army and one cannot imagine the heartache his mother, who had recently been widowed, must have suffered as she saw her youngest boy leaving for the Western Front, never to return.

On 14 July 1916 the 1st Battalion, Hertfordshire Regiment took over positions at Festubert from the 16th Battalion, The Rifle Brigade. Rowland was officially reported as Missing in Action on 23 July 1916 but the unit war diaries for the battalion and the 118th Brigade do not show any activity or casualties on that day. However, the Hertfordshire Regiment had been involved in a trench raid on 19 July, in which a total of 64 men – made up of 3 officers, 6 NCOs and 55 other ranks – attacked German positions with the intention of capturing prisoners for

Men of 'E' Company, 1st Battalion, The Hertfordshire Regiment, leaving for France in November 1914. The *Herts at War* project has identified a number of men in this photograph.

Private Walter Flanders. (*Supplied by Nancy Jack and colourised by Doug Banks*)

Lance Corporal Valentine Flanders. (*Supplied by Nancy Jack and colourised by Doug Banks*)

Lieutenant Colonel Arthur Martin-Leake (Centre) circa 1915.

Arthur Martin–Leake
Memorial at High Cross.

Sergeant Tom Gregory (Left) and Corporal Hamlet Bloxam (Right) with a comrade from the Hertfordshire Regiment. Hamlet Bloxam served with the Herts Regiment until May 1915 when failing health saw him transferred to the 575th Employment Company, Labour Corps. He eventually died from the effects of ill health on 22 May 1919 and is buried in the Vicarage Road Cemetery, Watford.

The Satterthwaite Collection discovered by the *Herts at War* Project.

The Satterthwaite brothers.

Private Edward Ernest
Ambrose Collection.

TOP IMAGE LOW RESOLUTION.

Left to right: Martin Powell, Mandy Wilson, Lesley Powell and Colin Wilson, visiting William Clements' grave on the 100th anniversary of his death.

Members of the Royal British Legion and Royal Observer Corps visiting the grave of Second Lieutenant Peter Francis Kent at the H.A.C. Cemetery.

Sergeant Frank Edward Young.

Rick and Richard Young at the precise location where Second Lieutenant Frank Edward Young VC met his death.

The grave of Second Lieutenant Frank Edward Young VC at Hermies Hill Cemetery, France.

Dawn Kite (second from the left), great niece of Elphinstone Chamberlain, Madame Lucile Delaye (centre), granddaughter of Madame Lucile Delaye, and Sheryl Kite (second from the right) great-greatniece of Elphinstone Chamberlain, where they met at Elphy's grave.

intelligence purposes. The raid got off to a good start but it appears the Germans were aware of the attack and were fully prepared. The raiders had to leave the German trench empty handed, suffering a number of casualties, with 3 officers wounded, 3 other ranks killed, 1 other rank missing and 12 other ranks wounded.

It is very likely that Rowland was one of the other ranks who were listed as killed or missing, his death most likely not being officially recorded until a few days later. Not only had her youngest son been reported as missing, but to make matters worse for his mother, his body was never to be recovered.

Rowland has no known grave and his name is recorded on the Loos Memorial, France. He was only 16 years old.

Grave of Private William Stoten at Essex Farm Cemetery, Ypres.

William Henry Stoten was the third son of Frederick and Jane Stoten of The Fleet, Baldock Street, Royston. Their eldest son, John, had joined the Hertfordshire Regiment prior to the Great War and had been a member of 'E' Company. He was with the regiment when it arrived in France on 5 November 1914 and was severely injured on 19 November 1914 by shell splinters during an artillery bombardment which claimed the lives of seven members of the company. John lost his right eye as a result of his injuries and was discharged from the army in October 1915. Just a few weeks later, 16-year-old William – perhaps looking for revenge for his brothers' injuries – enlisted in the

Private William Stoten.

Hertfordshire Regiment. He was posted overseas in October 1916, just in time to take part in the Battle of Ancre, the final British offensive on the Somme in 1916.

As winter drew in, William moved with the battalion to the Ypres sector and on 7 January 1917 was holding frontline positions near Hill Top, northwest of the village of Wieltje. At 2.45 am the positions were heavily shelled by German artillery and then raided by German infantry. Although the attack was driven off, three men were killed by a single shell in an attempt to render support to the men in the isolated frontline outposts; Captain Eric Butler Smallwood MC, Corporal Currell MM, and Private William Stoten. All three men are buried side by side in Essex Farm Cemetery, Ypres, a short distance from where they were killed.

Both Roland Newling and William Stoten are remembered on the Royston War Memorial.

Probably the most bizarre teenage loss was that of Second Lieutenant Digby Crunden Cleaver of 'Woodside,' Much Hadham, who was killed whilst flying on 29 December 1915. He had joined No. 1 Squadron just four days earlier and was asked to accompany Lieutenant George Frederick Prettyman on a flight to Hazebrouck, where they were to pick up a new machine. The idea was that Prettyman would fly them to Hazebrouck and collect the new machine, whilst Cleaver flew their original aircraft back to base.

Second Lieutenant Digby Crunden Cleaver of Much Hadham, killed in a bizarre flying incident.

As they approached Hazebrouck, Prettyman decided to give the young pilot a lesson in ground observation and as Cleaver was leaning out over both sides, it appears that the aircraft became uncontrollable, eventually turning on its back. Prettyman claimed that after getting the aircraft under control, he looked back to see the observer's seat empty and Cleaver falling to earth. Prettyman landed the aircraft and found that Second Lieutenant Cleaver was dead. He was just 17 years old. This is the official story, but there is some intimation that Prettyman was actually just showing off and Cleaver was not secured in his seat.

THE IMPACT OF WAR – PRIVATE SAMUEL RAW

The impact of war on the mental state of a soldier is far better understood today than it has ever been. The subject of 'shell shock' during the First World War was significantly studied, but much less is known about the effects of mental conditions such as depression and anxiety on soldiers on the front. Initially, statistics maintained by the medical services indicated over 20,000 cases of mental illness during 1915. As of 1916, a large majority of these cases were listed under a more general term of 'non-combatant casualties'. As the war drew on, a manpower crisis began to arise in the British Army as some of the combatants suffered the effects of psychiatric breakdowns. Soldiers who were evacuated from fighting positions as a consequence of mental health illnesses placed an enormous strain on resources, and doctors came under immense pressure to return soldiers to duty as quickly as they could. Often, where this could not be achieved, the soldier's condition was dealt with through military discipline, rather than continued medical treatment. Soldiers from all walks of life were evacuated to base hospitals, where treatments were varied and frequently experimental. Records show that one Hertfordshire soldier, Samuel Raw, a long-serving professional, was affected by a mental condition which appears to have been treated with little more than a temporary change of location. This is his story.

Samuel was born on 27 November 1889 as the son of Henry and Harriett Raw of 22 Green Street, Hertford. He attended St Mary's Church of England School in Ware and appears to have led a relatively normal life. He enlisted in the Bedfordshire Regiment on 7 December 1910, serving with the 2nd Battalion, which at that time was stationed in Bermuda. In 1912 the battalion moved location from the Caribbean to South Africa, where it had seen a great deal of action in the Boer War.

Having served much of his soldiering career in warm climates, Samuel arrived in a rain-soaked France on 3 January 1915, when the battalion was located in billets at Pont de la Justice. They remained in this location until early March 1915. He first saw action when the battalion took part in the battle of Neuve Chapelle, where it endured significant casualties. Just a few weeks later the battalion took part in the Battle of Festubert, where it again suffered a high level of casualties. For even the most battle-hardened soldier, the devastating losses, the poor living conditions in the frontline trenches and the minute-by-minute threat of death must have been a perpetual strain. Throughout the summer of 1915 the battalion continued to serve on the Western Front, and by September became involved in the Battle of Loos, where it again saw much action.

By 21 April 1916 the battalion had lost a total of 473 officers and men, and it appears that the events had started to take their toll on Samuel's health. On 22 April 1916, after 16 months at the front, he was admitted to No. 43 Casualty Clearing Station at Frevent, suffering with melancholia, a condition that was believed to have been a consequence of significant personal loss. Today of course, his condition would have been treated through medication, counselling and a programme of rehabilitation that would have helped address the way he was feeling.

Samuel's condition was deemed severe enough for him to be returned to the UK, where he was attached to the 3rd Battalion of the Bedfordshire Regiment, who were performing coastal defence work at Landguard Fort, near Felixstowe. It was thought to be somewhat of a miserable location; cold and damp, with a large number of tented facilities. It's not surprising, therefore, that it was from here that Samuel absconded on 3 November 1916, having then completed almost 10 years' service with the regiment. His name can be found in the *Police Gazette* dated 14 November 1916, amongst those listed as British Army Deserters and Absentees. It is uncertain as to whether Samuel was captured, or gave himself up but eventually he was returned to his unit and subsequently posted back to France, in preparation for the British offensive at Arras.

On 11 April 1917 the battalion was in positions near the village of Henin Sur Cojeul, their objective being to capture the German trenches that formed part of the Hindenburg Line. As soon as the attack got underway, the assaulting troops came under very heavy enfilade fire from the German positions, and were quickly forced to take cover. Although casualties were fairly light, Samuel Raw was amongst the few men who were killed in action. At the end of the day, as his body lay upon the battlefield, the battalion war diary recorded the situation as being *'a quiet night, but very cold with a heavy fall of snow'*.

Samuel's body was eventually recovered from the battlefield and rests, along with seven of his comrades, at the St. Martin Calvaire British Cemetery in St. Martin-Sur-Cojeul, France.

A VERY SHORT WAR – PRIVATE WILLIAM HENRY CLEMENTS

Throughout the First World War there were many stories that involved incredible bravery and heroism in the face of the enemy, but for the majority of infantrymen, life both in and out of the trenches was fairly routine and, in general, somewhat mundane. For a large part of his service, a soldier would find himself performing tasks such as training, cleaning and washing kit, maintaining equipment and performing everyday jobs that kept his surroundings as comfortable as possible. Units would rotate in and out of the frontline, usually spending no more than four or five days in forward trenches, where life – the dangers aside – could be extremely unpleasant and uncomfortable.

Grave of Private William Henry Clements New Military Cemetery, Vlamertinge, Ypres.

The men on the frontline were required to keep a watchful eye on the enemy and on occasions take part in trench raids and small assaults on their opponents' position. There was constant shellfire from enemy artillery and harrying machine-gun fire from fortified positions. A desire to deny the enemy any form of movement or comfort was often the everyday objective. Inevitably, most units of the British army suffered a number of casualties. Whilst the loss of a comrade could be hard to bear, it was seen by many as part of the job and, in general, soldiers accepted the possibility that they could be killed, wounded or captured. Most tragic of all, however, were the occasions when a soldier, after enlisting in the army and succeeding in his basic training, was posted overseas only to become a casualty without ever firing a shot in anger.

One such case is that of Private William Henry Clements, a young man from the town of Sawbridgeworth, Hertfordshire, who gave his life in the service of his country on 29 June 1917. It was a considerable honour, 100 years after his death, to be able to escort members of his family on a brief tour of the Ypres salient, where his short life was brutally extinguished in one of the world's most tumultuous conflicts. Life on the Western Front was to be short lived for William, who would only spend 42 days on the European continent before his service was brought to an abrupt and tragic end.

William Henry Clements was born on 1 November 1897 as the second child and first son of Joseph and Elizabeth Clements (née Harber) of High Road, Sawbridgeworth, Hertfordshire. His father worked as a domestic groom, a job that involved caring for horses, cleaning their stables and equipment, seeing that they were exercised, and attending to the carriages they were used to pull. His mother worked hard to raise a large family in a time of austerity; they had a total of eleven children. William was baptised on 6 February 1898 at the Parish church of St. Mary the Great, by the Reverend Henry Alcion Lipscomb, and by the time he joined the British Army, his family were living at 4 Church Street, Sawbridgeworth.

Records show that William left home on 29 January 1917 and travelled to the county town of Hertford, where he enlisted into the army. He was described as aged 19 years and 2 months, stood 5' 6¾" in height, had a 33½" chest and weighed 127lbs (9 Stone 1lbs). In civilian life, he had been employed as a nursery hand.

Initially, he joined the 1st Reserve Battalion of the Hertfordshire Regiment, known as the 2/1st Battalion, and went through a period of basic training, most

The original Record of Service for William Clements shows that he enlisted at Hertford on 29 January 1917.

likely at Halton Camp in Buckinghamshire, where new recruits were first put through their paces to ensure their suitability as a fighting soldier. The aim of this course was to build up physical fitness and confidence, instil discipline and obedience, and teach the fundamental military skills necessary to function in the army. After a few weeks of basic training, things began to become more advanced. Soldiers would start to learn the basics of movement in the field and were introduced to night operations and route marching. Later would come weapons handling, marksmanship and digging trenches.

Following the completion of his basic training, William was transferred to No. 3 Battalion of the Machine Gun Corps, and went on to train as a machine gunner, a specialist occupation. The equipment he would have to use was one of the most complicated pieces of weaponry on the battlefield. He would have to know by heart how to work, fire and maintain the weapon in some of the most adverse conditions in the world. The machine gun was a weapon that would take lives but also save lives; and to save lives, it had to work at all times and in all conditions.

It was on 12 April 1917 that William was given his initial vaccinations for tetanus, typhoid and smallpox in preparation for serving overseas. A few weeks later, on 29 May, he boarded a troopship which left Southampton, arriving later that day in Boulogne. Once he landed, he travelled 12 miles south to the town of Camiers, where he joined the Machine Gun Corps Base Depot. Here a majority of men were further trained on both the Lewis gun and the Vickers machine gun. He would have spent his time preparing for service on the frontline by going through advanced training and preparation. William remained at Camiers until he was posted to No. 153 Company, Machine Gun Corps on 8 June 1917 at Zudrove, a small French village just a few miles from the Belgian border. William was amongst 26 men who were drafted into the company on that date. The unit was part of the divisional troops for the 51st (Highland) Division.

Every unit of the British army was required to keep a daily record of their movements, locations and events, known as war diaries. It is quite unusual for these secret documents to contain the names of soldiers who were killed, wounded or missing. Most commonly, they recorded the names of the officers as they passed in and out of the unit for training or secondment purposes, or as a consequence of being killed or wounded. The war diary for the 153rd Machine Gun Company, covering the period from May to June 1917, lists the names of soldiers who were killed or wounded. It also gives reference numbers which refer to points on British Army trench maps. From these references, it is possible to visit the locations of former trenches and fighting positions in which the unit served during June 1917.

On 21 June 1917 the company left the village of Zudrove and marched 3 miles to Watten, where they boarded a troop train to travel the 23 miles to Poperinghe,

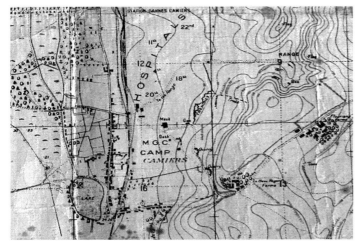

This original military map shows the location of the Machine Gun Corps Camp at Camiers. The area is almost unchanged, as can be seen in the photograph below.

(*Comparison Satellite Image*)

a central hub for Allied forces who were serving in the renowned Ypres salient. At the time of their arrival, the area was awash with men, munitions and equipment as the British army prepared itself for the forthcoming Third Battle of Ypres, commonly known as the Battle of Passchendaele. William and his comrades marched to billets at 'E' Camp on the outskirts of the town. They remained in the camp, continuing their training, until the night of 23–24 June 1917, when the entire company were ordered to move into the frontline area. No. 3 Section, which William was attached to, was then to wait in the transport lines on the outskirts of Poperinge.

On 28 June 1917 the men of No. 3 Section, who had been waiting for orders to move, marched into dugouts along the North Bank of the Yser Canal, on the outskirts of Ypres. That evening, German artillery units bombarded the area with

This trench map shows the location of the 153rd Machine Gun Company Headquarters, and the area that was heavily shelled by German artillery on 28 June, during which time William Clements was wounded.

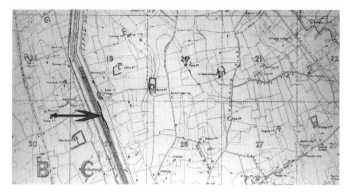

high explosive shells, killing 291604 Private Joseph Mair Aitken from Pittenweem, Fife, who was attached to the company from the 1/7th Black Watch. His name and his original unit are recorded on the Menin Gate in Ypres, Belgium. William Clements, 20150 Private Thomas Bremner and 89237 Private Alfred Waller were wounded. Sadly, Alfred Waller was not to survive the war and died of his wounds on 29 October 1918. He is buried in the St. Sever Cemetery Extension, Rouen, France.

The wounded men were taken to a dressing station in the village of Vlamertinge, where every effort was made to save their lives. William Clements could not be saved and he died as a consequence of his wounds, having been in sight of the enemy but not ever having the opportunity to fire a shot in anger. Burials were usually made in the original Military Cemetery, until June 1917, when the New Military Cemetery was begun in anticipation of the Allied offensive launched on this part of the front in July. Although the cemetery continued to be used until October 1918, most of the burials are from July to December 1917. On this basis, it is believed that William Henry Clements was one of the first men to be buried in this cemetery.

The medal roll for the Machine Gun Corps shows that William Henry Clements was entitled to the British War Medal and Victory Medal. The combination of a British War Medal and Victory Medal was fairly commonplace for men who joined the army after January 1916 and earned itself the nickname 'Mutt and Jeff'. A total of 170,500 officers and men served in the MGC, of which 62,049 were killed, wounded or missing.

In a tragic postscript, the reverend who baptised William was to lose his own son, Private Charles Hugh Pearson Lipscomb, who died of his wounds a few weeks before William on 18 April 1917 whilst serving with the 2nd Canadian Mounted Infantry. He was injured on 9 April 1917 with a shell wound to his arm, which fractured his humerus on the opening day of the attack on Vimy Ridge. He died at No. 2 Australian General Hospital in Wimereux, France. Both men have their names recorded on the Sawbridgeworth War Memorial.

The slip above was signed by Joseph Clements on 13 May 1920, when he took receipt of his son's medals.

British War Medal and Victory Medal, nicknamed 'Mutt and Jeff'.

William's army service record survives today, and a document within it indicates that his brother, Frederick Charles Clements, served in a prisoner of war camp at Clayhill, near Enfield. There are no records at this point to indicate which unit Frederick served with, but it is likely he was serving with the Royal Defence Corps, whose job was one of home defence.

PRIVATE CHRISTOPHER AUGUSTUS COX VC – A VICTORIA CROSS FOR ST. ALBANS

Christopher Augustus Cox was born on Christmas Day 1889 in Kings Langley. In 1912 he married Maud Swan with whom he eventually had eight children. After leaving school, he worked as a farm hand. Christopher enlisted in the Bedfordshire Regiment after the outbreak of war, joining 'B' Company of the 7th (Service) Battalion, a unit raised as part of Lord Kitchener's Army. After completing his training at Ampthill Park, he went to France, landing on 26 July 1915. His role within the battalion was that of a stretcher bearer, bringing in wounded comrades from no man's land – a particularly difficult and dangerous task. It was in this role that he was wounded in the leg on 1 July 1916

Christopher Augustus Cox VC.

when the 7th Battalion stormed not only the first two German trench lines but also took the Pommiers Redoubt. After recuperating from his wound, he was back with the battalion in time for the storming of Thiepval and the Schwaben Redoubt in September 1916 and served through the winter of 1916–17.

He survived the assault on the Miraumont trench system in February 1917 during the Ancre operations and earned his Victoria Cross in March 1917 when his battalion was one of the ones pursuing the Germans as they fell back to the formidable Hindenburg Line defences. On that day, 54th Brigade, which he was a part of, moved into the Loupart Line, with Christopher and the 7th Bedfords being south of Achiet-le-Grand. Although the Germans were withdrawing to the Hindenburg Line, they fought a controlled rear-guard action and held Achiet-le-Grand and Bihucourt villages strongly. The 54th Brigade had to advance 2 miles over open ground, which ultimately took five days and cost many casualties.

13 March saw him carrying several wounded Bedfords back to the dressing stations through a horrendous barrage and sustained machine gun fire. On arrival at the station each time, he did not hesitate to turn around and return to the battlefield in search of more wounded men. On 14 March, Cox's company were in reserve positions but stretcher bearers were called in for assistance. Having advanced straight through the barrage across open ground to the line of shell holes, the advance had been held up and the men gone to ground. Regardless of the danger, Christopher set about moving from hole to hole, dressing all the wounded men he could find. His task completed, he started carrying the most badly-hurt men back on his back, as there were no stretchers available. The first 200 yards were covered under intense, aimed machine gun fire but he dashed across the open, completely ignoring the fire as he went. Onlookers were amazed to see him return unhurt some time later, when he went back with a second man. This continued all day and into the night. About his actions on 15 March, Second Lieutenant Chapman is quoted as saying, '*I saw him wandering about in front of Hill 130 in the front wave, attending to the wounded. He showed absolute contempt of the volume of machine gun fire and heavy bombardment, although MGs opened on single targets. I previously saw him carry back a man on his back on three different occasions, and on withdrawing my company I found he had similarly treated six others, two of whom were wounded a second time while he was carrying them.*'

Incredibly, Christopher also ferried machine gun supplies to where they were needed the most when he returned to the battlefield, having dropped a wounded man off. Whilst carrying one man on his back, the wounded man was hit again but Christopher carried on, despite knowing he was being targeted by the efficient German gunners. At one point in the day Second Lieutenant Dealler saw him moving through a hail of machine gun fire being aimed at him, completely ignoring it as he did so. He arrived back with the officer, and having listed what work he had been busy doing, asked for any direction as to the next location of any wounded men. With no immediate reply being forthcoming, Christopher advanced back into the fire on his own initiative and disappeared over the brow of a hill, completely disregarding the attention of the German gunners who had so few targets to fire at. Once he found all the wounded Bedfords he could, he turned his attention to the Middlesex men who were next to them in the advance. Second Lieutenant Dealler added, '*He did not rejoin the company until about 12 hours after and although a very powerful man, whom I have never seen tired before, he was thoroughly exhausted.*'

Christopher Augustus Cox VC and his family on the occasion of his award.

16 March saw him ferrying the wounded back from the most advanced point through a hail of machine gun and artillery fire, transferring ammunition across the battlefield and marking out gaps in the enemy wire with tape in full view of the enemy gunners. When the advance was finished and the battalion was hurriedly digging in beneath an intense barrage, Christopher was one of the few men who could be seen above ground, where he was busily carrying on moving the wounded back to the aid stations to the rear.

17 March saw him advance to help the company in front of his own, as all their stretcher bearers had fallen. On passing through the gaps in the enemy wire whilst looking for wounded men, he paused to mark the passages that allowed following waves to move quickly through them later on. All told, Private Cox moved around 20 men from where they fell wounded back to the dressing stations despite intense fire and barrages. With so little movement taking place above ground, he was constantly a target for any German observer with a gun, yet he ignored the obvious danger and repeated the action time and time again. In addition, the number of men he must have dressed as they lay wounded in shell holes is another matter entirely and must surely measure somewhere between 40 and 60 men.

Unsurprisingly, for his outstanding bravery and courage under fire, Private Christopher Cox was recommended for – and received – the Victoria Cross. Six weeks later the 18th Division assaulted German positions around Cherisy during the Battle of Arras and the battalion was attacking south of the village. They advanced on the heels of the British bombardment only to find the wire uncut, after which the front waves had no option but to dig in and shelter from the crossfire and artillery barrage that rained down on them that day. During the advance, he received two wounds to his foot and had to be invalided home to Blackburn in Lancashire. Private Cox was unable to return to the front again after receiving his third wound, as he did not regain full fitness afterwards. Instead, he helped train the new recruits rather than being idle and of no use to his country and comrades.

Both of Christopher's brothers served in the war as well. Harry Cox served in the Navy and survived the war, but James Cox was killed in action in Belgium. After being wounded on 1 October 1916, he died two days later at No. 3 Canadian Casualty Clearing Station near Poperinghe. He is buried with over 10,000 others in Lijssenthoek Military Cemetery, Belgium.

Christopher Cox was presented with the VC by the King on 21 July 1917 at Buckingham Palace. His was one of 32 VCs presented that day. After the war, he returned to live in Kings Langley and loved to spend time in his garden. He worked for a few years for a builder and then worked for another 32 years as a maintenance labourer

Bedfordshire & Hertfordshire Victoria Cross recipients. Taken in 1956 at the 100th anniversary of the inception of the Victoria Cross. From left to right: Private Christopher Cox VC, Mrs Baron – sister of Private Samuel Needham VC, Lieutenant Colonel Tom Adlam VC, Mrs Hedges – widow of the then late Lieutenant Frederick Hedges VC and Corporal Alfred Burt VC. (*The Wasp*)

at the Ovaltine Factory. During the Second World War he served in the Home Guard and again showed his courage by entering the bombed-out Griffin Pub to search for the publican in the ruins. Unfortunately, Ted Carter was already dead; the only civilian killed in Kings Langley during the war.

After the war, Christopher was back at work in the factory, and in 1954, aged 64, he fell off the factory roof. This fall put him in hospital on and off for the rest of his life. He died 28 April 1959, aged 69. He was survived by his eight children.

DAY OF DAYS – THE HERTFORDSHIRE REGIMENT AT ST. JULIEN, 31 JULY 1917

Before the attack on the St. Julien position, which has since been given the name 'Battle of Pilkem Ridge', the 1st Herts, with other units of the 39th Division had to undergo a special course of training. On 21 June 1917 the battalion was billeted in the Moulle-Moulle-Seques area, about 7 km out of St. Omer on the Calais Road. In this district, a full-scale model of the sections of the line to be attacked had been prepared, woods being shown by branches of trees, and dummy trenches indicating the German positions. Day in and day out the troops were put through the part to be played by them in the attack, advancing first in artillery formation, then extending at a given point, which represented the crest of a reach at the southern edge of Kitchener's Wood, on which the famous Falkenhayn Redoubt was situated, and continuing in extended order to the line of the second objective, where in due course the barrage would be picked up.

The plan of attack for the 39th Division was as follows:

The section to be attacked was divided into three separate objectives, roughly the first, second, and third German defence systems, called the blue, black and green lines in operation orders. There was to be a very thorough artillery preparation for some days prior to the offensive, to be followed by the infantry advancing in leapfrog formation behind an impenetrable barrage. The 116th, and 117th Infantry Brigades were to capture the blue and black lines, and the 118th Brigade – composed of the 4/5th Black Watch, the 5th Cheshire Regiment, 1st Cambridgeshire Regiment and the 1st Hertfordshire Regiment – the green line.

This latter objective was rightly considered the most difficult, as it was not possible to give it the same amount of artillery preparation as the others, on account of a lack of direct observation and the distance it was situated from the guns. In fact, the brigadier in his address to the regiment on the day before the offensive was launched stated this, and added that 'Pride of Place' in the centre of the line had been allotted to the 1st Hertfordshire Regiment.

Intrepid German machine gunners might remain undercover and in action in spite of the barrage, and might possibly hold up the advance on a limited front until they could be dealt with by tanks or other means. As the action would be very local, it was not considered advisable to delay the general advance, especially as the success of an attack of this nature primarily depended upon the close proximity of the infantry to a creeping barrage. To fully appreciate the work performed by the battalion on 31 July, we must remember that all ranks had had it impressed on them, day after day for some time, that their part was to consist of merely walking behind the creeping barrage with slung rifles, and that no opposition would be met with other than an improbable machine gun nest, which if necessary, would be dealt with by tanks. In due course the battalion reached almost as high a state of perfection as was possible to expect in their training, and on 22 July, alongside the remainder of the 118th Infantry Brigade, it was moved by a motor bus to the camps near St. Jean Ter Biazin, preparatory to taking up the assembly positions for the battle. Routes to the line were arranged and one officer for each company went forward on 27 and 28 July to arrange for the assembly positions, which consisted of shell holes behind Hill Top Farm for the most part.

On the night of 30–31 July 1917 the battalion left the bivouacs near Vlamertinghe, which they had occupied on the previous day, and after a rather trying march across country through desultory shellfire and gas in the pitch dark, finally reached their assembly position just after midnight, having suffered only a few casualties.

The company officers were:

No. 1 Company: Lieutenant Hardy commanding, Lieutenants Walthew, Thompson and Scott.

No. 2 Company: Captain Lowry commanding, Lieutenants Ritchie, Head and Secretan.

No. 3 Company: Lieutenant Gallo commanding, Lieutenants Marchington, Francis and Edwards.

No. 4 Company: Captain D'Arcy Fisher commanding, Lieutenants Lake, Macintosh, Gilbey and King.

The following is a transcribed account of the action on 31 July 1917 as described by an officer of the 1st Battalion, Hertfordshire Regiment, Captain Bernard Gripper:

At 3:45 am on 31 July 1917, just as dawn was breaking, the barrage opened with a burst of flame along the whole line of the divisional front, the most intense barrage that had been put up to that period of the war. The 1st Hertfordshires were not due to move off for some time, so, as no reason for secrecy existed, fires were lighted and the men had breakfast. The weather, which had been fine practically throughout July, had broken on 28 July and during the whole of 31 July, low-lying clouds and drizzle rendered co-operation with the Royal Flying Corps almost impossible. The state of the ground was such from the rain, that progress of any sort could only be made with great difficulty, and it was this fact, more than anything else, which led to the comparative failure of the operation.

The Germans were well aware of the impending offensive and it transpired subsequently that they were also in possession of most of the details of it. They had accordingly withdrawn most of their guns in the forward area, and had apparently resigned any idea of holding their first system seriously; which was not surprising in view of the pounding it had received from our guns.

Hardly a shred of wire was to be seen, and what remained of the trenches was lightly held by inferior troops. The blue line gave little trouble, nor did the black line, although the Falkenhayn Redoubt on the southern edge of Kitchener's Wood needed the attentions of a tank before it succumbed. The 1st Hertfordshires left their assembly positions at about 5.00 am and advanced in artillery formation over the captured ground to the first

German line of defence, the blue line, where they took cover on account of the desultory shelling and a certain amount of machine gun fire. The latter was silenced shortly afterwards, by which time the 116th Infantry Brigade had reached the black line.

So far the attack had gone exactly to plan. While the 1st Hertfordshires were on the black line, bearings were taken in order to confirm that the battalion was keeping direction and to ascertain the position of

St. Julien, which lay over the crest of the ridge. The 1st Hertfordshires resumed their advance according to schedule, No. 1 and 2 Companies leading in artillery formation, followed by Nos. 3 and 4, being wished good luck by the 116th Brigade as they went through them. On gaining the crest of the first ridge, leading platoons came under machine gun fire; the signal to extend was immediately given, and the promptitude with which platoon commanders and NCOs got the men out of artillery formation saved many casualties.

The 'dead ground' west of the Steenbeek was reached and the battalion had to cross the stream by a plank bridge, owing to its swollen state. It was here that the battalion had their first disappointment, as the two tanks detailed to accompany them were both out of action. One got stuck irretrievably in a shell hole, and the other fell into the Steenbeek, and although its crew made gallant efforts to get it underway again, they could not do so. The battalion, after crossing the Steenbeek – having plenty of time to do so – reorganised in the dead ground on the far side of the stream. The colonel was full of optimism and the example he set kept everyone cool and collected. The Padre wandered from company to company – although shelling was pretty continuous – cheering the men up, giving them cigarettes and showing absolutely no fear; as calm as if such a thing as fear never existed.

The moment for the advance came, and although the intense barrage promised did not exist, as it appeared that only two 18-pounders and two 4.5-inch howitzers were in action on this part of the line, the Herts guards swept up the hill. Reconnaissance patrols from No. 1 Company were then extended along the St. Julien – Poelcappelle Road, but No. 4 Company was shortly afterwards compelled to withdraw a little, owing to 'shorts' from the two howitzers.

By this time the battalion was in touch with the Cheshires on the right, but there was no sign of the Black Watch, which had apparently got hung up in Kitchener's Wood. A battery of 77-mm guns had been discovered between the Steenbeek and St. Julien, which were duly appropriated.

The unpleasant features on the left of the line at this time were: no sign of the Black Watch and persistent machine gun fire from some pillboxes half left. At about 9.35 am a message was received from the officer commanding the left company of the Cheshire Regiment, intimating that the Germans were massing for a counter-attack on the Springfield – Winnipeg Road, and at the same time a reconnaissance patrol of the 1st Hertfordshires reported that the Germans were holding a line of old artillery dugouts about 400 yards east of the Poelcappelle – St. Julien Road.

This information was sent to battalion headquarters on the Steenbeek, and Colonel Page ordered the two leading companies to move up and man the latter road, with a view to forestalling any counterattack that might be in contemplation by the enemy. The road was manned and the enemy were in sight of the battalion for the first time in force that day. On the left the counter barrage was very heavy, and the left of the battalion was entirely in the air, and the ground was a very sticky, making the going very heavy.

The casualties on this flank were getting heavy, and still the promised intense barrage was conspicuous by its absence. During this advance Captain Lowry, commanding No. 2 Company, was killed. About this time, two German aeroplanes flying very low passed over the battalion, firing very light, and machine gunning the battalion, and shortly afterwards the Germans launched a counterattack. This was in some force, commencing with a line in extended order, which advanced up to the line of dugouts previously mentioned, when we joined up with about 100 others who were taking cover there, and who had opened heavy rifle fire to cover the advance.

At this point the counterattack was stopped by rifle and Lewis gun fire, mainly from No. 1 Company on the right. The heaviness of the enemy casualties at this point and also later in the day is vouched for by those of the regiment who were taken prisoner, Lieutenant Walthew estimating that he passed upwards of 150 German dead alone, on the ground over which the battalion advanced. At 10.10 am the intense creeping barrage was due to recommence in order to cover the advance to the third objective, the green line, but this completely failed to materialise on the battalion's front, owing – as it transpired later – to the impossibility of moving the guns up through the mud. Had this barrage been available, there is little doubt that the attack would have been entirely successful. Casualties up to this time – especially on the right – had not been heavy, and the men were in excellent spirits. The attack had to continue, and the men followed their officers without a moment's hesitation into a veritable hail of rifle and machine gun fire, proceeding from the shelters about 300 yards in front.

In spite of all their special training for this very attack in advancing at a walk in comparative safety behind a barrage, the battalion adopted the only possible course, namely open warfare methods of short sectional and individual rushes, with the greatest promptitude and gallantry. The casualties were at once devastatingly high. Lieutenant Gallo, commanding No. 3 Company and Lieutenant Scott of No. 1 Company were killed almost at once, and many officers including Lieutenant Hardy, commanding No. 1 Company, were wounded, but the battalion carried on, taking a heavy toll of the enemy, as was discovered when the position, about 400 yards east of the Poelcappelle – St. Julien Road, was taken at the point of the bayonet, together with some 70 or more prisoners.

By this time practically all of the supporting companies were on the frontline. On this position being captured, the Germans put down a very heavy barrage underlying about midway between it and St. Julien, thus entirely cutting off the battalion from any reinforcements which might have been supplied by the 1st Cambridgeshire Regiment, who were in reserve.

Lieutenants Francis, Thompson and Walthew on the right, with Lieutenants Ritchie and Head on the left and Lieutenant Secretan in the centre, went on with the remnants of the battalion. On the left, Lieutenant Ritchie and Head advanced on either side of a cross hedge with about five men each. Lieutenant Head advanced on the left side and was never seen again. Lieutenant Ritchie went on the right side of the hedge and found a row of pillboxes about 200 yards on, carrying his Lewis gun himself, he tried to get around them, but was knocked out, so Private Atkins went on with the three remaining men.

In the centre, Lieutenant Secretan was killed, and the final act of the battalion in the gallant fight can best be given in Lieutenant Francis' own words, who – with Lieutenant Thompson – was taken prisoner on the green line.

Our line was woefully thin by this time, consisting mainly of No. 1 Company, some of my own company, No. 3, and some of No. 4 Company. The remainder of No. 3 Company could be seen forming a second line, some 300 yards in the rear. It was here I met Lieutenant Thompson of No. 1 Company, the only other officer that could be seen. We had a hurried consultation: our left flank was bare, obviously non-existent: our right flank was in touch with the company of the Cheshires, but beyond them in the rear it could be seen that the cemetery was still untaken. Heavy fighting could be heard going on and the Germans showed their presence by the number of rockets being sent up. In front, we had a small creeping barrage, nothing to what we had seen earlier in the morning, we heard afterwards most of the guns had been unable to move owing to the mud. Everywhere around us was the cry, 'stretcher bearer wanted'.

We remembered our strict orders, 'Never mind your flanks, carry on with your job,' and decided to push on, taking advantage of the barrage and not waiting for our second line. The time now was somewhere around 12 noon. It was rather like leading lambs to the slaughter, as we had a pretty fair idea of what the Langmarck Line was going to be like though as yet we couldn't see it owing to the hedge lining the road in front of us, and also knew that beyond those few men in our second line there was no further help.

It cannot, therefore, be wondered at that our men, who had behaved up to now so magnificently, began to lose heart. It was just at this time that a private of the Cheshires came up to us, saluted as if on parade, and said, 'Connecting file Cheshires sir'. The way this man behaved was wonderful; he stuck to us the whole time and was eventually captured with us, he kept in front with Thompson and myself, shouting, 'There are Cheshires, come on the Herts'. I believe Thompson has his name, as he certainly deserved a medal.

We carried on at the walking pace keeping a good line, and having comparatively few casualties, until we reached the road. After going through the hedge lining the road, we had our first view of the green line, the great big trench on top of a rise, and what was worse, two thick lines of uncut wire in front, but it was our objective and the Germans in the trench in front of us could be seen running away. It was at this point that Sergeant Hammond came up to me with a broad grin on his face and said something about at last getting at the Bosche, and would he tell the men to get ready to go absolutely all out. Immediately afterwards, a private came up and reported Sergeant Hammond badly wounded in the leg; he died immediately I believe. I won't say much about Sergeant Hammond, as anyone who was out in France with the Hertfordshires knew him, but I should like it to be known that he died just as he had always carried on, absolutely fearless and looking as if there was no finer fun on earth than going over the top.

We were now faced with this terrible uncut wire, and the German fire was beginning to be particularly heavy again. Thompson and I managed to scramble through it with a few men, the remainder following. The Germans, unfortunately, who were leaving the trench looked round, saw how few we were, and from both flanks and from the front the most murderous machine gun fire was poured onto us. Those who had not yet reached the wire went back a bit, and the few who had got through went on a little way and finally took cover in a shell hole. Our little party was now reduced to about six men, including the two officers and the Cheshires' orderly. The Cheshire company on our right had been more successful and reached the trench and entered it. Our hopes were now centred on them.

Our barrage was now knocking the Langmarck Line about in front of us, it seemed deserted now immediately in front, though on the flanks it was obviously occupied. It was bitter to sit there and think that with a few more men and more ammunition, as small arms ammunition had mostly been used in St. Julien, the trench was ours for the asking. For a little while nothing happened, we lit flares for our aeroplanes, but they quickly went away, and a German one appeared flying low and firing on us. It may be mentioned that although our aeroplanes were obviously doing good work, we were hampered and worried ever since leaving St. Julien by low-flying German machines.

Germans could be seen well in our rear, both to the right and left of us, though our immediate rear was clear, and soon our men could be seen advancing again. They reached the wire and we tried to rejoin them. It was hopeless, the fire was too heavy. Three of the men with us were shot at once, so we sheltered again in a shell hole, and the men who had come up had to fall back. I gather that they were all wiped out as they were practically surrounded on all sides. We were still mystified as to what had happened to the Cheshire company but we quickly knew, as Thompson pointed out some Germans with some English coming out of trench on our right, and to our horror the English were the prisoners and were picking up the wounded and searching the ground. The Germans were now everywhere, the time being about 1.30 pm, and we were finally taken about 4.00 pm. It seemed to us we were the only two survivors of that awful day.

Corporal Oliver of No. 1 Company I believe, had been badly wounded getting through the wire and died very shortly afterwards. He had shown very fine spirit. I know little of what happened on the left. The Black Watch obviously failed early. No. 2 Company got held up at the pillboxes where Lieutenant Head was killed. No. 4 Company I do not remember seeing at all. After being captured, we crossed the Langmarck Line and were taken to Passchendaele. The Germans had evidently had a bad fright, as every arrangement for a hurried leave was obvious; guns left lying unattended in the fields and everything very much in confusion. There were, however, many battalions massed at Passchendaele ready to move up, and obviously very reluctant to do so.

What happened with the battalion headquarters is given from notes by the Reverend Edgar Popham MC, chaplain to the battalion and regiment, and Sergeant Major Tite DCM.

The reverend writes:

It was while we were at the Steenbeek that the doctor, Captain Charles, did such magnificent work, going from shell hole to shell hole, dressing wounds. After the battalion had advanced from the stream, a message came asking for reinforcements, and I lost sight of Colonel Page, hearing a few minutes later that he had been killed instantly by a piece of shell.

The Sergeant Major writes:

About 12.30 pm the adjutant, Captain Milne, was hit and died almost at once. I got together all available men, about 25, mainly signallers and officers servants, and formed a line in shell holes. We then opened fire and the enemy, who were advancing over undulating ground at about 500 yards' distance, were compelled to halt. We continued to hold them with the aid of a few stragglers who found their way back, and a sergeant and about 20 other ranks of the 14th Hampshire Regiment, but running short of ammunition, we had to retire to a partly-dug trench on the opposite side of the river. Just before this, I stopped a bullet in my left arm, which put that limb out of action, and a few minutes later Captain Charles, the medical officer, was hit in the thigh. The chaplain at once went to him, but I yelled to him to lie down.

I was later reinforced by Sergeant Ashwell, who turned up with a Lewis gun and one man carrying magazines. This was a great help and I placed him on our left flank where there was a gap of about 1,000 yards between us and the Black Watch. During the whole of the time the chaplain, with total disregard for personal safety, did all possible to aid the wounded, and when he retired, he was the last to leave and brought with him, almost carrying him, a man who was wounded in the leg.

About 6.00 pm Lieutenant Walker of the 1st Cambridgeshire Regiment arrived with half a company and took over command, ordering me to go back and get my arm seen to. This I did and after walking until nearly midnight, found our transport near Elverdinghe, where I reported to Major Phillips, afterwards receiving treatment at the Corps dressing station nearby.

The reverend also writes:

We had a few badly-wounded men in a pillbox; while I was with them, I heard that Captain Charles had been hit, and calling to him they found that his thigh had been shattered by a bullet. After making him as comfortable as we could, four splendid stretcher-bearers crawled down the hillside with him and eventually got him back; one of the bravest bits of stretcher work ever done by the Herts. I wish I could remember their names. By this time, we were numb with sorrow and also a bit anxious as we did not know where the British army was, but after a time RSM Tite managed to get in touch, and found that a company of the Cambridgeshire Regiment was waiting in our rear, and we felt easier. On arriving at the Cambs' trench, I found an officer in charge and our boys fighting happily, and as it was not the place for badly wounded man, I decided to try and take him back, and we managed to get to a dressing station at about 7.00 pm. The next morning, I found brigade headquarters and the brigadier asked me to take charge of the remainder of the battalion until Major Phillips could come up, which I did until relieved on the evening of 1 August.

The following extracts from Sir W. Beach Thomas letter, published in the *Daily Mail* on 15 August 1917, summarised the fighting in the area covered by the 118th Infantry Brigade.

The highest sacrifice in the third battle of Ypres was perhaps paid by the 1st Hertfordshire Regiment, who, with other territorials as gallant as themselves, took St. Julien and pushed forward deep into the enemy's country beyond. I have heard no more splendid or moving tale of gallant men going out to death and glory since the war began, not even that of the Lancashires told the other day. The achievement of some of the same troops in the final capture of Thiepval, St. Pierre Divion, and the Schwaben Redoubt a year ago went almost unrecorded. It would be a double injustice if this second and yet more heroic venture also were left unrecorded. Losing men all the time, but never checked, these troops pushed on a good 1,200 yards to the next line of German trenches. The men reached the approaches to a trench defended by 400 yards of uncut wire, 6 yards deep and running along a contour swept by machine guns from the left, front, and flank. Still they did not stop. Some made their way round, some hacked at the wire and forced a way over it. Somewhere about this time, the last of the officers in the Hertfordshire Regiment fell, and the Sgt, himself wounded, took command. Among the men still with them was a padre, a chaplain of many fights, who cheered them on and at the end, being the last man to cross a little stream, carried, and when he could no longer carry, dragged, a wounded man to safer quarters a mile or more to the rear. I write especially of a regiment known to me personally better than any regiment in the army, and one weighs words with special care in writing of friends. The fight was one of the stoutest fights of war, worthy of the guards at the first battle of Ypres. The men were 'Hertfordshire Guards' indeed, and homes should ring with this story of sacrifice and valour.

The 39th Division were supported by Nos. 132, 133 and 134 Field Ambulance of the Royal Army Medical Corps. Their records show that men of the Hertfordshire Regiment carried the wounded for a distance of 2.5 miles in appalling weather conditions in order to provide them with basic medical attention. Duhallow Advanced Dressing Station, believed to have been named after a southern Irish hunt, was a medical post 1.6 km north of Ypres, and today is the location of the Duhallow ADS Cemetery.

A GLIMPSE OF HUMANITY AMIDST DEVASTATION – PRIVATE PERCY BUCK

In terms of Great War history and the county of Hertfordshire, one day stands out above all others: 31 July 1917. On that day, in an advance made by the men of the 1st Battalion, Hertfordshire Regiment of a little over two hours, the 'Herts Guards' as they had become affectionately known, were to lose every one of their officers and more than 75 per cent of their other ranks – killed, wounded or captured.

Private Percy Buck.

Set into the context of the carnage seen that morning, one remarkable story emerged – forgotten since 1917 but rediscovered by the *Herts at War* project almost a century on. This is the story of Private Percy Buck. Percy was born in Peterborough, then in the county of Northamptonshire, in 1891 to a working-class family who made the move to the Hertfordshire market town of Hitchin soon after the turn of the century, making their home at No. 19 Baliol Road. It was in Hitchin that young Percy was raised and schooled, visiting St Mary's church each Sunday, where in his teens he became a Sunday School teacher. After finishing his education, Percy took up work locally as a printer's compositor and also joined the local Territorial unit, the Hertfordshire Regiment, in which he showed promise. He was promoted to the rank of Sergeant, serving as one of 'G' Company's musketry instructors. Percy Buck met and married local girl Bertha Stevens on 9 November 1912. Together they moved to Upper Culver Street, St. Albans, where Percy found better opportunities to further his career. On 15 August 1914, just days after the outbreak of war, Mrs Bertha Buck gave birth to a son, Cyril. Records today are unclear, but it appears that in the months before the outbreak of the war, Percy's time with the Territorials came to an end, possibly due to his move to St. Albans.

It should come as no surprise that when war was declared, feeling the pressure to support his young family, Percy did not immediately re-enlist into the army, although his time was to come. Surviving records tell us that after re-enlisting in the Hertfordshire Regiment on 10 January 1916, Percy began his initial training and by 12 August had achieved the rank of Lance Corporal. He was further promoted, to the rank of Corporal, on 23 September 1916 and – ready to play his part in the war – was held in the UK as part of a reserve battalion awaiting the opportunity for overseas service.

On 13 November 1916 the Hertfordshire Regiment, part of the 118th Brigade, 39th Division, took part in the last phase of the Somme Offensive, an action named the Battle of the Ancre. The battalion suffered a high level of casualties during this time and readily-trained replacements were soon sought from the reserves held in the UK. Percy Buck was amongst the replacements who arrived at Folkestone on 24 November to await embarkation for the Western Front. The following day, after a short hop across the English Channel, Percy found himself at the 17th Infantry Brigade Depot in Boulogne, and it was whilst here that Percy was regraded as a Private, probably due to the ranks of the Herts having their full complement of NCOs at the time.

During their time at Boulogne, Percy and his comrades were prepared for service at the front and on 7 December 1916 Percy, along with 51 other ranks, finally joined their unit in the field on the outskirts of Ypres. The battalion remained in this sector throughout the remainder of December, and spent Christmas Day in trenches along the left canal bank, where they had relieved the 11th Sussex Regiment.

On 7 January 1917, whilst the battalion was holding trenches in what was known as the hilltop sector, the Germans made a surprise trench raid, capturing three other ranks. During this raid, Captain Eric Smallwood MC was killed, along with two other ranks, Corporal Currell MM and Private Stoten.

When the Territorial Force was renumbered in 1917, men from the Hertfordshire Regiment were issued numbers in the range 265001 to 290000, the lowest number being issued to the man with the lowest number from the first series. Percy was given the regimental number 267098.

By June 1917 it was clear to all that a large offensive was building up in the Ypres Salient. Private Buck and his comrades were withdrawn from frontline service and drilled in the tactics to be employed in their part of the 'big push' of that year. The men spent days practising attacks over exactly marked out ground, learning their objectives and targets, leaving no stone unturned in their planning for the attack. In spare moments, men spent time in the local town or village, where often they would have photographs taken to send to loved ones at home. Percy and a group of unknown friends did just this in the village of Wormhout in June 1917.

On the evening of 30 July 1917 the Herts made their way back up towards the front via the towns of Vlamertinge to trenches on the northern side of the Ypres Salient, where they would attack the German-held village of St. Julien, the last of three objectives allotted to the 39th Division (of which the 1st Hertfordshire Regiment formed a part).

In the hours before the attack, survivors of the battle often commented on the light-hearted and nervous jokes that passed amongst the men. No doubt some were sombre, others thought of home and family, all wondered what was to come in just a few hours' time.

Private Percy Buck (Left) and a group of chums from the Hertfordshire Regiment.

The attack of that day was launched at 3.50 am with the Herts forming the reserve for the first phase, the support for the second phase, and taking the lead role in the third and final phase of that day. The first two phases of that morning were highly successful and by 8.30 am the Hertfordshire Regiment found themselves lined up along the Steenbeek River just 600 yards from their final objective.

At 10.10 am on 31 July 1917 Private Percy Buck and 620 comrades advanced from the Steenbeek River towards their objective. Within several hundred yards, they advanced into a hail of machine gun and artillery fire, effectively decimating the battalion. Several hours later, a bloody, exhausted group of men returned to the Steenbeek river, the survivors of a disastrous attack, and Private Percy Buck was not amongst them.

One of the most powerful of thoughts when looking back at the experiences of the Great War is to try to understand the impact felt at home when disaster struck on the battlefield. The fallout across Hertfordshire in the wake of the St. Julien attack was of an epic proportion. Every major town and village in the county lost at least one son that day, some many more. Some loved ones would hear the news that a husband, father or son had been killed or wounded immediately, and with predictable heartbreak. Others – perhaps less fortunate – such as Bertha Buck, would only receive the dreaded 'Missing in Action' telegram. Bertha and her 2-year-old son were simply told that Percy's whereabouts were not known; the silence must have been deafening and we can only imagine the anxiety Bertha must have felt each morning when seeing the postman walking down Balliol Road.

That silence was finally broken three months after Percy was last heard from, and in a most unexpected way. A letter arrived on the doorstep of 19 Balliol Road, postmarked from Geneva in Switzerland, the Headquarters of the International Red Cross.

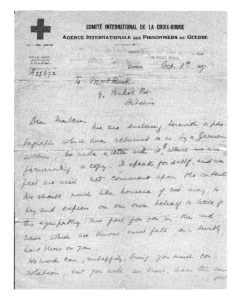
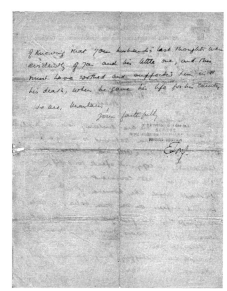

The original letter regarding Private Percy Buck.

Incredibly, the typed version of the original letter survives, a unique piece of history.

Receiving the astonishing letter from Gefreiter (Lance Corporal) Joseph Wilczek must have been the cause of very mixed emotions. Knowing that her husband would not be coming home would have obviously been devastating news for Bertha, but knowing for sure what she had probably feared all along may have also come as some kind of relief. Bertha may also have taken solace in that in his dying moments, Percy had taken the photograph of the two people dearest to him and held it for comfort in his final act. How she felt about the German soldier who was Percy's enemy,

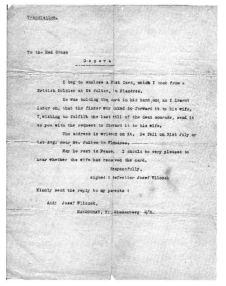

Original translation of the letter from Gefreiter Joseph Wilczek.

but who in the carnage of that day took it upon himself to perform a stunning act of humanity, we can but speculate. Today, with hindsight of a century, we can of course appreciate what Josef Wilczek did as a glimmer of human kindness on a catastrophic day.

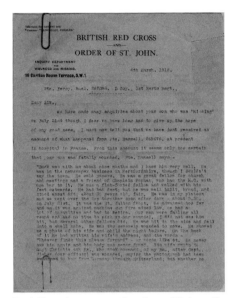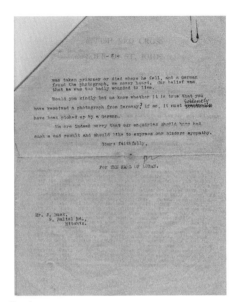

Red Cross letter regarding fate of Private Percy Buck

A few months after the end of the Great War, a comrade of Percy's who had been wounded and taken prisoner that day wrote a statement which was also sent to Mrs Buck, providing a little more detail about Percy's fate.

Private Percy Buck's body was never identified and he is today named on the Menin Gate Memorial to the Missing in Ypres.

The story of Percy Buck was forgotten in the years following the Great War until the *Herts at War* project uncovered a newspaper article detailing the event in 2014, and republished the story once more, this time with an appeal for information. The article was read by Christina Reynolds, granddaughter of Percy and custodian of a box of family artefacts including the original letter from Josef Wilczek and documents relating to this remarkable tale. Once more, after 100 years, the story of Percy Buck could be told again.

In November 2018 the final chapter of this incredible story came to light and can now be told for the very first time. After examining records, it was believed until 2018 that Gefreiter Wilczek did not survive the Great War, and that he, too, shared Percy's fate or was amongst the 'missing'. However, further research has proved that to be incorrect. In appealing to historians in Josef's hometown, it was possible to determine that there were only two Josef Wilczeks born in the right time period to serve in the Great War, and that only one of those men, born on 24 February 1897 had served in the German Army during the Great War.

Armed with Josef's date of birth, and with the assistance of German historian Immanuel Voigt, it was possible to trace records of the International Committee of the Red Cross, which showed that one Josef Wilczek, a Corporal with a Prussian infantry regiment was officially listed as 'Missing in Action' in September 1917 near Polygon Wood in the Ypres Salient.

A further report – this time British – shows that a man of the same name and the same date of birth was captured by British troops on 26 September 1917 and that he was wounded in both buttocks at the time of his capture.

Prisoner of War Record Entry for Joseph Wilczek.

Further research has since shown that after capture, Josef was taken back behind British lines and was admitted to hospital in Manchester just a week after his capture. Here he recovered from his wounds and probably wrote to his family for the first time to inform them that he was in fact alive, before being transferred to a prisoner of war camp in Hawick, Scotland, where he stayed for the rest of the Great War. Once it was absolutely confirmed that Josef survived the Great War, with the help of Polish interpreter Ania Marchwiak and a Polish historian in the modern city of Zabrze, it was possible to track down Mrs Ewa Pikulinksa, Josef's granddaughter, who until that date knew nothing of her grandfather's wartime experiences.

Ewa knew only that her grandfather had been a prisoner of the British, that he had 'nothing bad to say about them' and that he had bred rabbits whilst in captivity. However, she was also able to confirm that Josef returned to his hometown after the war, got married and had three children. He survived the incredibly turbulent times the region saw in the 1920s and during the Second World War, eventually dying on 15 October 1983, aged 86.

Finally, Ewa was able to provide one last piece to the puzzle: a photograph of Josef. Taken at a family marriage in the 1960s, the grainy image is the only known image of Josef Wilczek, late Corporal of the German Army and a truly honourable man.

Joseph Wilczek.

MURDER ON THE HIGH SEAS – EDWARD BADEN SHARP

Whilst the Hertfordshire Regiment suffered devastating losses on the fields of Passchendaele and many of the county's men were to lose their lives on this day of days serving with other units of the Commonwealth armies, death also visited those upon the high seas. For one young man, the fields of Flanders, which lay some 875 miles to the southwest, could not have seemed further away. Yet his fate at the hands of the same enemy, passing almost unnoticed, was no less than those who perished on the battlefields of Belgium.

The SS *Belgian Prince.*

Edward Baden Sharp, a 16-year-old apprentice serving with the Mercantile Marine, was the son of William and Frances Annie Sharp of 29 Watson's Walk, St. Albans. On 31 July 1917 he was aboard the SS *Belgian Prince*, which was carrying a load of blue clay bound for Newport News, Virginia. The ship had been built in Sunderland by Sir James Laing & Sons in 1901 for the Megnatic Steamship Company of Bristol and named *Mohawk*. The little steamer, after being sold twice, finally ended up with the Furness Withy Company and was renamed *Hungarian Prince*. In 1915 she was aptly renamed *Belgian Prince*.

The ship left Liverpool to undertake what was to be her last voyage. At about 7.50 pm she was some 175 miles from Tory Island, Ireland when, without warning, a torpedo hit her on the port side between the engine room and the No. 5 hold. The engines were quickly disabled along with the dynamo, which prevented the vessel from sending a distress signal. The ship took on a list and the crew abandoned her in three lifeboats. During this time, the *U-55* surfaced and began to shell the vessel with the intention of disabling the wireless. Oberleutnant zur See Wilhelm Werner, the commanding officer of the *U-55*, of course, had no way of knowing the wireless could not be used, so this action is understandable. For an unknown reason, *U-55* moved around to the starboard side and fired her machine gun at the ship. Werner then approached the three lifeboats which held the entire 42-man crew. They were all ordered to get out of the boats and taken on board the casing of the *U-55*. The master, Harry Hassan, was taken below while the men on deck were searched. They were asked if they had any weapons and were handled quite roughly by the German crew, according to the survivors.

What happened next can only be described as deliberate murder. The crew of the *U-55*, under orders from Werner, took the lifebelts from most of

Wilhelm Werner at the time he was serving on Reichsführer SS Heinrich Himmler's personal staff.

the survivors and threw them overboard. They then got into the lifeboats, took what they wanted and tossed the rest into the sea, removed the corks and further damaged them with axes to be sure they would sink. One small boat was kept intact and boarded by five of the Germans who took her to the damaged, drifting hulk.

According to Chief Engineer Thomas A. Bowman, one of just three survivors: *'When they boarded her, they signalled to the submarine with a flash lamp, and then the submarine cast the damaged lifeboats adrift and steamed away from the ship for about two miles, after which he stopped.'*

If the crew were taken aboard the *U-55* to be returned to Germany as PoWs, taking the men on board and destroying the lifeboats would be understandable – a U-boat captain did not want to leave any evidence floating in the water that would indicate that a ship had been sunk, lest his boat be discovered, and drifting lifeboats were the best evidence. However, this time the *Belgian Prince* had not sunk and Werner even had some of his own men on the ship.

The *U-55* crew then went below and closed the hatch, and the boat got underway on the surface. Werner sailed about two miles then submerged the *U-55* with the forty-one survivors still on the casing of the boat. Chief Engineer Bowman stated: *'About 10.00 pm the submarine dived and threw everybody in the water without any means of saving themselves, as the majority of them had had their lifebelts taken off them.'*

Having taken their lifebelts and destroyed their lifeboats, Werner now decided to simply drown the entire crew; a clear act of cruelty and outright willful murder, and this was not the first time he had done this. Werner had carried out a similar act with the crews of the *Torrington* on 8 April 1917 and four days later on 12 April to the crew of the *Toro* – despicable acts of murder on the high seas. The men in the water had little chance of survival and all but three died.

The three who survived were able to tell the tale of what happened to their fellow crewmen after they were picked up by a British patrol boat later in the day. Able Seaman George Silessi swam back to the *Belgian Prince* and reboarded her; he was on board when a U-boat came alongside of the ship the next morning. He said several Germans boarded the stricken ship and looted her – lucky for him, the Germans did not see him and he jumped off the ship and got into a small boat which was nearby. The third survivor was an American, Second Cook William Snell of Jacksonville, Florida. He survived by hiding his lifebelt under his clothes. After the *U-55* went under, he also headed for the only place he could, the *Belgian Prince*. He got within a mile when he saw the *Belgian Prince* explode and sink. Silessi stated the U-boat fired two shots from her deck gun and the *Belgian Prince* sank stern first at about 7.00 am on 1 August 1917. Thirty-nine crewmen died in the North Atlantic, courtesy of Wilhelm Werner and the crew of the *U-55*, but what happened to the ship's master? It is unclear if Harry Hassan was brought back on deck or kept as a PoW, but I have been told by a family member that *'he was never seen or heard from again by his family.'* Bringing the total lives lost to forty.

The KTB (Kriegstagebuch), which is the submarines' war diary, mentions little of the event, and Werner makes no mention of the name of the ship or the fate of the crew. He also makes no mention of taking the Captain prisoner – a clearly evasive entry in the log of the boat to keep this crime a secret. In Germany the public were told that what the British press had reported was nothing but a lie.

Nevertheless, it can be confidently asserted that the story of the German sailors taking the crew of the sunk ship on deck and then submerging and washing them into the sea can only be a low lie and calumny. If our U-boat men had wanted to let the foreign crew perish, they did not need laboriously to take them aboard. The idea that Germans out of sheer devilry pretended to save the men, only in order to let them perish, could not possibly occur to German sailors.

In Holland, the press mocked the Germans by publishing a pastoral letter which was read at Protestant churches in Germany, including the cathedral attended by the Kaiser. The letter was published next to the story about what happened to the men of the *Belgian Prince*. It read in part: *'We will comport ourselves as Christians toward our enemies and conduct the war in the future as in the past with humility and chivalry.'*

Wilhelm Werner sank a considerable amount of shipping and in 1918 he torpedoed and sank HMHS *Rewa*, a fully lit and marked hospital ship. Fortunately only four people were killed. He tried to sink another hospital ship, the *Guildford Castle*, but because of a dud torpedo and a misfire, he failed in this endeavour. He was charged with war crimes but fled Germany and never faced trial.

Werner lived in Brazil and later returned to Germany, where he joined the NSDAP. He later joined the SS and rose to the rank of SS Brigadeführer serving on Reichsführer SS Heinrich Himmler's personal staff. He never answered for his crimes and he died on 14 May 1945.

MY SISTER SAVED MY LIFE – CORPORAL WILLIAM TAYLOR MM

Perhaps one of the most common terms to be linked with warfare – and particularly survival in battle – is 'luck'. Of course, skill, ability and proficiency at one's job goes a long way to help chances of survival, but sometimes it is a slice of good old-fashioned luck that saves the day. Corporal Bill Taylor embodied many of the attributes mentioned above; a brave and proficient soldier, skilful and – in terms of battle at least – lucky. Bill was 23 years of age when war was declared in 1914 and was serving with the Hertfordshire Regiment Territorials. In civil life he worked as a gardener and was a mild-mannered and gentle man. He was also incredibly brave. Throughout the first two years of the Great War, Bill served as a stretcher bearer. He took part in the First Battle of Ypres, The Battle of Festubert, Loos and served on the Somme. It was for tireless work saving lives of British wounded and German prisoners over a 48-hour period in November 1916 during the Battle of the Ancre that Bill was to receive the Military Medal for his exemplary work in the field.

Corporal William Taylor MM.

Rather unusually, Bill's role changed between 1916 and 1917 so that by mid-1917 he was no longer carrying a stretcher, but instead had swapped this for a high-powered Lewis light machine gun. Ironically, even though he had used a stretcher to save lives on the Somme, he would use a Lewis gun to do the same the very next year at Ypres.

Bill was one of the 620 men of the Hertfordshire Regiment to take part in that fateful attack on St. Julien on 31 July 1917, on this occasion leading a Lewis gun team with No. 4 Company on the northern flank of the battalion's advance. It was as he ran into a withering machine gun and rifle fire at the furthest point of the battalion's advance, that Bill felt a sharp pain in his chest – he was struck by shrapnel. Fortunately for Bill and his comrades, the shrapnel had struck one of his most treasured possessions, a thick leather wallet, tightly packed with photographs of his family. The shrapnel had pierced all layers of the wallet and each photograph in turn, before finally embedding in a photograph of Bill's sister. It did not penetrate his body (although it broke several ribs in the process), the photographs amazingly saving Bill from serious injury or even death.

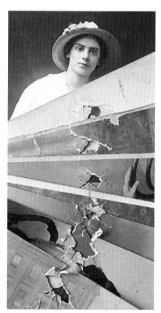

The photographs that saved Corporal Bill Taylor's life when they stopped shrapnel from penetrating his body.

This miraculous escape meant that Bill was able to continue the fight when he was most needed. Each with a Lewis gun, it was Bill Taylor, along with another soldier, Private John Goodwin, who volunteered to cover the withdrawal of the men of the Herts when two German counterattacks threatened to cut them off and annihilate them. Pouring fire into the German attackers, the two men managed to hold off the Germans long enough for the few survivors of the Hertfordshire Regiment to return to safety. To the north, Corporal Taylor was able to safely withdraw and make his way back to friendly lines, although to his south, Private John Goodwin was not seen again. His body was found several months later where he had last been seen – he was killed in action on his 39th birthday.

For his bravery that day, Corporal Bill Taylor was to receive a Bar to the Military

*It's your December Birthday
And too nice a time to miss
Wishing "Happy Birthday, Merry Christmas"
To the one who's reading this!*

Happy All Year, Too!

From C+m Winch 18.12.75.

Many thanks for helping to save my life on the Somme Nov 12 1916. Also I know you did the same for many others

Bill Thanks

Yours Sincerely C Winch

A greeting from a Private Cecil Winch, whose life he had saved on the Somme in November 1916.

Medal. Bill survived the war – having been wounded three times in the process – and returned home to Hertford. He got married in 1927, although tragically his wife died just a few years later, giving birth to their twins, who Bill was left to raise alone.

Back in civilian life, Bill returned to his gardening job, which he continued until retirement. As testament to the esteem in which he was held, every single year Bill would receive a greeting from a Private Cecil Winch, whose life he had saved on the Somme in November 1916. The final one that was sent before his death in the late 1970s is treasured by Bill's grandson. Bill served as an air raid warden in the Second World War and died in 1979 at the age of 88. Today he is remembered proudly by his grandson David, who kindly loaned Bill's wartime collection to the *Herts at War* project.

THE BRAVE ROYSTON DOCTOR – HAROLD ACKROYD VC MC

Harold Ackroyd was born in Southport, Lancashire on 13 July 1877 the son of Edward Ackroyd, who was the chairman of the Southport & Cheshire Lines Extension Railway Company. He was first educated at Mintholme College in Southport and later attended Shrewsbury College. He then went to Gonville and Caius College, Cambridge where he achieved his BA in 1899 and subsequently proceeded to his BSc in 1903, MA and MB in 1904 and finally finished his MD in 1910. He was, for some time, at Guy's Hospital in London and later was the house physician at Queen's Hospital, Birmingham but was never in private practice. He went on to spend a period of time as house surgeon at the David Lewis Northern Hospital in Liverpool. He then returned to Cambridge, where after securing a British Medical Association Scholarship, he was engaged in research work. Harold married in 1908 and moved from Southport to Brooklands in Royston.

Harold Ackroyd VC & his daughter Ursula in 1916.

In February 1915 Harold was commissioned as a temporary Lieutenant in the Royal Army Medical Corps and was soon promoted to the rank of Captain. He went to France in August 1915. He was present during heavy fighting in Delville Wood in July 1916 which was a real shambles. The wood was strewn with the dead and wounded bodies of British, South African and German troops. It was during this bitter fighting on 19 July 1916 that Harold would end up performing bravely. Captain G.H.F. Nichols, author of *The 18th Division in the Great War*, writes:

> *The fighting was so confused and the wood so hard to search that the difficulties in evacuating the wounded seemed insuperable but Ackroyd, bespectacled and stooping, was so cool and purposeful and methodical that he cleared the whole wood of wounded British and Bosche as well.*

After eleven separate reports were received regarding his actions during the fighting, he was recommended for the Victoria Cross but was ultimately awarded the Military Cross instead, for his conspicuous gallant efforts as the battalion medical officer. The official citation states:

> *He attended the wounded under heavy fire and finally, when he had seen that all our wounded from behind the line had been brought in, he went out beyond the frontline and brought in both our own and enemy wounded, although continually sniped at.*

A sensitive and dedicated man, Harold found the carnage and waste of human life deplorable, and in August 1916, following his award, he was invalided home for a period after suffering from what was described as a 'breakdown', Nichols writing that 'his nerves gave way.'

In November 1916 Harold returned to France and later went with the battalion to the Ypres Salient. It was here, at the Menin Road, between 31 July and 1 August 1917 that his work as the battalion doctor earned him the Victoria Cross. A staggering twenty-three separate reports were received regarding his courageous behaviour.

The 18th Division history once more provides a powerful description:

And in all that hellish turmoil, there had been one quiet figure, most heroic, most wonderful of all. Doctor Ackroyd, the 6th Berkshire's medical officer, a stooping grey-haired, bespectacled man, rose to the supremist heights that day. He seemed to be everywhere; he tended and bandaged scores of men... But no wounded man was treated hurriedly or unskilfully. Ackroyd worked as stoically as if he were in the quiet of an operating theatre.

The citation reads:

Utterly regardless of danger he worked continuously for many hours up and down and in front of the line tending the wounded and saving the lives of officers and men. In doing so he had to move across the open under heavy machine gun, rifle and shell fire. He carried a wounded officer to a place of safety under very heavy fire. On another occasion, he went some way in front of our advanced line and brought in a wounded man under continuous sniping and machine gun fire. His heroism was the means of saving many lives and provided a magnificent example of courage, cheerfulness and determination to the fighting men in whose midst he was carrying out splendid work.

He was slightly wounded on 31 July but remained on duty but sadly, Harold would not live to receive his award. On 11 August 1917 at 'Jargon Trench' near Glencourse Wood, Harold was carrying out his usual work with total disregard for his own safety when he was killed by a sniper.

Corporal Scriven wrote to Mrs Mabel Ackroyd several days later and informed her of the circumstances surrounding her husband's death.

The medals of Harold Ackroyd VC on display at the RAMC HQ in Millbank, London.

I was acting orderly corporal and on hearing the news I took a party of stretcher bearers but on arrival I found he was dead. There were six other poor fellows in the same shell hole who had met the same fate, it was a perfect death trap. He was visiting each company about 150 yards ahead of us to see if there were any wounded to attend to and was shot in the head by a sniper.

His wife and young son were presented with the medal at a ceremony in the Quadrangle of Buckingham Palace on 26 September 1917. A replica of the VC along with his MC and other war medals are on display at the RAMC HQ in Millbank, London, along with a painting of him winning the Victoria Cross.

Harold Ackroyd is buried in Birr Cross Roads Cemetery, Zillebeke, Belgium.

A REMARKABLE LIFE – GEORGE RANDOLPH PEARKES VC, DSO, MC, CdG

Official records indicate that 619,636 men and women enlisted with the Canadian Expeditionary Force during the Great War. Of these, approximately 424,000 served overseas with 59,544 losing their lives.

There were many acts of gallantry and heroism amongst the Canadians, with a total of seventy men receiving the Victoria Cross, nine of which were awarded for participation in the Second Battle of Passchendaele. One of these was a Hertfordshire man, who – rather than follow in the footsteps of his father and grandfather – opted to 'go west' and build a life in Canada. His new life was soon interrupted by the spectre of war, and his return to the old country was to bring about a story of amazing personal courage and tenacity in the face of the enemy.

George Randolph Pearkes was born in Watford, Hertfordshire, on 26 February 1888 as the eldest son of George and Louisa Pearkes. His father and grandfather ran a successful drapery business in Watford High Street, but this was not to be the life for George.

He attended the Berkhamsted School and later described how his time there made a significant impact on the remainder of his life:

I'm certain that my public schooldays influenced my whole life, more than anything else that I can think of. I am sure that the idea of playing for a team, for the school, influenced all my life and I see, the further I look back, why the sense of duty in the war to your battalion, to your men and even when one goes through to Parliament, why you have your Constituency, and so forth. The sense of doing your duty was inculcated to you in those very impressionable days.

At Berkhamsted, Pearkes trained in the school cadet corps and hoped to enter the Royal Military Sandhurst Academy to prepare for a career in the military, but these hopes were dashed when his father suffered financial difficulties and could not afford a university education for his son, so George decided to emigrate to Canada. What lay before him, he did not know, but whatever he might accomplish, he would have to do it by his own efforts.

In May 1906 he headed west to Red Deer, Alberta, Canada, where he began working on a farm which was run by the Berkhamsted School Headmaster, Dr Thomas C. Fry, with the intention to help students prepare for a farming career. George remained there for two years then took a job at a nearby farm to gain more experience. In 1909 he set up his own homestead near Dovercourt, Alberta, and

Major George Pearkes VC wearing the ribbon to his Military Cross and four wound stripes on his uniform.

a year later his brother Edward, who had also been at the Berkhamsted Farm, joined him on the homestead. Later that year their mother and sister also moved to Canada, whilst their father remained in England.

Despite the best efforts of this quiet and unassuming man, it was clear that George was not suited for farming and in 1911 he joined the Royal North West Mounted Police and served in the Yukon region until the outbreak of the First World War. He asked to purchase his discharge from the RNWMP and his request was granted. Constable William 'Willie' Kellock McKay, a fellow Britain, noted in his diary how when he went to Whitehorse on 23 February 1915 to wish George 'au revoir', it was –28 °F (–33 °C)!

George Pearkes enlisted in the 2nd Canadian Mounted Rifles on 3 March 1915 and was destined to become an expert bomber. After being promoted to the rank of Corporal, he embarked for France on 22 September that year, arriving the following day to begin a period in his life that would see heroism, suffering and outstanding leadership, which was to be indicative of his remaining years.

In a letter to his mother, dated 2 October 1915, George gives a very succinct overview of how life was in the trenches for the average soldier during the Great War. His description, which could have been written at any point of the war, is reflective of conditions for most of the combatants on the Western Front.

My dearest Mother,

At last I have the opportunity to drop you a few lines. No doubt you have received various post cards from me, saying that I am well, I can't tell you very much news even now as all outgoing mail has to be censored by our officers and just at present the censor is very strict. Almost hourly in the day time we would see either one of our aeroplanes or one of the German's shelled by the anti-aircraft gun, the shells would burst all around the aeroplane but I have never seen one hit yet. When the shell bursts, one can see from the ground the fire and the smoke hangs like a cloud for ten or fifteen minutes. The aeroplanes fly at a great height and as a rule are out of range.

It is the custom here for troops to take turnabout in the frontlines of trenches, one regiment taking a number of sections of the front trench for three days then moving back to the second line for another three days and then back to the third line, then back again to the frontline. About once in six weeks they come back to the reserve lines for a rest. I have been up into the frontline and just came back yesterday, conditions are not exactly pleasant there, but one feels they are doing their bit and finds out what our troops had to put up with during the past seven or eight months. How some of them have stood it, I don't know. All the time that we were in the frontline we were submitted to fire from the hostile guns and riflemen.

The trench was very narrow, just room for two men to push by each other. In front of each trench is a parapet made of sandbags, these are more or less bullet proof, but afford little protection from shell fire. The height from the top of this parapet to the bottom of the trench is between six and seven feet and the trench at the bottom is not more than four feet wide. There is a small ledge along the front on which one stands in order to fire over the sandbag, and cut into the rear of the trench are the dugouts, these are small caves with room enough for two men to lie down in, there is space enough to sit up in one of these but not enough to stand up in. The men's duty in the trenches are [sic] to keep up a more or less continuous fire on the German lines, which are about 150 yds away, and to pick off any of their men that show up, also to be ready to resist any attack that may be made. All night and every night, every man has to stand by, none is allowed to sleep or to be in the dugouts, during the day one man in every three has to be on duty, taking their turn in shifts of two hours, this gives each man four hours of so called rest, but during this four hours one has to cook and feed yourself, clean out the trench and do any other fatigue, from this you will see that there is very little time for sleep, indeed, when one comes out of the frontline they are just about all in. The mud and wet are awful, there was just about a foot of water in the bottom of our trench and it rained all one day and night. Anyway, all the boys we met were fit, none hurt. Maddocks wishes to be remembered. Will write again first chance. Love to Hilda and the others I know, good luck to you at Mt. Tolmie.

Yours most affectionately,

George

It was not until 28 November, when the 2nd Canadian Mounted Infantry arrived at Messines, Belgium, that George had his first real taste of combat, participating in a rather unsuccessful raid on a German roadblock situated on the Messines – Ploegsteert Road. Keen to get to grips with the enemy, George was both disappointed and frustrated when the officers leading the raid decided to withdraw from the assault after the raiders had revealed themselves to the enemy. However, George did have the opportunity to throw some of his grenades at the offending obstacle and enemy soldiers who held it. Their response was to throw grenades back, later giving George the opportunity to reflect on the folly of the assault.

Constable George Pearkes of the Royal North-West Mounted Police at Whitehorse, Yukon Territory.

By 3 March 1916, George had been promoted to the rank of Sergeant, and was wounded for the first time on 23 March, when the battalion was in trenches in the vicinity of Hooge, near Ypres. At 3.30 pm that afternoon, in a series of bombing and counter-bombing exchanges, a German assault struck the Canadian positions, killing two men and wounding sixteen others, including Sergeant Pearkes. He was hit by grenade shrapnel in the head and left arm and was soon passed along the evacuation chain to hospital. He wrote home to his mother a few days later, displaying the kind of feelings for his men that he would come to be known for:

Dearest Mother,

I am afraid you will have heard that I have been wounded so am writing a note to tell you that it is really nothing. I asked the Chaplain to do so too as I came through the dressing station. I am wounded very slightly in the arm and head, caused by a German bomb when they attacked our out post on Friday.

The bombers did fine work and drove them out again at once. I do feel proud of the boys, my section has all the work to do and they did it like heroes, although they are only young chaps. Losing these boys hurts more than anything and they were my best friends but we gave the Huns more than they gave us. Now don't worry dear, I'm alright in the Canadian General Hospital and shall soon be out.

Goodbye dear. George.

George found himself back at the front by 30 April, having been declared fit enough to return to his unit. He had, by this time, been recognised as officer material, and after being interviewed by both the brigade and divisional commanders, George was promoted in the field to the rank of temporary Lieutenant. He was made the acting battalion bombing officer, the previous holder of the post, Lieutenant Maguire, having been seriously wounded in an artillery attack whilst George was in hospital. However, it was not long before George would again return to hospital.

At 11.00 pm on the night of 19 May 1916, German infantry bombed the battalion positions at Halfway House near Hooge, wounding the new bombing officer and five other ranks. On this occasion, George was again struck in the head. A jagged piece of wood from the handle of a German 'potato masher' grenade was seen sticking out of his head 'like a horn'. Despite being stunned and blinded by blood, his company drove off the attackers and George survived the ordeal. He eventually found himself at No. 14 General Hospital in Boulogne to receive treatment. On leaving hospital he was sent to No. 6 Convalescent Depot at Etaples, where he was given the opportunity to rest and recover.

On his return to his battalion, George found that many of his old comrades had been killed or wounded during the fight for Mount Sorrel. The battalion then spent a period of time training and preparing the reinforcements for service at the front. In July they returned to Sanctuary Wood, where the fighting had become more aggressive as each side attempted to dominate no man's land by both day and night. Here, George was involved in a number of aggressive bombing patrols where he, and those men with him, spent a majority of the time crawling on their stomachs in an effort to get close to the enemy positions. Although he was recommended for an award on more than one occasion, none of them were ever granted.

In August 1916 George Pearkes left the 2nd Canadian Mounted Rifles and was attached to the headquarters of the Canadian 8th Infantry Brigade, commanded by Brigadier General James Harold Elmsley. Here, he was placed in the role of the brigade bombing officer, being responsible for the training of all the brigade bombers. George, however, longed to be in the thick of the fighting and only held this post for a few weeks. He was posted to the Pozières – Courcelette sector of the Somme, where the 8th Canadian Brigade had taken over positions from the ANZAC Corps close to Mouquet Farm.

The Battle of Flers-Courcelette, the two-army assault launched by Sir Douglas Haig on 15 September, was fought on a wider front than its name suggests. The two villages are three miles apart, but the battle area extended for ten miles from Combles on the French left, to Thiepval, overlooking the east bank of the Ancre. The Canadian 2nd Division, making the main effort astride the Albert – Bapaume road, attacked the defences in front of Courcelette. On the left, Major General Lipsett's 3rd Canadian Division – its front held by the Canadian 8th Brigade –

were charged with providing flank protection. It was in this action that the use of tanks would be seen for the first time, but with limited success.

In a chalk quarry, some 300 yards from Mouquet Farm, George Pearkes was placed in the Brigade Bombing Headquarters. The Canadians had driven out the enemy in the area with apparent success and captured the farm on 16 September. As it turned out, however, the German garrison – far from being annihilated – had taken refuge in tunnels and brought in fresh troops to hold the maze of trenches immediately east of Courcelette. The farm was lost to a German counterattack before being recaptured by British forces on 26 September 1916.

On 27 September 1916, as the Battle of the Somme raged on, George was given the Command of 'C' Company, 5th Canadian Mounted Rifles, a unit made of men from the eastern townships of Quebec, with many being French-Canadians. They were tasked with assaulting a series of fortified German trenches, the first of which was named Zollern Graben, the second, Hessian Trench and the final one, Regina Trench. Throughout a series of attacks and counterattacks, the Canadians fought a bitter struggle with the enemy.

Two German counterattacks achieved initial but short-lived success as Canadian bombers, led by George Pearkes, regained ground temporarily lost to the enemy. Two hundred yards of Hessian Trench still in German hands fell the next afternoon. George Pearkes was awarded the Military Cross in *The London Gazette* dated 19 December 1916 for his part in the action. The citation reads as follows:

> *For conspicuous gallantry in action. He led a bombing party with great courage and determination, clearing 600 yards of trench and capturing eighteen prisoners. Later, although wounded, he remained at duty until the battalion was relieved.*

This section of the trench was bisected by the Grandcourt Road. It lay over a low ridge of ground, and in order to see how far the thick barbed wire in front of the trenches had been cut, patrols were sent out on the night of 30 September. The assault began the following day and was deemed a disaster. Short-falling artillery plastered the jumping-off positions and the preparatory barrage failed to hit the German lines, and the majority of the German wire was not cut. Canadian casualties were heavy during the assault as machine gun fire laced into entire assault companies caught up in no man's land. The few survivors who managed to reach Regina Trench were driven out or overwhelmed by German counterattacks, and half the assault force was dead or wounded by the end of the day with no gain to show for their efforts. George Pearkes was slightly wounded in this assault but remained on duty. He would live to fight another day.

Following their involvement in the Battle of Courcellete, the 5th Canadian Mounted Rifles left the Somme at the end of October and moved to what was deemed to be a quieter area, the Vimy/Arras Sector. Here Pearkes got to know his men and they got to know him. Nicknamed 'Pearksy' by his troops, George was well liked as they knew he would never ask them to do something that he himself was not prepared to do. He exuded both confidence and cheerfulness, which helped to boost morale when faced with the incessant drudgery of the trenches and the presence of fear and death during combat. One NCO said of him:

As a commander and leader of men, he proved to me he had no fear whatsoever and I would follow him anywhere. I was one of the first men in our company to go on patrol into no man's land with him, and got to the enemy frontline barbed wire. We could hear the Germans talking. I felt safe with him. He was also a generous officer by giving money as prizes in sports and to section NCOs for the best warfare training while out for a rest. He offered to carry a man's pack whilst the man rode his horse on a route march from one town to another. This was the kind of officer he was.

On the night of 29–30 October 1917 his battalion was located on the outskirts of the village of Passchendaele, their objective being the capture of enemy positions at Vapour Farm. The plans for the attack had been relayed in detail to all company commanders but a setback occurred during the night, when intense artillery fire from both the Allies and the Germans resulted in the commander of 'D' Company, Captain Leonard Carl Eaton, being killed and two other officers wounded.

The attack commenced at 5.50 am and George, leading 'C' Company, was wounded in the opening moments of the attack. He later recalled:

As I stepped out into the open, there was a good deal of illumination at the time with rockets and flares going up, both German and our own. Although it was hardly daylight you could still see glimpses of men clambering out of the trench. We'd hardly got out when that counter-barrage came down. At that time, I was hit in the thigh by shrapnel and was knocked down. I rather thought, 'Now I've got it.' There seemed a little uncertainty among the men immediately alongside me, whether they should go now I'd been hit. For a moment I had visions of going back wounded and I said to myself: 'This can't be. I've got to go on for a while anyway, wounded or not.' So, I clambered to my feet and I found a stiffness in my thigh but I was able to move forward and the rest of the company came forward.

The assaulting companies, 'A' and 'C', soon reported that apart from heavy machine gun fire from the German positions, they were also suffering from the effects of shellfire from the Canadian artillery, which was falling short. Despite this, both companies pushed forward in the muddy morass, and observers – their view largely obscured by intense smoke – reported that heavy hand-to-hand fighting was taking place, with the enemy falling back in large groups.

The company came under intense fire from locations known as Source Farm and Vapour Farm. Pearkes and his men continued to advance and as they did, the fire grew more intense. Eventually, he reached Vapour Farm with no more than about 30 men, and they came under fire, particularly from snipers. Pearkes knew he needed support and at one point a member of his company was killed whilst carrying communication pigeons. On witnessing the man's death, he wrote out a message and tied it to a pigeon's leg with a fibre from a sandbag.

> *Germans are digging in on top of ridge about 200 yards away. I have 8 2nd C.M.R. and 12 5th C.M.R., all very much exhausted. Ammunition running short. Do not think we can hold out much longer without being relieved. Both flanks still in the air.*

Pearkes had no idea if his message would get through, but it did. The battalion commander ordered an artillery strike on Vanity Farm, where the German counterattack was forming, and caused many casualties and great havoc amongst the enemy troops. In the meantime, efforts were made to get ammunition and men up to Pearkes, who was determined to hold on to the ground gained, as he knew it had cost the lives of many of his men. This proved to be a difficult task, and many of those sent forward to relieve the men of 'C' Company were cut down – a sight that George would never forget. Despite this, he continued to encourage his men as he crawled from shell hole to shell hole. It would be 48 hours before relief would come.

The men of 'C' and 'D' companies of the 2nd Canadian Mounted Rifles would be the ones to eventually relieve Pearkes and his men. In gathering darkness, they moved out, often knee-deep in mud, to reach Source and Vapour Farms. They gathered up the men, with Pearkes insisting that he did not leave until all his men had been removed. There were just 35 men to be relieved and all but a few of them had been wounded.

For George Pearkes – weary from two days without sleep, his leg stiff and numb from his wound, and sad at the loss of so many good men – there was a sense of duty done despite tremendous odds. He later said: *'We had got on, where nobody else had got on. We had survived and we were all thankful.'*

Major Pearkes was awarded the Victoria Cross for his actions and leadership at Passchendaele, Belgium on 30–31 October 1917. His citation explains further:

For most conspicuous bravery and skilful handling of the troops under his command during the capture and consolidation of considerably more than the objectives allotted to him in an attack. Just prior to the advance Maj. Pearkes was wounded in the left thigh. Regardless of his wound, he continued to lead his men with the utmost gallantry, despite many obstacles. At a particular stage of the attack his further advance was threatened by a strongpoint which was an objective of the battalion on his left, but which they had not succeeded in capturing. Quickly appreciating the situation, he captured and held this point, thus enabling his further advance to be successfully pushed forward. It was entirely due to his determination and fearless personality that he was able to maintain his objective with the small number of men at his command against repeated enemy counterattacks, both his flanks being unprotected for a considerable depth meanwhile. His appreciation of the situation throughout and the reports rendered by him were invaluable to his commanding officer in making dispositions of troops to hold the position captured. He showed throughout a supreme contempt of danger and wonderful powers of control and leading.

Later, in a scathing post-action report, it was stated that the Canadian Artillery had caused significant number of casualties amongst their own men before they had even left the trenches, and their performance was described as 'generally faulty and unsatisfactory'. It is quite possible that George's wound was actually caused by friendly fire.

On 30 November 1917, after recovering from the wound he received at Passchendaele, George was posted to the 116th Battalion, Canadian infantry. He served with them throughout the winter of 1917–18 and would lead them through the German Spring Offensive and in the final months of victory, as the Allied armies left the trenches behind and moved into open ground. For his masterly handling of the battalion at Hamon Wood, George was awarded the Distinguished Service Order. The citation reads:

Lt.-Col. George Randolph Pearkes, V.C., M.C., 116th Bn., Can. Infy., 2nd Cent. Ont.Regt.

This officer handled his battalion in a masterly manner, and, with an enveloping movement, completely baffled and overcame the enemy, who were in a very strong position. He then captured a wood, the final objective, which was about 5,000 yards from the start. Before this, however, the men were becoming exhausted, on observing which he at once went into the attack himself, and, by his splendid and fearless example, put new life into the whole attack, which went forward with a rush and captured 16 enemy guns of all calibres up to 8 inches.

On 17 September 1918 George was wounded for the fifth time. The battalion was in billets at Guemappe, which was still within German artillery range. As the men of one of the companies were queuing for a meal, a number of shells fell among them, causing devastation. George, who was at battalion headquarters, heard the commotion and went to investigate. As he did so, a second barrage of shells came down, killing and wounding many more men, including George Pearkes, who was seriously injured. As he was loaded into an ambulance, it was unlikely that he would survive. A few days later, however, a fellow officer wrote to George's mother:

> *In the Field, Sept.22nd. 1918*
> *Dear Mrs. Pearkes:*
> *You have already received word that your son, Lieut-Colonel Pearkes, V.C. M.C. Croix de Guerre, has been severely wounded. We have also sent word that the operation he has had has been very successful, and he continues to improve every day. I was speaking to him this morning and he asked me to let you know his present condition. He is quite bright, anxious to see everyone who comes in and talks quite cheerfully. It will be a matter of weeks before he will be able to be out of bed, but as far as we can see at present, there seems to be no occasion for worry as he appears to be now quite past any danger.*
> *He was wounded through the body by a small piece of shrapnel which also went through his arm above the elbow. This was removed and it was found that no vital organ had been injured, so that is all in his favour. He is receiving the very best of care, and I have no doubt in a few days he will be writing you himself.*
> *With sympathy and my best wishes, A.B. Coty, Capt. 116th Bn.Can.*

George – although weak – survived again. He spent many weeks in hospital and was eventually evacuated to a London hospital. It was whilst he was here that the Armistice was declared and the war came to an end.

The medical records for George Pearkes make very sombre reading. He was wounded on five occasions, suffering injuries to his left arm, head, knee and left buttock. His spleen was removed after it was described as being 'shattered', several ribs were removed and he had numerous scars where shrapnel had entered his body. Pieces of artillery shell had to be removed from his flesh and some of his internal organs. However, he managed to survive these devastating injuries, thus enabling him to continually rejoin his unit and resume his role as commanding officer.

After the war Pearkes returned to Canada where he continued his military career. In the summer of 1924, while on furlough in Victoria, visiting his mother and sister, Pearkes met and fell in love with Constance Blytha Copeman. They

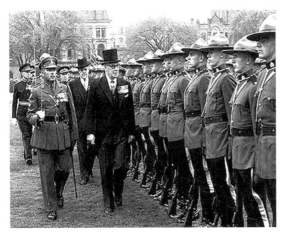

Hon. (Major General) George Pearkes VC, PC, CC, CB, DSO, MC, CD., Minister of National Defence at a parade on Parliament Hill in September 1957, inspecting men of his beloved RCMP.

George Pearkes & Constance Blytha Copeman

got engaged and were married in August 1925. Their daughter, Priscilla Edith ('Pep'), was born in 1928, followed by their son, John Andre, born in 1931. Sadly, Pep suffered an infection in the hospital not long after she was born, which led to a succession of illnesses, and she died as a young child.

George Pearkes commanded the 1st Canadian Infantry Division in the UK during the first part of the Second World War (1940–42), and then returned to Canada to become the General Officer Commanding, Pacific Command. He resigned after a disagreement with the government over conscription in 1945 and entered federal politics as a Conservative, representing Nanaimo (1945–53) and later Esquimalt-Saanich. He became Minister of National Defence (1957–60) during a critical period when production of the Avro Arrow aircraft was halted, the BOMARC Missile was introduced, and the use of atomic warheads by Canada's armed forces was hotly debated. George Pearkes was appointed Lieutenant Governor of British Colombia in 1960, and retired in 1968. He died on 30 May 1984 aged 96. A remarkable life for a draper's son from Watford.

Quick Fact

The Commonwealth War Graves Commission records the names of 78 men from Hertfordshire who served with Canadian Forces and are commemorated within the Commission cemeteries and memorials. The reality is that a great many more men from across the county lost their lives whilst serving in Canadian units during the Great War.

TRENCH RAIDER – GEORGE SIDNEY CARTER MC

George Carter was born in Weston, Hertfordshire, on 16 May 1898 as the youngest son of John and Clara Carter. After completing his education, he became a gardener and would have remained so, if it had not been for the onset of war.

On 8 September 1914 George, who was now living at 3 Huntingdon Road, Stevenage, was attested at Hitchin for service in the Bedfordshire Regiment and was immediately accepted for military service. He was only 16 years old, but he gave his age as 19. This small matter appears to have been of no consequence to the recruiting officer and he was whisked off for a period of basic training. Once his training was complete, he was

George Sidney Carter MC.

transferred to the 11th Battalion, East Surrey Regiment on 31 October 1914. This was a reserve battalion stationed at Dartmouth and it was here that he was promoted to Corporal a few weeks later, on 12 December. Two weeks later, on Boxing Day 1914, he was promoted to Sergeant. George remained with the battalion until the summer of 1915, when it moved to Colchester.

On 25 August 1915 he was transferred to the 8th Battalion, East Surrey Rifles and the following day he left for service in France. He remained in France until 28 January 1916, when he was shipped home. George remained in England throughout the spring of 1916 until he was posted to the 2nd Battalion, East Surrey Rifles on 28 August. The battalion was serving in Salonika at the time and he remained with them until January 1917, when he returned home to undertake a commission. During his service in Salonika, George had completed his will, which left all his estates to his mother. After returning to England, he was accepted to No. 19 Officer Cadet Battalion in Pirbright and on 15 March 1917 an excited George arrived at Kingston Station under railway warrant number 660395 to begin his new career. After the completion of his training, he was posted to the 9th Battalion, East Surrey Rifles and returned to France on 25 August 1917.

It had been some eighteen months since George had been on the Western Front and by now it had become a living hell of mechanised destruction and death. On 20 November 1917 the battalion was situated 2,000 yards west of Bellicourt, midway between Cambrai and St Quentin, when a trench-raiding party was organised. The objective was for the raiding party to capture or kill any enemy troops on the frontline and blow up any dugouts that were situated in a sunken road just beyond the frontline. There were five parties, and George Carter, commanding 'A' Company, led No. 1 Party, which contained six other ranks.

At 6.30 am they set off at the eastern end of a trench known as Fish Lane to enter the enemy frontline and 90 seconds later they were at the entrance to the enemy trenches, where they encountered a coil of concertina wire. He cut a gap through the wire, and as he did so, two Germans threw several grenades towards the party. This killed one of the raiders and wounded George, his senior NCO, Sergeant Bell, and a private. At this point, two privates, Mortimer and Bell, picked up George Carter and under enemy fire, carried him back to the British trenches. Sergeant Bell – although wounded – then attacked the German grenade throwers with his own grenades and killed them both. He then returned to the parties and reorganised them to continue the raid but was ordered to withdraw. The battalion commander, Major Thomas Hutchinson Sabine Swanton, believed that the raiders may have been spotted as they assembled for the attack and commended all those involved for their efforts. Three of the raiders, Lance Corporal Henry Millard, Private Frederick Prested and Private James Hunt, were killed during the action.

George Carter was evacuated to No. 13 Field Ambulance with multiple wounds and later transferred to No. 8 General Hospital in Rouen. A telegram was sent to his parents informing them of his condition, and his mother was given permission to visit him in hospital. George died of his wounds at 2.00 am on 28 November 1917. The officer commanding the hospital handed his personal effects to his mother. He was posthumously awarded the Military Cross on 25 April 1918 and the citation in *The London Gazette* read:

> *For conspicuous gallantry and devotion to duty during a raid. Whilst cutting the wire on an enemy parapet he was very seriously wounded by a bomb. Although completely crippled, he continued to cheer on his men till he saw that they had entered the enemy trench.*

George Carter is buried in the St. Sever Cemetery, Rouen, France. He was aged 19 and was entitled to the Military Cross, 1915 Star, British War Medal and Victory Medal.

GOD'S WORK THIS DAY – BRITISH ARMY CHAPLAINS

The role of the British Army Chaplains in the Great War is one that is often surrounded by myth, misrepresentation and misunderstanding. At the outbreak of war, there were an estimated 116 chaplains in the Regular British Army.

By 1918 there were over 3,000 in France alone, every man a volunteer. Many chaplains had entered the armed forces with little or no training and were often ill prepared for what they were about to witness. Despite this, chaplains would very often seek out the wounded and the dying in no man's land, dragging them back to the trenches for treatment and prayer. They would spend time in makeshift hospitals, often with little rest or sleep and they went doggedly about their business despite the dangers from both the enemy and the dark sense of humour of the British Tommy. Records show that 179 chaplains were killed on active duty.

For those chaplains who served with county regiments, the link was often a tenuous one. Their years of ecclesiastical training were carried out far from home and chaplains very often found themselves serving with men with whom they had little in common apart from their faith. Yet they were at the very centre of the everyday lives of the men they served with, sharing trenches, holding religious services prior to combat, arranging and attending funerals, and being one of the few men present at military executions.

Laid To Rest, At Last – the Reverend John Richard Duvall

It is often said that one of the most complex – perhaps even bizarre – but less known theatres of the Great War was that of the Salonika campaign. Serbian forces defeated the Austrian aggressors in 1914 but the following year the Germans sent a substantial force to support the Austrians and Bulgarians in their fight against the Serbs. For their part, the British and French sent an initial two divisions to Salonika in an effort to support the Serbs, but it

The Reverend John Richard Duvall.

was too late. The Serbian army had been defeated and the King, along with his government, had been forced into exile. A new Greek government was soon in power and the Allied commander, French General Maurice Sarrail, was now faced with a far less cordial relationship, but Salonika was to remain an Allied enclave for the rest of the war.

Sarrail commanded a multinational force that by the beginning of 1917 included Serbian, Russian and some Greek formations, as well as those of the French and British. Both the geography and logistical demands of the operation were seriously questioned by army commanders who believed that the Allied troops involved would be better employed on the Western Front.

Amongst the British troops serving in Salonika was the Reverend John Richard Duvall, the only son of John William and Anna Duvall of Walton Road, Ware, Hertfordshire. He had attended Selwyn College, Cambridge, and Ely Theological College, and was ordained on 21 December 1913 by the Bishop of Liverpool, Francis James Chavasse, who would have four sons serving in the army during the Great War himself. Major Christopher Maude Chavasse MC was a chaplain with the 62nd Division; Lieutenant Francis Bernard Chavasse served with the Royal Army Medical Corps; Lieutenant Aiden Chavasse served with the 17th The King's (Liverpool Regiment) and was killed in action in the Ypres Sector on 4 July 1917; and Captain Noel Chavasse was the only soldier to be awarded the Victoria Cross on two occasions during the First World War, as well as a Military Cross. He died from his wounds in the Ypres Sector on 4 August 1917 and his grave remains one of the most visited on the Western Front to this day.

On 23 August 1915 the Reverend John Duvall, serving with the 12th Cheshire Regiment, was declared fit for service overseas by a medical officer of the Royal Army Medical Corps and the following day signed a form of engagement for service with the British Expeditionary Force, which – as a 4th Class Chaplain to the Forces – brought him the princely sum of 10 shillings (50p) a day plus any appropriate allowances. In addition, he would be provided food and lodgings, as well as free transport to and from any theatre of war in which he may serve.

On 4 October 1915 the Reverend John Duvall was issued with a field service communion set – the property of His Majesty's Government – and was posted to Salonika, where he arrived in December 1915. By this time, the Allied forces had taken up defensive positions under the assumption that the Bulgarian forces would attempt to advance into Greece. The expected invasion never took place and instead, the Bulgarians dug in along the Greek – Serb border from the coast of Albania to Doiran Lake and the Bulgarian border.

In 1916, Allied troops in Salonika advanced against the Bulgarian defensive line. The British Salonika Force (BSF) took up positions at Doiran and advanced into the Struma Valley to the east, driving out Bulgarian forces during September. The French, supported by Russian, Italian and later Serbian troops, captured the strategic town of Monastir in November 1916.

It was on 4 July 1916, whilst serving with 13th Manchester Regiment, that John Duvall renewed his contract for duty overseas.

In April 1917, the Allies launched a major offensive. The main thrust was made by French and Serbian forces to the west, with the British launching a diversionary attack at Doiran. Both these attacks failed, and the campaign settled down to a stalemate until September 1918, when Serbian forces broke through the Bulgarian lines. Bulgarian resistance quickly crumbled and on 30 September an armistice came into effect.

In October 1917 all eyes were focused on the Western Front as the third battle of Ypres drew to its ghastly conclusion. The Allies, despite their horrific losses, deemed themselves to be victorious over the German forces, whose losses simply outstripped those of the victors. For the Reverend John Duvall, having now sufficiently recovered from his bout of malaria to rejoin his unit, life in the Balkans campaign dragged on ominously.

It was on 6 October 1917 that the Reverend Duvall, attached to the 7th Battalion, Wiltshire Regiment was struck by pieces from an artillery shell. Seriously wounded, he was transported to No. 78 Field Ambulance, where every effort was made to save his life. Sadly, he succumbed to his injuries later that day and was initially buried in the British Cemetery at Baisili.

On 12 May 1919 the Director of Grave Registrations and Enquiries wrote to John's father, advising him that for a variation of reasons, his son's body had been exhumed and reburied in the Janes Military Cemetery in Greece. This, however, was not the only time that John's body would be relocated. The cemetery at Janes was on low ground, and under the normal conditions of the region, it was found difficult to approach and almost impossible to maintain in good order. So, in February 1921 the 560 bodies that were buried in the cemetery were exhumed and moved south to Sarigol Military Cemetery, Kriston, Greece. His name is recorded on the Ware war memorial.

The final last resting place of Chaplain 4th Class The Reverend John Richard Duvall, aged 28, at Sarigol Military Cemetery, Kriston, Greece.

THOMAS JASPER SHOVEL – CHAPLAIN 4TH CLASS

Thomas Jasper Shovel was born on 2 August 1884, the son of Thomas and Ellen Shovel of Upton Cross, Linkinhorne, Cornwall. His father was the chairman of the Liskeard Union Board of Guardians, whose role was to administer the workhouses within the parishes of the Liskeard area.

Thomas Jnr. was the eldest of four sons and whilst he and his brother George Cloudsley Shovel, were destined to become Wesleyan ministers, his younger brother Ernest George would become a journalist and eventually would go on to be the London subeditor of the *Western Morning News*. Ernest served as an officer in the 10th Battalion, Duke of Cornwall's Light Infantry and saw action on the Western Front from 1917 to 1918. His youngest brother, Leslie Owen Shovel, worked on the family farm most of his life.

Thomas entered the ministry in July 1905 and worked in the Hitchin and Stevenage area under the watchful eye of the Reverend John Pellow, taking services in the Methodist Church situated on Stevenage High Street. The 1911 Census shows that Thomas Shovel was living just a short distance away at No. 18 Green Street, Stevenage, a property that still stands today.

Thomas Jasper Shovel.

He was ordained in July 1912, after which he was given charge of the English Wesleyan Methodist Chapel in Holyhead from August 1914 until March 1916, when he departed for Preston, Lancashire. At this stage of war, he offered his services to the Wesleyan Army & Navy Board, but was told there was no vacancy for him. Not satisfied that he was in the right sphere of labour, he wrote to the chairman of his local board and said that unless he was offered an Army Chaplaincy, he would enlist directly into the army as a private.

He joined the Royal Army Chaplains Department on 16 January 1918 as a Chaplain 4th class (Captain). After a short introduction to army life, the Reverend Shovel embarked from Folkestone on 29 January 1918 to go to France, where he was attached to the 2/2nd Wessex Field Ambulance on the Western Front.

On 5 October 1918, described in the brigade war diary as a 'quiet day', the Reverend Shovel was walking with a field ambulance medical officer, Major Harold Cotterell Adams, when a shell exploded near them. Adams was wounded and Thomas Shovel died from shrapnel injuries. He was originally buried near Louverval Chateau, but in 1927 was reinterned in the Louverval Military Cemetery, Doignies, France. (Row A. Grave 6.)

Although his name is not recorded on the Stevenage War Memorial, it is inscribed on the Holyhead County School Great War Memorial, the Upton Cross Methodist Chapel – which was part of the Liskeard and Looe Methodist Circuit – the Linkinhorne War Memorial, Cornwall, and on the east wall at the Royal Garrison Church of All Saints in Aldershot – the Memorial to the Royal Army Chaplains Department. Thomas was entitled to the British War Medal and Victory Medal.

The grave of Thomas Jasper Shovel at Louverval Military Cemetery, Doignies, France.

Chapter Five

1918 – Victory & Defeat

By the end of 1917 the Russian Army had collapsed amid the events of the Bolshevik Revolution and thus relieved of pressure on the Eastern Front. The German Army, under the command of General Erich Ludendorff, now turned its attention to forcing a decision in France. The German High Command began to amass and train a considerable fighting force in preparation for a massive offensive on the Western Front which would rely on a new tactic using shock troops supported by highly mobile groups of light artillery. A formidable army of seventy-four divisions took up position along the 80-km front from Bapaume to Saint-Quentin. Ludendorff aimed to break through the Allied lines defended by thirty British divisions, and advance to the Channel in order to seize the ports used by the British before American reinforcements could arrive in any great number.

Ludendorff called his offensive *Kaiserschlacht*, the 'Emperor's Battle', although it was code-named 'Operation Michael'. The assault began at dawn on 21 March 1918 with a devastating artillery barrage, the likes of which had never been seen before on the Western Front. In a lighting infantry attack, the Germans quickly penetrated the British defences, forcing them into a hurried retreat.

Losses were high, with the British suffering 38,000 casualties and 20,000 prisoners on the first day. After a month of fighting, Ludendorff decided to halt the attack after the Germans had progressed more than 60 km into the Allied lines in some areas, but their troops were exhausted and their supply lines could not keep pace. After a pause lasting several days, and a return to trench warfare along makeshift lines, Ludendorff decided to restart the offensive in the form of limited, tactical attacks on certain sectors of the front. One of these, Operation Georgette, saw the German Army fight its way along the Lys Valley to Béthune between 9 and 19 April, sweeping aside the Portuguese Expeditionary Force and flattening the town's centre with heavy shelling. French and American forces finally brought the German thrust to a halt in May 1918.

In July, the front began moving in the opposite direction, propelled by a powerful and coordinated counterattack by the Allied armies. On 8 August 1918 the Allies began an offensive along the length of the front, which Ludendorff described as the German Army's 'Black Day'. This offensive, named the 'Hundred Days Offensive', also known as the 'Advance to Victory', was a series of Allied successes that pushed the German Army back to the battlefields of 1914. It was a period of fast-moving warfare with tanks, planes, troops and artillery working closely together. Beginning with the Battle of Amiens, the offensive sought to push the Germans out of France, forcing them to initially retreat to the Hindenburg Line.

The main German defences were anchored on the Hindenburg Line, a series of defensive fortifications stretching from Cerny on the Aisne River to Arras. Before the Allies' main offensive was launched, the remaining German salient west and east of the line were crushed at Havrincourt and St Mihiel on 12 September, and at Epehy and Canal du Nord on 27 September. It was during a German counterattack on 18 September that Second Lieutenant Frank Edward Young of the Hertfordshire Regiment was to be awarded a posthumous Victoria Cross for his actions at Havrincourt.

On 26 September French and American Expeditionary Forces launched an offensive in the Meuse – Argonne region at the southern end of the Hindenburg Line, which involved attacking over difficult terrain. Two days later, the army group under Albert I of Belgium, which included the Belgian Army, the British Second Army and the French Sixth Army, launched an attack near Ypres at the northern end of the Hindenburg Line. This is now known as the Fifth Battle of Ypres. Both attacks made good progress initially, but were later slowed down by logistical problems.

On 29 September the central attack on the Hindenburg Line commenced with the British Fourth Army attacking the St. Quentin Canal and the French First Army attacking fortifications outside St Quentin. The Allies broke through the entire depth of the Hindenburg defences over a 19-mile (31 km) front and subsequently, the British First and Third armies broke through the Hindenburg Line at the Battle of Cambrai on 8 October. This collapse forced the German High Command to accept that the war had to be ended. Throughout October the Allies continued to press the Germans back, forcing them to abandon increasingly large amounts of heavy equipment and supplies, and reducing their morale and capacity to resist. Casualties remained heavy for the Allied fighting forces as well as in the retreating German Army, and the dreaded telegrams notifying the next of kin of the death and injury of their loved ones continued to arrive on many Hertfordshire doorsteps.

On 30 October 1918 the Armistice of Mudros was signed between the Ottoman Empire and the Triple Entente aboard HMS *Agamemnon* in Mudros port. Ottoman operations in the active combat theatres ceased. Eventually, after 100 days of fighting, the Great War on the Western Front ended in a victory for the Allies with the Armistice being signed on 11 November 1918, bringing a welcome conclusion to the slaughter.

British dominance of the sea and the indirect pressure that the Grand Fleet brought to bear on the German war effort – particularly through the blockade – were vital to the Allied victory. On 21 November 1918, in accordance with the recently signed armistice, much of the German High Seas Fleet sailed into the Firth of Forth in Scotland to surrender. The Great War was over.

A QUESTION OF DISTINGUISHED CONDUCT – PRIVATE HENRY CHARLES FORDER

Throughout the Great War there were many examples of brave and gallant deeds. Many of these went unrecognised but for some, their actions would result in the award of a gallantry medal. A local newspaper report in 1918 indicates that one Stevenage soldier, Henry Charles Forder, had been awarded the ribbon to the Distinguished Conduct Medal. Henry was an experienced and long-serving soldier who had seen much action, but official records show no recognition of such an award. This is his story.

Henry Charles Forder was born on 27 January 1887 as the son of Henry Charles and Susan Forder of North Road, Stevenage, Hertfordshire. On 12 November 1904, at the age of 17 years and

Private Henry Charles Forder.

10 months, Henry – then employed as a labourer – joined the Bedfordshire Regiment at Hitchin, Hertfordshire. He served with this battalion in India, Aden and Bermuda before returning to the UK for Home Service.

Following the outbreak of the Great War, Henry was posted to France on 16 August 1914, where the battalion moved by train to Le Cateau. They then marched a further 5 miles to billets in Pommereuil. After suffering from the effects of a sprain to his right foot on 6 September 1914, Henry was evacuated to the UK. He remained in hospital until 8 November, when he was posted back to France, joining the 2nd Battalion at Bailleul on 12 November 1914. He served with the battalion throughout the winter of 1914–15, eventually being promoted to Sergeant by 25 September 1915. He was admitted to No. 97 Field Ambulance on 28 March 1916, suffering from laryngitis and was sent to the 30th Division Rest Station to recover, where he remained until 2 April, when he was posted back to his unit.

It was on 11 July 1916 that Henry was wounded at Trones Wood on the Somme but remained on duty. The battalion was in position by 1.30 am and had formed up in lines, with an interval of five paces between each man, and a distance of 150 yards between platoons. Orders had been received that the battalion was to enter the wood at 3.27 am, so the leading line commenced to advance at 3.10 am towards the southeastern edge of the wood. Since it was dark, the advance was not observed until the leading line was 400 yards from the wood. Then enemy machine guns opened fire and quickly got their artillery to work. The battalion suffered many casualties on entering the wood, but by 3.45 am the whole battalion had reached the inside of the wood. However, owing to machine gun and shell fire, they had entered rather too far at the southern end and due to the denseness of the undergrowth, it was not possible to see more than a few yards in front of you, so the companies had great difficulty keeping in touch. It was found that the wood was strongly held and full of trenches and dugouts. After a lot of fighting inside the wood, some members of 'B' Company reached the northeastern edge and commenced to dig in. As no British troops were holding the northern end of the wood, this party became isolated and the enemy was seen advancing from the direction of Longueval. Organising troops in the wood was very difficult owing to heavy casualties and the denseness of the undergrowth but the battalion managed to hold its own, and by 7.00 pm on the evening of 11 July most of the remnants of the battalion had dug themselves in on the southeastern and southwestern sides of the wood. However, all companies had been reduced by the many casualties, including Henry Forder.

It is at this point in his military career that a strange event occurred. Henry, a much-needed NCO, was reduced to the ranks as a result of inefficiency on 15 August 1916, whilst the battalion was in billets at Lestrem. There currently appears to be no explanation for this event.

On 25 February 1917 Henry was admitted to No. 96 Field Ambulance suffering with dyspepsia and, again, found himself at the 30th Division Rest Station. His condition grew worse and he was then sent to No. 22 General Hospital at Camiers on 10 March 1917. On 15 March Henry boarded the hospital ship *Gloucester Castle* and returned to the UK. He was admitted to the Welsh Metropolitan War Hospital in Cardiff and on 28 March 1917 was subject of a medical board, where it was determined that he was suffering from pulmonary tuberculosis (TB) and he was no longer fit for war service.

Henry was discharged from the army on 18 April 1917, was awarded the Silver War Badge and returned to civilian life. His condition grew worse over the following months and eventually, after being admitted to the Ware Hospital, he died on 21 January 1918 from TB. A local newspaper report claimed that his death was the consequence of the effects of gas and exposure during war service. It also claimed that Henry was awarded the Ribbon to the Distinguished Conduct Medal in January 1918 but official records do not substantiate this claim. Henry is buried in the St. Nicholas Churchyard, Stevenage, and his name – along with the award he was not entitled to – are recorded on the Stevenage War Memorial.

A TEMPORARY POSTING – SECOND LIEUTENANT PETER FRANCIS KENT

One of the more iconic buildings within the county was that of the Kent Brushes factory at Apsley.

The family-run business, which has been in existence since 1777, is a renowned purveyor of quality brushes; a tradition that continues today. In 1901 Kent Brushes built factories alongside the River Gade in Apsley, where goods were able to be delivered to their own wharf.

By the time of the Great War, the factory was employing many local people and were producing a variation of brushes for both civilian and military use under the guidance of Ernest Neild Kent. In a soldier's kit, you would find no less than seven Kent products; hair, tooth, shaving, cloth, shoe-blacking, shoe-polishing and button brushes. They also produced large quantities of horse brushes for the army.

Second Lieutenant Peter Francis Kent.

With a prosperous business, the future seemed bright for Ernest Kent and his wife, Lilian Margaret. The couple were married in June 1892 and their first son, Humphrey Neild, was born on 2 November 1893.

Their second son, Peter Francis, was born on 14 September 1898, and it is him we focus on here using material supplied by the David Good collection.

Peter's initial education began at Bengeo College, Hertford, after which he followed his father and brother as a pupil of Clifton College, Bristol, where he achieved a rather average academic record. He then began an engineering apprenticeship – most likely to aid him in the running of the family business. In October 1915, the St John the Baptist church in Aldenham produced a Roll of Honour, in which 16-year-old Peter Kent is listed as being involved in munitions work.

Just twelve months later, on 9 October 1916, listing his occupation as apprentice engineer, Peter enlisted in the Royal Flying Corps as a cadet, with the regimental number 68219, and the rank of Airman 3rd Class. No doubt, with his engineering background and the rapid development of military aviation, his imagination was captured. The fact that an aerodrome had been built on the outskirts of the village of Shenley, meant that Peter would have seen a great deal of flying activity and, like so many young men, was attracted to this exciting new technology.

Destined for greater things, Peter was discharged from the ranks on 27 February 1917 in order to take up a temporary commission as a Second Lieutenant. Initially, he was attached to the General List, and was later appointed to a temporary commission in the Royal Flying Corps. His introduction to flying – at a time when there were a great many accidents due to the precarious nature of the machines involved – began at Oxford and later progressed to Farnborough. Following his basic pilot training, he was attached to the School of Special Flying at Gosport.

Peter arrived in France in December 1917, initially on a six-week temporary posting, being attached to No. 3 Squadron, Royal Flying Corps. It appears he was given a series of menial flying tasks by his squadron commander, who then sought permission for him to take up combative duties.

On the afternoon of 6 February 1917 Major Raymond-Barker led a close offensive patrol after being informed that 'Richthofen's Circus' was airborne. The only pilots available to Raymond-Barker were Captain Charles Sutton, Lieutenant Augustus Grey Dixwell Alderson – a 19-year-old who hailed from St. Leonard's-on-Sea, Sussex – and Second Lieutenants William Dennett and Peter Kent. The pilots quickly ran to the hangar at Warloy Aerodrome, threw on their flying suits but didn't bother about field boots, and were soon airborne in their Sopwith Camels. The squadron patrolled the Western Front between Arras and St Quentin, flying at a height of around 2.5 miles. During the flight, Second Lieutenant Dennett was forced to turn back with engine trouble, reducing their fighting capability. Then they spotted the enemy Albatross aircraft at around 1,500 feet above their position.

A deadly dogfight soon commenced and Captain Sutton disappeared. His tailplane had been badly damaged but he managed to nurse his stricken aircraft back to Warloy. Major Raymond-Barker could now only see the aircraft of Gus Alderson and Peter Kent, who managed to shoot down two Albatrosses between them. However, the remaining four enemy aircraft were too much for the pair and they were soon shot down.

In a letter to Peter's father dated 7 February 1918, the squadron commander provided some detail of what had happened to the pilot.

My Dear Mr Kent,

It is with every regret I have to inform you that your son 2/Lt P.F.Kent went on a patrol yesterday afternoon and has not returned. Here is the story.

A patrol of four went out, one of whom later returned with engine trouble. The remaining three ran into a formation of six Huns. In the ensuing fight, our leader was first sent down out of action with his fin so badly damaged he could hardly keep his machine in control. He eventually struggled home, though badly shot about. Our remaining two stuck to their job, and one of the Huns promptly went down in flames. A second Hun followed a minute later. One of our two machines went down in flames, and the last went down out of control, but recovered at about 2,000 feet, and was seen to land on the other side. The pilot of this machine was probably wounded, and recovered himself in time to get control of his machine. Which of the two machines your brave son was flying, it is impossible to say. We are dropping messages over and as soon as we get any more definite news, I will of course let you have it at once.

There is still hope, though not of the best. It is the cruellest of fortune that we should lose your son especially now. He was, as you know, attached to us from Gosport for six weeks and during that six weeks he did whatever jobs were going like everyone else. He then applied to me to remain on, and until the question was settled I sent him off on various flying jobs that did not necessitate war flying.

Still there was a delay, and he begged to be able to do the ordinary jobs again. I got permission. Be proud of him. Those two, even if the worst happened, died game to the last. The batteries in the frontline reported it was the finest show they had ever seen. They were my two best.

With every sympathy to you and yours in your present anxiety.
Major Richard Raymond Barker

In the heat of battle, Major Raymond-Barker had been unable to ascertain which pilot had been shot down and survived a crash landing. Research, however, shows that the second pilot was in fact Augustus Grey Dixwell Alderson and he had been injured by enemy fire. His right leg shattered, he lost consciousness and tumbled earthwards out of control, crashing into a tree. Miraculously, Alderson survived the crash and was captured by German soldiers, who took him to a field hospital well behind enemy lines. He regained consciousness a week later as a prisoner of war.

When Gus Alderson was repatriated after the war, the first people he went to see were Peter Kent's parents and evidently struck up a very close relationship with them. He married Edith

Augustus Grey Dixwell Alderson.

Mary Doig, a native of Barnet, on 18 August 1919 and the couple named their son after Peter Kent. Gus Alderson passed away in Maidstone, Kent in 1996.

In a final letter to Peter's mother Major Richard Raymond Barker wrote:

My dear Mrs Kent,

I was very sorry to hear your news, though I knew that one of those brave two never came back. It almost seems useless my offering you and yours any consolation in your bereavement, but there is one thing that can always be remembered to your son's glory. He could not have had a braver end, against very heavy odds, almost with his back to the wall so to speak, they eventually got him down not before he had already finished off at least one of the enemy. Us fellows out here ever hope for a finer end. On my next leave, though that may be some time yet, if I may I will try and call on you myself.

With my deepest sympathy, and that us all, yours very sincerely,
Major Richard Raymond Barker

On 20 April 1918 Major Richard Raymond-Barker MC was flying a Sopwith Camel (D6439) in the vicinity of Bois de Hamel, and would be the very last victim of Manfred von Richthofen, the 'Red Baron'. In his very last combat report, the German ace wrote:

With six planes of Jasta 11, I attacked a large enemy squadron. During the fight I observed that a Triplane was attacked and shot at from below by a Camel. I put myself behind the adversary and brought him down, burning, with only a few shots. The enemy plane crashed down near the forest of Hamel where it burned further on the ground.

The following morning Manfred von Richthofen was shot down and killed.

In a tragic postscript to Peter's story, a document contained in his service record shows how the War Office made a devastating error. A few weeks before Peter's arrival in France, on 20 November 1917, another pilot of No. 3 Squadron, Second Lieutenant Thomas John Kent, was shot down near Cambrai and was taken prisoner. His mother waited desperately for news on her son's fate, and was eventually informed that her boy was in captivity. One can only imagine her initial horror when late on the evening of 15 February 1918 a telegram arrived

Manfred von Richthofen.

at her door informing her that her son was reported missing on 6 February 1918. Her response was swift and courteous but it took the War Office a full week to respond to her letter, apologising for their error and offering a somewhat pitiful explanation for their actions. One wonders how many other mothers, wives and loved ones suffered the pain of anxiety as a consequence of administrative errors.

For Peter's parents, however, the pain must have been worse with the absence of any further information from the War Office. It was not until 18 March 1918 that they were officially told the news. By this time, they were already fully aware that their son was dead. Ernest wrote to the War Office pointing out that he already knew more about Peter's death than they did, and suggested they could improve upon their casualty notification system.

Peter Kent was originally buried in the Lecluse Churchyard, but on 3 March 1925 his body was removed from its grave by local labour under the supervision of Mr C. Rutter of the Imperial War Graves Commission, and re-interred in the H.A.C. British Cemetery at St. Main, where it remains to this day.

It was an extreme pleasure and a great honour to guide veterans of the Royal British Legion and the Royal Observer Corps to the site of Peter Kent's last resting place as part of the Great War centenary commemorations.

THE COURAGEOUS WOUNDED – CORPORAL HORACE BAVINGTON DCM

Horace Leonard Bavington was born on 10 March 1896 as the fourth son of William and Harriett Bavington (née Faulkner), who were living in Queen Street, Hitchin at the time. His father was employed by the Great Northern Railway at Hitchin as a porter and a wood cutter.

William and Harriett, like so many other Victorian families, suffered the loss of three of their children at a very young age. Alice, who was born in 1887, died in her first year. Henry, who was born in 1891, died at birth, and Arthur, who was born in 1889, died when he was just 4 years old. Therefore, it must have come as a great relief to see their remaining children, William, Horace, Harold, Elsie and Lilian, grow older.

Corporal Horace Bavington DCM.

Horace went on to attend the British School in Hitchin and at the age of 15 became an errand boy for the Premier Meat Company. By the time he was 16 years old, Horace worked as a clerk for the Great Northern Railway, like his father. On the 10 March 1913, his 17th birthday, he enlisted in the Hertfordshire Regiment. Standing at 5 feet 5 ½ inches, and with a 34-inch chest, Horace was declared fit for service in the 1st Battalion, with the regimental number 2145. He was embodied into service on 5 August 1914, the day after the Great War broke out, but it was not until 21 January 1915 that he was posted to France, becoming a member of No. 4 Company. After just two days with the company, he was sent to No. 4 Field Ambulance suffering with inflamed tonsils but after treatment, he returned to duty on 9 February.

It was on 3 July 1915 that Horace was admitted to No. 5 Field Ambulance. This time he was suffering from pyrexia, which is a form of fever. He was transferred to No. 6 Casualty Clearing Station, where he remained with an undiagnosed condition until 9 July. On that date, he returned to his unit so it must be presumed that his fever had passed.

On 15 September 1915 Bavington was attached to a trench mortar company and was granted proficiency pay (Class I), on 30 May 1916 he was made acting Lance Corporal, and on 11 September 1916 he was promoted to Corporal.

On 13 November 1916, near the village of Thiepval on the Somme, Horace distinguished himself in action; he played a leading role during the Hertfordshire Regiment's attack as part of the Battle of the Ancre. That morning, in a dense fog, the men of the Hertfordshire Regiment – led by Horace's No. 4 Company – left their 'jumping-off positions' in a captured German trench system known as the Schwaben Redoubt, to attack down a sloping valley towards the Ancre River. In leading one of two bombing parties, Horace managed to get into the well-defended German Hansa Line and proceeded along its length for a distance of some 400 metres, throwing grenades ahead of him as he went, apparently personally dispatching a number of enemy soldiers as he did so. Once Horace and his comrades reached their objective, Mill Road Trench – an impressive 1,600 yards from their start positions – they began to consolidate against the expected German counterattack. During this time, the captured dugout Horace was in was hit by an enemy shell, collapsing it on the occupants. Over the next hour, his comrades worked feverishly to free the trapped men, eventually bringing Corporal Bavington out unconscious. Fortunately, 30 minutes later he regained consciousness. He refused to be evacuated for medical treatment, preferring instead to aid with the defence of their hard-won gains.

On 10 January 1917 he was admitted to No. 46 Casualty Clearing Station, again with an undiagnosed condition. Eventually, on 18 February 1917, he returned to duty. It was during this period that he learned he had been awarded the Distinguished Conduct Medal for his actions on 13 November. The award was officially announced in *The London Gazette* on 26 January and read:

> *For conspicuous gallantry in action. He led a bombing party with great gallantry, and rendered valuable assistance in the consolidation of the position. He has at all times set a splendid example.*

It was also at this point, under Army Council instructions, that Horace was allocated a new regimental number, 265306.

On 9 May 1917 Horace was wounded on duty. He was admitted to No. 133 Field Ambulance then returned to duty on 30 May. It was on 25 June 1917 that Horace returned home on leave for 14 days, and this would be the last time his family would see the Horace they knew. He returned to the frontline on 6 July and was wounded – this time seriously – a few days later. A large piece of shrapnel from an exploding shell struck Horace on the left side of his head, causing devastating injuries.

On 16 July 1917 Horace underwent an operation and on 24 of July 1917 he was transferred to the Croydon War Hospital for further treatment. A report dated 17 September 1917 states the following:

> *On the left side of the forehead is a semi-circular scar. Just above the left eyebrow is a scar, not quite healed, where a drainage tube was inserted and from which brain substance came away for about six weeks. The left eye has been excised, parts of the left frontal bone have gone, including the orbital plate and there is a distinct injury of the brain over the left frontal region. The left socket still discharges slightly. An x-ray shows a small object lying on the right – bone. He is deaf in the left ear but there is no paralysis of any limb.*

Horace died as a consequence of his injuries on 21 February 1918 despite months of treatment and more than a dozen operations in an attempt to stabilise his condition. He is buried in Hitchin Cemetery, Hertfordshire. Horace was 22 years old. In addition to his Distinguished Conduct Medal, he was also awarded the 1915 Star, British War Medal, Victory Medal and a Silver War Badge with the number 135527.

Sadly, like a great many other Hertfordshire families, this was not the last time that the effects of war would devastate the Bavington family. Horace's nephew, Arthur Henry Bavington, was to lose his life during the Second World War.

WAR OVERCOMES AN ADDICTION – SERGEANT GEORGE MAJOR MM

Our view of the soldiers who served in the Great War is that they were often either enthusiastic volunteers or subjugated conscripts. What is sometimes forgotten is that many battalions within the British Army, particularly in the early months of the war, were manned by 'regular soldiers' – paid-by-the-day professionals, who were either still

Medals of Sergeant George Major MM.

in service or had been rapidly recalled from the reserve army to fight for King and Country. Within their ranks were men who had served for a considerable amount of time and were wholly accustomed to military life and its disciplines. These tough Edwardian soldiers who had signed up for a minimum seven years of service in the army plus a further five years in the reserve army, were used to a lifestyle that not only subjected them to harsh discipline but also often elicited drunkenness, violence and an urge to indulge in the many excesses that became available to them. One such Hertfordshire soldier was George Major of St. Albans, a man who could readily be described as a typical 'pre-war regular', but whose character was to see an unexpected change with the outbreak of the Great War. This is his story. George Major was born in 1888 as the son of George and Esther Major of Titus House, St. Albans, Hertfordshire. He was one of ten children. After leaving school, George worked as a straw hat blocker in St. Albans, and it was at this stage in his life that he decided to join the military. The strain on the regular army stationed on garrison duty around the world necessitated the use of a civilian army that could be called upon in a time of crisis to provide trained support. Despite the fact that he had flat feet and four bad teeth, George was accepted for enlistment in the 4th Battalion, Bedfordshire Regiment (Herts Militia) on 27 January 1906 and was given the regimental number 5533.

A little over a year later, on 15 April 1907, George, whose civilian occupation was now recorded as a painter's labourer, enlisted in the Bedfordshire Regiment. He was aged 19 years and 2 months and described as a muscular youth with light brown hair, blue eyes and standing at just 5′ 5″ (1.65 metres) tall. After undergoing a form of basic training in the United Kingdom, which supplemented his militia training, George was quickly shipped off to help protect British interests around the world.

Now with a new regimental number, 8995, his first posting was with the 2nd Battalion, Bedfordshire Regiment, to the crown colony of Gibraltar, where he arrived on 29 August 1907. His service record, which covers an extensive period, shows that on 5 February 1908 he was disciplined for drunkenness and being outside the fortress after first evening gun fire – a sound that signified the closing of the gates to the town. A few months later, on 8 July 1908, he found himself in trouble again; this time for being absent from evening gun fire. These incidents saw George being punished with confinement to his barracks for four and three days respectively. Seemingly not having learnt his lesson, a further incident followed just a few weeks later, but this time it was for being drunk and creating a disturbance in his barracks. Again, George found himself confined to those selfsame barracks for another three days. Eventually, his period of service on 'Gib' complete, George left the fortress island on 27 January 1910 and returned to the United Kingdom, where he was attached to the 1st Battalion, Bedfordshire Regiment, who were stationed in the county depot at Kempston Barracks, Bedford.

It would appear that being at home was probably the worst thing for George. He found himself disciplined on no less than ten separate occasions between May 1910 and September 1912. The transgressions occurred in a number of military garrisons, such as Colchester and Aldershot, and saw him charged with offences such as drunkenness, resisting arrest by the military police, being absent, overstaying his pass and damaging an army canteen – including the smashing of beer glasses. The punishments varied in their severity but included confinement to barracks, loss of pay and eventually, imprisonment. His company commander was fully aware that George had a significant drinking problem, but his general behaviour and performance as a soldier was deemed to be very good and as such, his offences appear to have been treated relatively lightly.

During his time back in the United Kingdom, George found himself the subject of another condition that greatly affected Edwardian soldiers: syphilis. This was claimed to have been contracted in the London Borough of Chelsea, the location of a large barracks serviced by numerous public houses in the vicinity and all the trappings that were associated with them. Treatment was rudimentary, and George's record lists a significant number of occasions when mercurial treatments were applied. This, of course, did not appear to have been a deterrent for the young soldier and his name would soon be as well known to his medical officer as it was to his company commander.

By 8 January 1913 George found himself in South Africa, back with the 2nd Battalion. However, it wasn't long before he was, once again, brought before his company commander for a variety of similar offences, mainly concerning drunkenness. Surprisingly, his performance as a soldier never seems to have been in question despite all his transgressions, and appears to typify many of the service records of pre-war soldiers of that period. He is described by his commanding officer in October 1913 as *'clean and respectful, honest and hard-working'*. At this stage, George had been employed as part of the Garrison Police, as well as being the company cook.

However, a significant change was about to occur for the British Army with the outbreak of the Great War. For George, too, there would be extensive change, not only in his circumstances but also in his character. With the commencement of hostilities, the 2nd Battalion, Bedfordshire Regiment, were hurriedly posted back to the United Kingdom, arriving home on 20 September 1914. Just a few short weeks later, on 3 October 1914, they were posted to the Western Front. George was to see action with the battalion in all its major actions in the early stages of the war. His service record demonstrates a dramatic change in his behaviour. Gone were the instances of drunkenness and absenteeism. Instead, a steadfast and reliable regular soldier stepped up to the plate in the face of an onslaught by a determined enemy.

On 27 September 1915, whilst the battalion was holding a German trench near the French town of Hulluch, George was wounded in the buttock by shellfire. He was evacuated to No. 14 General Hospital in Rouen, after which he was transported back to the United Kingdom, where he soon fell into his old ways once he was on home soil. Whilst stationed at Kempston Barracks, he found himself disciplined on two occasions within a five-day period for being absent, most likely related to being drunk on the previous night. George remained at the depot until he was fully fit to return to the front. On New Year's Eve 1915, he was shipped back to France, only to discover that he had been transferred from the 2nd Battalion, Bedfordshire Regiment to the 2nd Battalion, Border Regiment. There is no indication within his service record why this action was taken, but it is most likely an interdivisional transfer based on manpower requirements. Some, however, may say that his commanders felt this hardworking but troublesome soldier may benefit from a period of service amongst a thousand Scotsmen!

Undeterred, George, now with the regimental number 10/20973, returned to France and joined the 2nd Border Regiment in their billets at Buigny-L'Abbe, near Abbeville. He served with them throughout the winter and spring of 1916 as the battalion, part of the 20th Brigade, 7th Division, saw action in what was deemed to be the quieter Somme Sector. The battalion soon found itself preparing for its involvement in the forthcoming 'Big Push' on the battlefields of the Somme Valley, and it was here that George was to gain a medal for gallantry.

On the night of 30 June 1916 the battalion moved up from Morlancourt and took up positions in a location known as the B2 Subsector of the trenches, with all troops being in position by 1.30 am. At 7.27 am the battalion advanced from its positions in four lines, making for its first objective, named Danube Support trench. At this stage the battalion began to move to the left as it had been ordered to do, and casualties were relatively light. Their advance continued towards their second objective, a trench named Apple Alley, which was reached by 8.30 am. The brave Scotsmen bombed and bayoneted their way forward, as the enemy – realising that some of the trench system had been captured – attempted to create a new frontline by joining up shell holes and communication trenches. Throughout this period, the battalion was subjected to intense machine gun and rifle fire, with the addition of artillery shrapnel as they followed closely behind the British barrage, as well as retaliatory fire from German artillery.

By the end of the first day, the battalion had suffered a total of 92 men killed, 246 wounded and 4 missing. George Major was amongst those who had been wounded, but whose outstanding bravery in the face of continual enemy fire was to see him be awarded the Military Medal and secure a promotion to Corporal. He was wounded in the right arm by shellfire and was initially evacuated to No. 23 Field Ambulance at Morlancourt, before being passed on to No. 34 Casualty Clearing Station at Vecquemont. After some rudimentary treatment, George was transported to No. 10 General Hospital at Rouen, and on 8 July 1916, he returned to Blighty aboard the hospital ship *Salta*.

George remained in the United Kingdom until he was fit enough to return to his unit. During this time, he married his sweetheart, Emily Maud Hawes of Harpenden, at St. Saviours Church in St. Albans on 2 September 1916 and saw his award of the Military Medal announced in *The London Gazette* of 11 November 1916. Then, declared once more to be fit enough for active service, George was posted back to France on 25 April 1917. He would not see home again.

Upon his arrival at Etaples on 26 April 1917, George Major was held at No. 25 Infantry Base Depot until 17 May, when he rejoined the 2nd Battalion, Border Regiment. He was promoted to Sergeant on 22 March 1917, and was no doubt ribbed continually by the men of his company about him being 'Sergeant Major', whilst not really being a Sergeant Major.

On 4 October, in a steady drizzle of fine rain, the battalion – who were located near to the edge of Polygon Wood in the Ypres Sector – moved into forward assault positions. They had been ordered to take part in an attack in which their role was to leapfrog the 8th Devonshire Regiment, whose objective was known as the red line, and then move onto the next objective close to Journal Wood, named the blue line. They were also tasked with mopping up any prisoners in the area between the two objectives. It was during this assault that George was wounded again; he was shot in the right foot. He was evacuated to a nearby field ambulance, and then to No. 2 Canadian Casualty Clearing Station at Remy Siding. The following day, in a demonstration of the efficiency of Allied medical services at the time, George found himself at No. 22 General Hospital at Camiers. After three weeks of convalescence, he was posted, again, to No. 25 Infantry Base Depot and rejoined his battalion in the field on 31 October 1917, where they were resting in billets at Renescure. Little did he know that in just a few short weeks he would be leaving the dreaded Ypres Sector to serve on an entirely different front, from which he would not return.

On 24 October 1917 a combined Austro-Hungarian–German attack took place against Italian positions at Tolmino. The assault, greatly aided by misty conditions, took the Italians completely by surprise. A heavy artillery barrage and the use of gas and smoke saw the joint force break through the Italian lines almost immediately. By the end of the day they had advanced a remarkable 25 km, using infiltration tactics and exploiting breaches in the Italian line with the use of grenades and flamethrowers. The German secondary attacks on either side of the main offensive were, however, far less successful and made little progress. Nevertheless, the Germans' sweeping success in the centre endangered the majority of the Italian forces at the River Tagliamento. In order to ensure that this significant defeat did not lead to Italy withdrawing from the war, the Allies organised a joint Franco-British force to support their allies. The British Expeditionary Force (Italy) came under the command of General Herbert Plumer with the principal units being the 5th, 7th, 23rd, 41st and 48th Divisions.

On 17 November 1917 the 7th Division, including the 2nd Border Regiment, was ordered to leave France and move to the Italian Front, where they were to face the combined Austro-Hungarian and German force. Apart from the lengthy journey and a welcome change in scenery, there was an immense change in the weather. The troops, now in the thinner mountain air of the Asiago region, were faced with freezing weather conditions, much worse than those experienced on the Western Front. Of course, for many men of the Border Regiment, these conditions were not unlike those seen in the Scottish Highlands, but for a man from St. Albans, such conditions must have been particularly taxing.

The transportation of ammunition, rations and stores proved extremely difficult. Tracks were difficult to maintain and the rocky ground meant that the digging of trenches was almost impossible. Sangars, constructed from stones, had to be built to provide shelter. Water was a constant problem and life for the troops was, on the whole, unpleasant and uncomfortable. It is not surprising therefore, that some of them sought solace in the local communities. The Italians were described as 'surprisingly friendly' by one soldier, who also warned of the dangers of the local 'Vino Rosso', advising that it was to be greatly respected in comparison to the 'thin wines and beers of France'.

In this environment, sadly, Sergeant George Major saw the old demons return and on 22 March 1918 he was arrested by the Military Police. Four days later he was brought before a Field General Court Martial, where he was charged with the following:

1. *When on active service – Drunkenness.*
2. *When on active service – Conduct to the Prejudice of Good Order & Military Discipline.*

i.e. Striking 29282 Lance Corporal Norman Wellox. (Service record incorrectly states Willcox.)

After being found guilty of these actions, George was sentenced to take rank and precedence as if his appointment to the rank of Sergeant bore the date of 27 September 1917. This appears to be somewhat of a lenient outcome for a serious offence, given that it took place whilst on active service. There appears to be no explanation for the leniency of the court.

By the beginning of August 1918, the battalion were training at Bassano. On the night of 6–7 August they were ordered to carry out a raid on Stella Fort, an enemy-held position near the village of Canove. The following is an extract from a report written by the battalion commanding officer, Lieutenant Colonel Hugh Alexander Ross DSO, in which he describes the raid.

The object of the raid was to capture the enemy front and support lines from about Stella House westward to and including Stella Fort, to capture prisoners, obtain identifications and do as much damage as possible. The Battalion of the Manchester Regiment raided by my immediate right. For the purpose of the raid I used 'B' and 'D' Companies, one Lewis gun section of 'B' company to form a left flanking party.

From 9.45 pm onwards the whole party was covered by and under the observation of the regimental scouts. The raid was under the command of Captain J W Little MC. At 10.00 pm the Battalion Scouts moved out to cover the frontage, to gaps in the wire and to lay the tapes marking the forming up position and lines of withdrawal. The night was dark and still and ground conditions favourable. At 10.35 pm, the raiding party moved out through the tunnels, 'B' company through the left, 'D' company through the right tunnel.

At 11.45 pm, the raiding party had formed up and at zero-hour, 12 midnight, the barrage came down and the raiding party moved forward as ordered. Two small parties of the enemy were seen running back but very little opposition was met until raid headquarters had been established at Stella House and number four line was in position. At map reference H304.501, Nos. 1 and 2 Lines came upon a line of wire running north to south, covering Stella Fort; this wire held up the advance and fairly heavy machine gun and trench mortar fire was opened up on the party here. Nos. 1 and 2 Lines were ordered to get around this obstacle and to re-form on the other side. After slight delay this movement was accomplished and the lines advanced into Stella Fort and rushed and captured.

In the fort the enemy put up a strong resistance especially on our right flank; this was overcome and several prisoners collected. They were in marching order and wearing full equipment and packs. No. 2 Line had reinforced No. 1 at this point and the line proceeded forward. Defensive points were formed and the enemy were bombed to the western end of the fort, while mopping up continued. No one would come out of the dugout in the fort and they were bombed.

No. 3 Line was successful and Gwent trench was quickly cleared and held by the left platoon. The right platoon failed to discover the trench mortars reported about E 307.512 (these were not active) but rushed a single trench mortar at about H 308.508 (map reference), destroyed the team and burst three Mills No. 5 in the trench mortar which was seen to be effectively destroyed. The raiding party withdrew in good order to their re-forming position where they were almost at once sent back to the checking posts at raid headquarters on Stafford Hill as owing to the successful counter battery work the hostile barrage was very indifferent. The searchlight proved of great worth, while it was in operation, but unfortunately at the most difficult part of our task it failed. The enemy were very stubborn and fought with a good deal of determination. I forwarded a large number of identification discs and other identifications to headquarters.

One officer and 20 other ranks were handed over to the military police. Two machine guns were captured, the third machine gun sent back by Captain Little from Stella House with one prisoner and escort of two men failed to reach raid headquarters, though the escorted prisoners were brought in, they were killed by a trench mortar bomb near Holla North. Finally, I would like to bring to your notice the work of the Royal Artillery. Nothing could have been better or more accurate than the assistance they gave to my raiding party.

I have the honour to be, sir, your obedient servant,

Lieutenant Colonel H. A. Ross

Commanding 2nd Battalion, Border Regiment.

Sadly, Lieutenant Colonel Hugh Ross was killed in action just a few weeks later, on 27 October 1918. Records show that George Major was one of twenty fatalities suffered that night, half of whom have no known grave.

George Major served in the British Army for 11 years and 27 days, was disciplined on no less than 23 occasions, contracted syphilis, was wounded on several occasions and survived some of the worst battles of the Western Front. He endured the endless drudgery and horror of trench life and bravely faced the enemy, where his behaviour had been outstanding, resulting in the award of

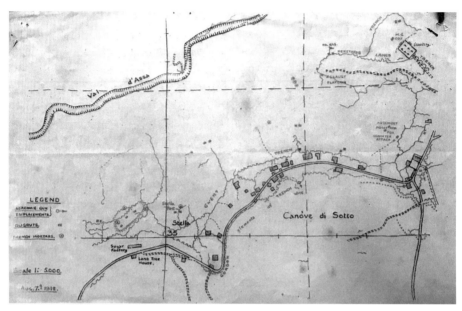

A contemporary trench map shows the location of the attack by the 2nd Border Regiment on the night of 8–9 August 1918.

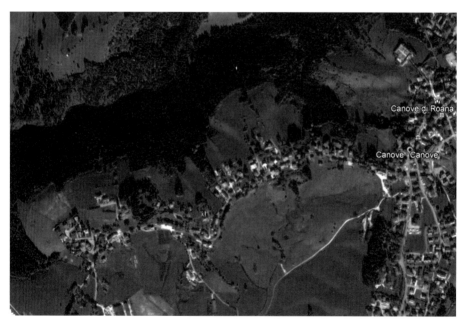

A modern satellite image of the same area still shows the scars of war close to the town cemetery, where trench lines can still be seen.

The Giavera Memorial and Cemetery, Italy

the Military Medal. His name, and that of his comrades'who shared the same fate, are recorded on the Giavera Memorial, Italy. Sergeant George Major was entitled to the following awards: Military Medal, 1914 Star, British War Medal and Victory Medal.

Whilst George was only married to Emily for a short time, she never remarried following his death. Records show that her life was quite ordinary. She worked mainly as a domestic servant in different parts of the country for the rest of her days. It was only as her life drew to a close that Emily returned to the family home at 49 Longfield Road, Harpenden, where she passed away on 4 October 1948 at the age of 60 as a consequence of heart disease. On her death certificate, she is described as the widow of Sergeant George Major of an unnamed regiment.

A VERY SHORT WAR – PRIVATE FRANK SMITH

Frank Smith was born in Back Lane, Stevenage, Hertfordshire, on 4 May 1899 as the eldest son of George and Kate Smith. His siblings included his elder sister, Lily, and three younger siblings, Florence, Ernest and Oswald. Their father worked as a cowhand on a local farm and by 1911 the family was living in Fore Street, Weston, Hertfordshire.

A service record for Frank has not survived but it is most likely that he was conscripted into the army after his 18th birthday. He joined the army in Hitchin, and records show that he initially trained with the 51st Royal West Surrey Regiment, being given the regimental number TR/9/15025.

Following the completion of his training, Frank was posted to the Western Front and arrived in France on 20 March 1918, first being held at an Infantry Base Depot close to the coast. The day after his arrival on the continent, the Germans began their Spring Offensive in the Somme region and Frank was quickly prepared to join a battalion in the field.

He was posted to the 2/2nd Battalion, London Regiment, Royal Fusiliers (City of London Regiment) and given the regimental number GS/75926. Frank joined the battalion in the field at Besmé, France on 28 March 1918 as part of a draft of 114 reinforcements after the battalion had suffered heavily in the initial German assault, losing 21 officers and 650 other ranks.

Private Frank Smith.

The location is about 22 miles south of where the German attack had begun on 21 March. On the night of their arrival, Frank and the rest of the battalion marched to positions east of the Manicamp Sector, about 1.5 miles south of Abbecourt, where they relieved the French 18th Entrenching Battalion.

On the morning of 2 April 1918 the battalion was relieved by the French 246th Infantry Regiment and moved to Blérancourt and then onto Audignicourt, where they spent the night resting in caves. The following morning, they marched to Ambleny and after an overnight rest, wearily marched to Dommiers, 6 miles southwest of Soissons.

On 6 April the battalion marched to Longpont, where they boarded trains to take them to Longeau, and on arrival, the men of the battalion undertook a further 5-mile march to a copse 3 miles north of Gentelles Wood, where they moved into bivouacs and were held in brigade reserve. At this stage, the battalion consisted of 10 officers and 250 other ranks but were later reinforced by three companies of the 12th Battalion, Middlesex Regiment. The battalion remained at Gentelles Wood for the next two weeks, where they were engaged in repair work on the reserve line, east of the wood, where it straddled the Amiens–Albert Road.

As the German Spring Offensive gained momentum, the action at Hangard Wood, south of Villers-Bretonneux, close to the Somme River, would form part of the larger, second battle of Villers-Bretonneux. Taking place on 24 April 1918, this was a significant event, as it was the first tank on tank battle in history.

On the morning of 24 April, a very determined attack was made by the Germans upon the front of Third Corps in the area of Villers-Bretonneux. This small town is of great importance, as it stands on a curve of the rolling downs from which a very commanding view of Amiens is obtained, the cathedral especially standing out with great clearness. Already the city had suffered great damage, but the permanent loss of Villers-Bretonneux would mean its certain destruction. The attack was undertaken by four German divisions and was supported by tanks, which did good work and broke through the British line, held mainly at this point by the 8th Division, which had hardly recovered from its services on the Somme.

There were fifteen German tanks, so their presence was a formidable one, the more so in a mist which was impenetrable at fifty yards. The British now experienced the full horror that tanks can bring. Even the bravest heart trembles as they loom up out of the haze bringing to bear all their hideous firepower.. The 2/4th London Regiment were driven back to the line Cachy – Hangard Wood on the south of the village, so the battalion closest to them – the 2/2nd London Regiment – had to fall back or risk being cut off.

The 2/10th London Regiment counterattacked at once, however, and penetrated Hangard Wood, helping to ease the situation. The 2nd Battalion, Middlesex Regiment and the 2nd Battalion, West Yorkshire Regiment were overrun by the tanks and even the historical and self-immolating stab in the belly was useless against these monsters. The 2nd Battalion, Rifle Brigade was also dislodged from its position and had to close up on the 2nd Berkshires on its left. The 2nd Battalion, East Lancashire Regiment also had to fall back but after coming in touch with a section of the divisional artillery, they were able to rally and hold their ground all day with the backing of the guns.

The 2nd Battalion, Devonshire Regiment – in reserve on the right – was also attacked by tanks, the first of which appeared suddenly before Battalion Headquarters and blew away the parapet. Others attacked the battalion, which was forced to move into the Bois d'Aquenne. By chance there were three heavy British tanks in this quarter, and they were at once ordered forward to restore the situation. Seven light Whippet tanks were also given to the 58th Division. These tanks then engaged the enemy's fleet, and though two of the heavier and four of the lighter ones were put out of action, they silenced the Germans and drove them back. With these powerful allies, the infantry began to move forward again, and the 1st Battalion, Sherwood Foresters, carried out a particularly valuable advance.

Shortly after noon the 173rd Brigade of the 58th Division, in which Frank Smith was serving, saw the Germans massing behind their tanks about 500 yards east of Cachy, with a view to attacking. There were three British Whippets still available, and they rushed out and did great work, catching two German battalions as they were being deployed. The 58th Division had good support on their right flank in the shape of the Moroccan Corps, a unit which was second-to-none in the French Army for attack. These were not engaged, but under the orders of General

Debeney they closed up on the left so as to shorten the front of General Gator's division, a great assistance with the British ranks being so depleted. His troops consisted largely of 18-year-old lads like Frank Smith, sent out to fill the gaps in the severely depleted British units. Nothing could exceed their spirit, though their endurance was not equal to their courage.

58th Division Memorial at Chipilly, Somme.

On the evening of 24 April, General Butler said, *'The battle is lost. There is time to win another one.'* The Germans not only held Villers-Bretonneux, but they had taken Hangard village from the French and held all but the western edge of Hangard Wood. The farthest western point ever reached by the Germans on the Somme was on this day, when they occupied the Bois l'Abbé for a time. They were driven out in the afternoon by the 1st Battalion, Sherwood Foresters and 2nd Battalion, West Yorkshire Regiment. The Germans did not reach Cachy, which was their final objective, but nonetheless it was very necessary that Villers-Bretonneux and the ground around it should be regained instantly before the Germans took root. For this purpose, a night attack was planned on the evening of 24 April and was carried out with great success.

For the purposes of the attack, the 13th Australian Brigade was placed under the 8th Division and was ordered to attack to the south of Villers-Bretonneux, while the 15th Australian Brigade made a similar advance in the north. Each of these was directed to pass beyond the little town, which was to be cleared by an independent force. On the right of the Australians was the balance of the British 8th Division, which had to clear up the Bois d'Aquenne.

The attack was carried out at 10.00 pm, with the infantry having white armbands for identification in the darkness. There was no

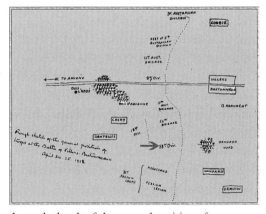

A rough sketch of the general position of troops at the Battle of Villers-Bretonneux, 24–25 April 1918. The part played by the British in this battle is very often overshadowed by the achievements of the Australian forces.

artillery preparation and the advance was across unknown country, so it may be considered as one of the most hazardous operations in the war.

The operation was predominately an Australian one and from the onset, the machine gun fire was very severe, especially against the Australian 51st Battalion. However, the admirable individuality of the Australian soldiers was of great service to them, every man getting forward through the darkness as best he could. The weather was ideal, for there was sufficient moon to give direction, but not enough to expose the troops to distant fire.

The German flares were a help to the attack by defining the position. The Australian front got as far forward as Monument Wood – level with the village – but the British 173rd Brigade on their right was in some difficulty; they themselves were badly enfiladed from the town, so they could not maintain their more advanced position. The 2nd Battalion, Northamptonshire Regiment, attached to the 13th Australian Brigade, had been told to take the town itself, but both their colonel and their adjutant were killed during the assembly, and some confusion of orders caused the plans to miscarry. On the north of the town, the 15th Australian Brigade with the 22nd Durham Light Infantry attached had been an hour late in starting, but after some confused fighting, entered Villers-Bretonneux after dawn. The area was cleared up by the 2nd Berkshires, aided by a company of the Australian 58th Battalion. The German tanks had done good work in the attack, and some of the British tanks were very useful in the counterattacks, especially three that operated in the Bois d'Aquenne and overcame the obstinate German resistance in front of the 8th Division. Daylight on 25 April found the British and Australian lines well up to the village on both sides, and a good deal of hard fighting – in which the troops got considerably mixed up – took place.

Frank Smith only served on the Western Front for four short weeks, but it was a period of intense military activity, with the German Army achieving its deepest advance since 1914. The British lost 178,000 men between 21 March and 29 April 1918, with 15,000 killed and 90,000 missing – most of whom had been taken prisoner. The French suffered 92,000 casualties and the German figure is estimated to be approximately 348,000 casualties.

Frank Smith has no known grave and his name is recorded on the panels of the Pozieres Memorial, which contains 14,691 names of those men of the British and South African forces who were lost on the Somme between 21 March and 7 August 1918.

Frank Smith was entitled to the British War Medal (Left) and the Victory Medal (Right).

A LIFE TAKEN – CORPORAL PHILIP EDWARD KINGHAM MM

For a great many visitors to the battlefields of the Western Front, the high point of their tour may be a visit to one of the many cemeteries maintained by the Commonwealth War Graves Commission. Here the visitor will find row upon row of neatly tended graves; the last resting place of men and women whose lives were lost to the ferocity of war, the ravaging effects of disease, or the unfortunate outcome of an accident. There are of course a great many military graves within the shores of the United Kingdom. Some are maintained by the Commission but many are under the care of the local authority. There are those, too, whose lives were taken from them as a consequence of military courts of justice or

Corporal Philip Edward Kingham MM.

– some might say – injustice. Arguably, the most poignant, however, are those graves that are filled with the bodies of individuals who believed that the only option for them was to take their own life.

In the Hatfield Road Cemetery on the outskirts of St. Albans there are 147 First World War graves. Of these, 93 form a neatly maintained plot with the remainder spread out across the cemetery. One of these is the burial place of Corporal Philip Edward Kingham, a holder of the Military Medal.

One of the original members of the Hertfordshire Regiment who landed in France on 6 November 1914, Philip was the son of William Randolph and Jessie Kingham of Russell Avenue, St. Albans. He served with the regiment throughout the Great War and fought in the various locations in which the battalion found itself. There is no service record available for Philip, as it was destroyed during a German air raid on London in 1940, so it is not possible to provide a detailed background to his military career. There is no doubt that as a private soldier, he endured the depravations of trench life suffered by so many of his chums during the time that his regiment served along the Western Front.

In November 1916, following the Battle of The Ancre River, Philip Kingham, now a corporal, was awarded the Military Medal for his part in *delivering key messages across open ground, despite being seriously wounded in the leg*.

By the time he was 21 years old, Philip Kingham had become a veteran of the battlefront and had survived the ever-increasing ferocity and inhumanity of trench warfare. In the spring of 1918, following the German offensive on the

Somme, Philip Kingham was wounded in the right knee. His injury was bad enough for him to be evacuated back to the UK and following his recovery, he was attached to the 3rd Battalion, Bedfordshire Regiment, who were performing Garrison duties on the East Coast.

At 4.15 am on Sunday, 19 May 1918 Lance Sergeant Alfred Cook heard an unusual noise, and on entering the ablutions, he found Corporal Kingham lying on the floor in a pool of blood, with a rifle by his side. Sergeant Major Luke Flint, a witness at the coroners hearing, said that the rifle had been fired, and he extracted an empty cartridge case from the chamber. Dr Herbert Harrison, a Captain in the Royal

The grave of Corporal Philip Edward Kingham MM at Hatfield Road Cemetery, St. Albans.

Army Medical Corps, stated that the Kingham's left jaw was fractured and, in his opinion, death was instantaneous. He took his own life and was just 22 years old.

THE CAPTIVE HERO – CAPTAIN JULIAN ROYDS GRIBBLE VC

Julian Royds Gribble was born on 5 January 1897, the son of George James and Norah Gribble (née Royds) of Kingston Russell House, Dorset. He was educated at Eton School and when the First World War began, he transferred to the officers' training school at Sandhurst. In early 1915 Julian was commissioned as a Lieutenant in the Royal Warwickshire Regiment and was posted to train recruits at Albany Barracks, Parkhurst on the Isle of Wight. He remained on the island for a year, sometimes taking drafts of newly trained troops as far as the French ports.

Captain Julian Royds Gribble VC.

In April 1916 Julian was ordered to France. Over the next six months he was in the thick of the fighting during the Battle of the Somme, with no leave. In October he was sent home as sick with 'trench fever'. Although it was recommended that he took a three-month rest, he reported back to Parkhurst after just four weeks.

From there he was posted to the 10th Battalion with the rank of Captain. At a time when the average life expectancy of British army officers at the front was 17 weeks, Julian was already a veteran. He spent the winter of his 20th birthday in the mud, frosts and floods of Flanders, and served throughout the Battle of Passchendaele.

In the darkest hours of 21 March 1918, the unsuspecting British Third and Fifth Armies were shocked by the most intense barrage of the war. In eight hours 6,500 German guns delivered 1.16 million poison gas and high explosive artillery shells into the British defences. Supported by the close fire of over 5,000 mortars, the barrage moved forward 200 metres every four minutes, annihilating defences and leaving the surviving defenders deaf and stunned. It was the beginning of the German Spring Offensive, code named Kaiserschlacht (the Kaiser's Battle). The 10th Battalion, Royal Warwickshire Regiment, was in reserve with the Third Army when the German barrage began. Behind the creeping barrage, 76 German divisions – equivalent to the entire British Army in France – advanced. They were led by 'Stormtroopers' armed with wire cutters, grenades and flamethrowers. Behind them came large battle groups of infantry with field artillery and heavy machine guns, followed by more masses of marching infantry.

The four infantry companies of the 10th Battalion hastily dug in along 1,600 yards of Hermies Ridge behind the rearmost British defences with orders to hold the position to the last man. The battalion was supported by its own battery of field artillery, flanking infantry, and further batteries of artillery and heavy machine guns.

On the second day of the offensive, the Germans began to shell these new positions, and the command structure of the British Third Army began to break down as it joined the Fifth Army in a fighting retreat. The next morning, as Julian reported that the Germans were massing to attack, the battalion's artillery were galloping away under conflicting orders. As the German attack intensified, more supporting artillery and infantry retreated. The battalion found itself increasingly isolated and surrounded. Even the HQ staff and any retreating stragglers they could rally were thrown into the desperate fighting. They held on for three hours but by 12.30 pm only 'D' Company was left holding on to the top of the ridge. When it became obvious that he was the last officer standing, Julian finally allowed his men to retreat, keeping six with him. Private Madeley was one of them. He said, *'I got hit and I am glad to say I broke through, but not with the Captain.'* Julian was last seen emptying his revolver into the final assault. *'I saw him go down under about seven big German brutes and that was the last I saw of one of England's finest officers.'* The Kaiser's Battle lasted just two weeks and 425,000 men fell on all sides in a battle that is now often overlooked.

The citation for his part in this action is found in *The London Gazette* dated 25 June 1918:

For most conspicuous bravery and devotion to duty. Capt. Gribble was in command of the right company of the battalion when the enemy attacked, and his orders were to 'hold on to the last'. His company was eventually entirely isolated, though he could easily have withdrawn them at one period when the rest of the battalion on his left were driven back to a secondary position. His right flank was 'in the air,' owing to the withdrawal of all troops of a neighbouring division. By means of a runner to the company on his left rear he intimated his determination to hold on until other orders were received from battalion headquarters – and this he inspired his command to accomplish.

His company was eventually surrounded by the enemy at close range, and he was seen fighting to the last. His subsequent fate is unknown. By his splendid example of grit, Captain Gribble was materially instrumental in preventing for some hours the enemy obtaining a complete mastery of the crest of ridge, and by his magnificent self-sacrifice he enabled the remainder of his own brigade to be withdrawn, as well as another garrison and three batteries of field artillery.

The gravely wounded officer was robbed by German troops and left for dead, but later it was discovered that he was actually alive. He began to make a good recovery in a hospital in Germany but found himself on the losing side in the terrible final months of the war. The Allied blockade of Germany was so effective, that the whole country was in a state of starvation. When Julian arrived at the new officers' prison in Mainz Castle, he and his fellow inmates suffered six weeks of starvation before the first Red Cross parcels arrived. In May 1918 Julian heard that he had been awarded the Victoria Cross for his stand on Hermies Ridge. The other officers saw the letters 'VC' on the envelope and carried the embarrassed man about the barrack square on their shoulders. The First World War finally came to an end after the Kaiser's abdication in October 1918. Eight days before the Armistice, Julian fell ill. On the morning of 24 November his fellow prisoners were released and boarded the train home. Julian was left alone in the castle hospital. He died shortly after midnight. His last words were to dismiss his nurse: '*Go away gnadiger Frau* (gracious lady).' The following day the French Army arrived with food and medicine, but it was too late for Julian.

He is buried in the Niederzwehren Cemetery in Germany, and his name is recorded on the war memorial in Preston, Hertfordshire.

TO BE FRANK – A FATHER & SON IN THE HERTFORDSHIRE REGIMENT

It is not uncommon to read about siblings serving together in the Great War, but it is much rarer to find a father and son who were serving in the same regiment. One of the most remarkable stories relating to Hertfordshire is that of Frank Young and his eldest son, also named Frank.

The officers' service record for Frank Young Senior was heavily weeded in April 1964 and many documents appertaining to his service were lost forever. The following details have been obtained from what remains of his record and from other military and genealogical sources. In an effort to aid with the confusion of detailing the service life of two men with the same name, their stories have been separated, beginning first with Frank Young Senior.

He was born as Frank Fensome on 27 March 1874 in Houghton Regis, Bedfordshire. His mother, Sarah Fensome, was the daughter of George Wilson, the landlord of the Five Bells in the High Street. In later life, Sarah married James Young and Frank's surname was changed.

Frank attended schools in Houghton Regis, Dunstable and Chapel Street, Luton, and on 16 November 1889 – at the age of 15 – he joined the army, enlisting in the 1st Battalion, Bedfordshire Regiment. His first posting with the battalion was in February 1890, when they moved from England to the garrison island of Malta. They remained there for the rest of the year, and in December 1890 the battalion sailed for the Indian continent, where they relieved the 2nd Battalion, Bedfordshire Regiment.

On his 17th Birthday, 27 March 1891, he was promoted to the rank of Lance Corporal and quickly achieved the rank of Corporal by April of that year. In November 1892 Frank attained the rank of Lance Sergeant, but he only held this for a short while, as on 16 March 1893 – not long before his 19th birthday – he became a fully-fledged Sergeant.

The British Army in India had two major roles, that of internal security and that of defence against invasion. The popular potential aggressor was Russia, seeking a way to the sea through Afghanistan and the northwest frontier buffer zone. This area was sparsely inhabited by fiercely independent tribes. All the

The Three Bells, Houghton Regis, the birth place of Frank Fensome, whose name was later changed to Frank Young.

1918 – Victory & Defeat   181

males were armed, and the females disposed of the prisoners. When the tribes did not quarrel between each other, they would launch raids on villages in India. The Peshawar Division was ready to form columns according to the situation at the time, whether it be for resupply of the garrisons or punitive operations.

The terrain was mountainous with steep-sided hills with many convex upper slopes producing false crests, making troops on the highest point invisible to supporting arms in the valleys. It was easy for an enemy to conceal themselves amongst the loose rocks and boulders. Movement of formations and animal transport were only practicable along the valleys, so movement along ridges parallel to the valleys was not possible. Digging trenches was impossible. Protection against enemy fire was, therefore, provided by building sangars (circular walls of stone).

The tribesmen were highly mobile in their territory and were quick to exploit an unguarded vantage point. The movement of columns, therefore, had to be somewhat ponderous. This, perhaps, gives an indication of the terrain faced by Sergeant Frank Young and the men of the Bedfordshire Regiment as they entered the region to help quash intertribal fighting in January 1895.

The siege and relief of the fort in Chitral in the remote mountainous region beyond the Northwest Frontier of India, held by Sikh and Kashmiri soldiers and their British officers from 3 March to 20 April 1895, is one that caused a stir in late Victorian Britain. On 14 March 1895, the Government of India ordered the mobilisation of the Peshawar Division based in Peshawar, in view of the situation and the incursion into Chitral by Umra Khan, the Khan of Jandol and Dir. The division was placed under the command of Lieutenant General Sir Robert Low KCB. The base for the division was moved to Nowshera, and concentration started on 26 March 1895. Within two and a half weeks, 15,000 troops with followers and transport animals, were assembled at Hoti Mardan and Nowshera.

The division comprised:

First Infantry Brigade: Brigadier General Kinloch, 1st Bedfordshire Regiment, 1st King's Royal Rifle Corps, 15th Sikhs, 37th Dogras and 2 field hospitals.

Second Infantry Brigade: Brigadier General Waterfield, 2nd King's Own Scottish Borderers, 1st Gordon Highlanders, 4th Sikhs, the Guides Infantry and 2 field hospitals.

Third Infantry Brigade: Brigadier General Gatacre, 1st Royal East Kent Regiment (the Buffs), 2nd Seaforth Highlanders, 25th Punjab Infantry, 2/4th Gurkha Rifles and 2 field hospitals.

Divisional Troops: 11th Bengal Lancers, Guides Cavalry, 13th Bengal Infantry, 23rd Punjab Pioneers, 15th Battery, Royal Artillery, No. 3 Mountain Battery,

Royal Artillery, No. 8 Mountain Battery, Royal Artillery, No. 2 (Derajat) Mountain Battery, 3 companies, Bengal Sappers and Miners, an Engineer Park, 3 field hospitals and a veterinary field hospital. The 34th Punjab Pioneers joined the division at the end of March 1895.

<u>Lines of Communications Troops:</u> 1st East Lancashire Regiment, 29th Punjab Infantry, 30th Punjab Infantry, No. 4 (Hazara) Mountain Battery, 2 field hospitals and a veterinary field hospital.

The Relief of Chitral was the first expedition to take the Indian and British armies over the Malakand Pass into Swat and Jandol. The British had little information on the country that lay to the north of Mardan. There were no roads, only tracks over the mountains. The first range of border hills was 3,000 to 6,000 feet in height. Beyond were further ranges of high mountains and three substantial rivers without bridges; border hills, then the Swat River; Laram Range up to 6,000 feet, then the Panjkora River; Janbati Range and the Dir Valley; and the Lowarai Pass into the valley of the Kunar River. Until roads could be built, the force would have to rely on pack animals to move supplies. Some 30,000 mules and camels were used in support of the force. No tents were taken and the baggage allowance was 40 lbs for officers and 10 lbs for soldiers, including a greatcoat. The weather was snowy, windy and rainy mixed with fierce sunshine.

The 2nd Brigade was given the task of clearing out the enemy. However, the entrenched enemy was in a strong position and the brigade was unable to capture the pass. The divisional commander instructed the Bedfordshires to strengthen the attack by outflanking the enemy through an 'east-about move'. The battalion made the move successfully; their subsequent attack surprised the enemy and they fled the field of battle. The battalion followed up the routed enemy for a further 4 miles, right into the village of Khan. Unfortunately, the remainder of the division was unable to reach the location in what remained of daylight, and the battalion was forced to spend the night without supplies. Despite this, the battalion was successful in its task, the campaign came to an end in May 1895, and the men started their journey back to India.

Frank received the Indian General Service Medal for his part in the campaign, with a bar reading 'Relief of Chitral 1895'.

Frank Young married Sarah Ellen Burgoyne in 1894 and their first son, Frank Edward Young,

The Indian General Service Medal with Relief of Chitral Clasp.

was born on 10 October 1895, following his return from the Chitral campaign. The couple would have two more children whilst living in Punjab: Isabella and Louisa. On 5 May 1899, Frank, who had held the rank of Sergeant for over six years at this point, was promoted to the rank of Colour Sergeant – a rank he would hold for almost 16 years. By 1905 the family returned to Bedfordshire as a consequence of Sarah's ill health, and here a further four children would be born to the couple: Albert, Percy, Leslie and Marjorie.

In 1908 the 1st Battalion returned to England to be stationed at Aldershot. Under the Territorial and Reserve Forces Act 1907, a part of Haldene's reforms, the Territorial Army was created and the Bedfordshire Regiment's two militia units were renamed and reorganised. By 1909 the Hertfordshire Battalion had left the regiment, becoming the 1st Battalion, Hertfordshire Regiment, based in Hitchin. Frank and his family lived at the Drill Hall, Verulam Road.

It was at this point that Frank Jnr., now at the tender age of 14, enlisted into the Territorial Army on 26 November 1909, joining his father's regiment as a boy recruit with the regimental number 1285. He trained rigorously with the regiment, and a great deal would have been expected of him as the son of a Colour Sergeant. Frank Jnr. fared well and was deemed to be an outstanding young soldier, of whom his father must have been very proud.

Following the outbreak of war on 4 August 1914, Frank Snr. and the men of the 1st Battalion, Hertfordshire Regiment, were mobilised and made ready for overseas service. The following day the Regiment was embodied into the British Expeditionary Force and both Frank and his son were mobilised.

This small contingent of less than 1,000 men were to be one of the first Territorial Army units to be posted overseas but Frank Jnr. – although he had volunteered for service abroad – was not among them, after a physical disability prevented him from going overseas.

In the meantime, on 5 November 1914, the battalion embarked at Southampton aboard the merchant vessel *City of Chester*, arriving in Le Havre the following day, where they then marched to No. 2 Rest Camp. Over the next few days the battalion travelled by train, bus and foot across France and Belgium until they reached the town of Vlamertinghe. After a long and wet journey, they marched

Frank Young (Snr) on the left and Frank Young (Jnr) second left, just before the outbreak of the Great War. (*Paul Johnson Collection*)

through Ypres to reach their final destination, a location known as Kilo 3, just on the outskirts of the village of Hooge. The battalion was part of the 2nd Division, whose Headquarters were located in Hooge Chateau.

On 12 November, the weather began to change, with freezing rain and light snow making an uncomfortable situation even worse for the troops. As the Germans commenced a major attack, the battalion moved about 2 miles along the Ypres–Zonnebeke railway, where they entrenched themselves in a wood. Here, they would begin to move in and out of the frontline and experience severe shelling from German artillery.

On 20 November the battalion marched some 20 miles on foot to the town of Meteren. It was here that they first joined the 4th Guards Brigade and were proudly inspected by the King and the Prince of Wales. They left Meteren on 22 December 1914 and marched to the town of Bethune, a distance of some 15 miles. Here they spent Christmas 1914 in the trenches at Rue Du Bois, and there were certainly no hints of fraternisation with Germans. In fact, Christmas Day 1914 was to bring tragedy for the battalion when Private Percy Huggins was shot by a sniper and killed on Christmas morning. Incensed by the enemy's actions on this holy day, Lance Sergeant Tom Gregory ran forward and killed the German sniper. Unknown to Tom Gregory, a second German sniper was in position close by and quickly responded to the death of his comrade by ending the Lance Sergeant's life with a single shot.

A major change occurred for the battalion when on 19 January 1915 they were reorganised, using the double company format preferred by the Guards Battalions. Just ten days later, on 29 January 1915, Frank was promoted to the rank of Company Sergeant Major, and a week later was made an acting Regimental Sergeant Major. The battalion spent much of the month moving in and out of the line in the Rue Du Bois area. The winter of 1914–15 was wet, cold and miserable, and the troops suffered considerable deprivations, and as a consequence, many men suffered with a variation of medical issues relating to the weather.

By this time, Frank Jnr. had joined the battalion and therefore both father and son were together at the front for a time. The battalion's first offensive battle took place on 6–7 February 1915 when the 4th Guards Brigade attacked the brickfields at Cuinchy. The attack began early in the morning with the 1st Irish Guards to the right and the 3rd Coldstream Guards to the left. The attack was relatively successful, even though the Coldstream Guards had difficulty in capturing their objectives, and the brigade was fortunate in suffering relatively few casualties. The Coldstream Guards lost 1 officer and 20 other ranks, the Irish Guards lost 1 officer and 7 other ranks whilst the Hertfordshires lost 3 other ranks.

The next three months were spent in the routine of trench warfare, digging and repairing trenches, putting up wire and patching up damage caused by the endless shelling. The battalion continually moved back and forth; sometimes on the frontline, sometimes in support and occasionally in reserve. There were also periods of rest in or near the town of Bethune.

On 17 May the Hertfordshires moved into trenches east of Rue L'Epinette to support the Irish Guards in the Battle of Festubert, which commenced the following day. The 4th Guards Brigade was ordered to attack a location near Ferme Cour d'Avoue, known as Post 14. At 4.30 pm the Irish Guards attacked on the left of the brigade front, but were met by heavy rifle and machine gun fire and men began to fall rapidly. No. 1 Company of the Hertfordshires, under the command of Major Page, went forward to reinforce the Irish Guards, but little progress could be made. Only 300 yards of ground had been won when orders came to dig in on the position held. Major Page, with about 20 men, managed to advance a further 200 yards, quite close to their objective, but had to come back in line with the remainder of the attackers as no supports could reach them.

It was not until midnight that the Irish Guards were relieved by the men of the Hertfordshire Regiment. They fell back to trenches 800 yards behind a new line. The attacking company, under the command of Major Page, were at first just in the rear of the Irish Guards, and the remainder of the battalion were behind breast works still more to the rear. All day long the men of Hertfordshire were under heavy shellfire. Soon after the attack was launched, a messenger of the Irish Guards reported to Colonel Page-Croft that all his officers had been hit and that he could not find his commanding officer. The colonel immediately sent another company of the Hertfordshires up the line to support the Irish Guards. Arrangements were made for the relief of the Irish Guards, and as it was dark, two fresh companies of the Hertfordshires went out and started to dig a new line.

While digging went on, the stretcher bearers and volunteers from the companies not digging, conveyed all the wounded to the rear. At dawn on 19 May the trench along a 350 yard front was down to an average of 4 feet and well traversed. It was a good piece of work but the men suffered for it, as the new trench was heavily shelled while the the Hertfordshires held it that day. As soon as it was dark, the Germans redoubled their barrage and the shellfire was so heavy that the 2nd Battalion, Coldstream Guards, had to wait two hours before they could relieve the Hertfordshire Regiment.

Over the two days of 18 and 19 May 1915 the battalion saw 6 officers wounded, 17 other ranks killed, 7 other ranks dying of their wounds, and a further 86 other ranks being wounded. To quote Colonel Page-Croft's words, the battalion *'was a weary but proud crowd, and they were glad to reach billets at Le Touret at 12.30 am on 20 May'.*

The men of the battalion entered billets in the town of Bethune on 20 May and later moved to the town of Noeux Les Mines. It was on 6 June 1915, that the men of No. 2 Company moved to billets at Cambrin Headquarters. They remained here until 20 June when they moved to Sailly La Bourse, where they took over positions from the Irish Guards. The following day they relieved the men of the 2nd Battalion, Grenadier Guards in the trenches about 2 miles northeast of Vermelles, where they remained until 23 June. Throughout the entire period, the battalion spent a great deal of time working alongside the Royal Engineers, deepening and repairing communication trenches and performing minor construction works.

The battalion remained in its billets at Bethune until 6 July, when two companies relieved the 5th Battalion, King's Liverpool Regiment at Cuinchy. The two other companies remained in brigade reserve at Annequin. The men of the battalion were to spend the month of July moving in and out of the frontline, and held positions at Cuinchy, Givenchy and Cambrin. When they weren't in the line, they were in billets at Le Quesnoy and Bethune.

Throughout the month of August, the battalion continued in their rotation in and out of the frontline. On 19 August, described as a sad day for the battalion, the 4th Guards Brigade left the 2nd Division to form part of the Guards Division. The men of Hertfordshire now transferred to the 6th Infantry Brigade in the 2nd Division. The troops were kept busy – again digging a new trench, which was named Wolf's Road.

Throughout early September 1915 the battalion continued with its work in building, maintaining and repairing trench works. However, on 25 September things changed dramatically for the men of Hertfordshire, as they became embroiled in the Battle of Loos. At 6.30 am that morning, the men of No. 3 and No. 4 Companies were in support of the 1st Battalion, King's Liverpool Regiment as they went into the attack. The men of Liverpool failed to reach the German trenches and were held up by heavy machine gun fire. As a consequence, the Hertfordshires were ordered not to advance. Throughout that night they helped bring in the casualties the Liverpool's had suffered. On 30 September the battalion moved back to billets at Bethune. Their casualties throughout September were: 3 officers wounded, 4 other ranks killed, 2 other ranks dying of their wounds and 35 other ranks being wounded.

On 5 December 1915, Frank Snr. submitted an application to attend Officer Cadet Training. At the time, he was an Acting Regimental Sergeant Major with the Hertfordshire Regiment. He was interviewed by Brigadier General Arthur Crawford Daly, who commanded the 6th Infantry Brigade, and Frank was recommended for a commission in the Hertfordshire Regiment. By this time, he had seen over 26 years of service with the colours and was about to embark on a career as an officer.

As 1915 drew to a close, Frank found that he had been mentioned in despatches and his name recorded in *The London Gazette* of 31 December 1915.

In April 1916, the battalion, which had recently transferred to the 118th Brigade, part of the 39th Division, were in billets at Robermetz, near Merville and it was here that Frank Young left the 1st Battalion and returned to Blighty to take up a role as an officer and an instructor. Frank became a Second Lieutenant as of 4 August 1916 and was posted to the 3/1st Battalion, Hertfordshire Regiment.

By 17 April 1917 Frank had been promoted to Lieutenant and was posted to the port town of Folkestone, Kent. In 1915 a number of properties in the area of Marine Parade and Marine Terrace were acquired to create the first rest camp (No. 1 Rest Camp). Containing a large cookhouse, the camp could accommodate 2,200 men and was overseen by a camp commandant. In May 1916 this was supplemented by No. 2 Rest Camp, which could accommodate 1,000 men. In early 1917 it was decided that further expansion was required given the high volume of soldiers passing through the area, and several properties were obtained along The Leas, near Clifton Crescent. These were to become No. 3 Rest Camp, a significantly larger camp which could accommodate 5,000 officers and men. It was here that Frank Young was posted. He would have seen many young soldiers pass through the camp, including those from the Hertfordshire Regiment. During this period, he was also to become Deputy Town Commandant for Folkestone.

Frank was admitted to the Shorncliffe Military Hospital on 6 August 1918, suffering with a swollen face and ankles. He was diagnosed as suffering with albuminuria, a condition where the protein albumin is abnormally present in the urine. He remained in hospital for a month and on his release returned to his duties at No. 3 Rest Camp, where he found he had been promoted to the rank of temporary Captain.

It was here, on 19 September 1918, that Frank learned his eldest son, Second Lieutenant Frank Edward Young, was missing in action. It was an anxious two weeks

before the news that everyone feared would be confirmed, when a party of men from 1/5th Manchester Regiment found a body on the edge of Havrincourt Wood. Whilst there is no doubt that Frank would have been very proud of the fact that his son died doing his duty and was awarded the country's highest military decoration for his actions, there would have been very little to be said or done to help Frank and

Frank Young Snr (Standing Centre) at the time he was commandant of No.3 Rest Camp, Folkestone.

his family overcome the feeling of anguish and grief surrounding the loss of a child.

After being called before a medical board on 8 April 1919, it was found that Frank's disability was rated as 50 per cent and he was informed that he was fit for Home Service only. He was now aged 45 and was demobilised from the army on 18 November 1919, exactly 30 years after he first entered service. He was eventually retired by the War Office on 27 May 1921 and given permission to retain the rank of Captain.

Frank was awarded the following medals:
India General Service 18951902, 1 clasp, Relief of Chitral 1895 (3292 Sergt. 1st Bn. Bedford. Regt.); 1914 Star with clasp (3292 C. Sjt., 1/1 Herts. R.); British War and Victory Medals, M.I.D. oak leaf (3292 A.W.O. Cl. 1st Herts. R.) and Army Long Service and Good Conduct Medal EVIIR (3292 C. Sjt. Bedford. Regt.)

Frank Edward Young (Frank Jnr.), having completed his education, joined the staff of W.B. Moss & Son in Hitchin and remained with them for 12 months. In the spring of 1910 he was appointed to the rank of bugler and a few weeks later attended his first annual training camp at Ipswich. He left W.B. Moss and took up a post at the Orleans Gentlemen's Club in St. James Street, London, where he remained for a year before returning to Hitchin in 1911. He then started on what looked like a promising career at Hitchin Electric Power Station in Winbush Road with the intention of becoming an electrical engineer. During this time, Frank continued in his father's footsteps and faithfully attended the regiment's annual camps, as well as regular training sessions. Life looked set to remain fairly predictable but fate decreed otherwise and in August 1914 with the outbreak of war, he found himself summoned to another sort of destiny.

During the first week of the war, as he walked to the station to join his unit, loaded with his kit and equipment, Frank Jnr. met the Reverend John George Williams, the curate of St. Saviours in Hitchin. *'This is war,'* he told the clergyman, *'we are now in for the real thing. We have been playing at soldiers, now we must go and be soldiers.'* The Reverend Williams said that Frank showed no sign of regret that it had come to that, no impetuous eagerness to go out and do great things, only a quiet determination to do his duty.

Frank was to be disappointed. A physical disability prevented him from going overseas, but before the end of the year he underwent an operation to remedy the matter. After his recovery, he was posted to the 2nd Battalion, Hertfordshire Regiment, where his experience led him to quickly be promoted to the rank of Sergeant, and he soon became one of the battalion scouts.

On 21 January 1915 Frank, now fit for overseas service, set sail for France with the 1st Reinforcing Draft for the 1st Battalion of the Hertfordshire Regiment. The battalion was now part of the elite 4th (Guards) Brigade, serving with the 2nd Division, and young Frank joined the unit in a very sticky sector of the front, opposite a place known as La Bassée. It was from this point that both father and son were to serve together for a short period of time, seeing action with the Hertfordshire Regiment at Festubert, Cunichy and the Loos. Frank returned to Hitchin for a spell of leave and in January 1916, having already achieved something of a reputation as a bomber, he volunteered for training as a bombing instructor. This resulted in his leaving the battalion to join the staff of the Central Bombing School at Rouen.

On 3 April 1916 Frank was admitted to No. 9 General Hospital in Rouen, suffering from scabies. He remained there until 9 April, when he was discharged, but unfortunately he was soon back, returning to the hospital on 13 April. A further infection of impetigo and suspected tuberculosis resulted in him being invalided home on 4 May 1916, when he was admitted to the Welsh Metropolitan War Hospital in Whitchurch near Cardiff, where he remained for three months.

After his release from hospital at the beginning of August 1916, Frank was posted to the 3/1st Hertfordshire Regiment – a reserve battalion – stationed in Halton Camp near Wendover, Buckinghamshire at the time. While he was there, Frank was recommended for a commission and on 3 January 1917 he was posted to No. 6 Officer Cadet Battalion for induction training. After the completion of his training, Frank was discharged to a commission on 25 April 1917 as a Second Lieutenant in his old regiment at Halton.

Like so many of the best young officers, he was thrilled by the exploits of the Royal Flying Corps. The young officer, fresh from completing his training, applied for a transfer to flying training. Frank Jnr. was excited when the posting came through and he was sent on a six-week ground training course at Reading. From here he went to Sleaford, Lincolnshire to begin his flying training. Unfortunately, one of his flights ended in an

Second Lieutenant Frank Edward Young. Believed to be the last formal photograph taken of him.

awkward crash, in which he was badly shaken. This ended his brief flying career and in July he rejoined the Bedfordshires at Crowborough.

Time was now running out for Frank Young Jnr. He was posted to the 3/5th Bedfordshire Regiment on 10 July 1918, which was combined with the 1st Hertfordshire Regiment the following day. Frank went home to Hitchin for the last time on 48 hours' leave at the beginning of September 1918. His father, now a Captain and the assistant commander of No. 3 Rest Camp at Folkestone, saw his son for the last time as he embarked at Folkestone on 5 September. After a few days at a base camp, Second Lieutenant Young joined his unit at the front on 12 September. The last communication from him was a field postcard dated 17 September, reporting that he was well. The following day he was reported missing.

According to Private Gould, Frank's batman, two stretcher-bearers were in a dugout when two Germans took them prisoner. *'2nd Lieutenant Young saw them being marched away one German in front and one behind. Without hesitation he leapt out of his outpost, shot the leading German with his revolver and hit the other on the jaw with his fist and knocked him out.'*

The two stretcher-bearers then made good their escape and Young returned to his post. When Private Gould ran out of ammunition, Frank ordered him back and stayed on to face the enemy alone. When he got back to the main British trench, Gould's rifle was nearly red hot.

A citation published in *The London Gazette* dated 14 December 1918 describes how Second Lieutenant Frank Edward Young attained the country's highest accolade for bravery and gallantry, the Victoria Cross:

For most conspicuous bravery, determination and exceptional devotion to duty. On 18 September 1918, southeast of Havrincourt, when during an enemy counterattack and throughout an extremely intense enemy barrage he visited all posts, warned the garrisons and encouraged the men. In the early stages of the attack he rescued two of his men who had been captured, and bombed and silenced an enemy machine gun. Although surrounded by the enemy, 2nd Lt. Young fought his way back to the main barricade and drove out a party of the enemy who were assembling there. By his further exertions the battalion was able to maintain a line of great tactical value, the loss of which would have meant serious delay to future operations. Throughout four hours of intense hand to hand fighting Second Lieutenant Young displayed the utmost valour and devotion to duty, and set an example to which the company gallantly responded. He was last seen fighting hand to hand against a considerable number of the enemy.

On 27 September 1918 a party of men from 1/5th Manchester Regiment found a body of a soldier on the edge of Havrincourt Wood, who – by the body's condition – appeared to have died instantly following a shrapnel wound to the head. Through correspondence found in his pockets, they were able to identify the body as that of Frank Young. The party then buried the body where they found it, and a rough cross was placed over the grave.

Lieutenant Males, the man who discovered Frank's body went on to write home to his family:

> *I sought and obtained permission to remove the remains to a more fitting resting place in a certified British Cemetery. This was done by a selected party of our men under my personal supervision. The remains were removed on a limber covered with a Union Jack and reinterred with all the*

Second Lieutenant Frank Edward Young.

respect due to our gallant Hertfordshire hero in Hermies Hill British Cemetery. *The original cross was replaced at the head of the grave and this noble and well-loved officer and soldier now rests in a sacred plot of British ground in the centre of France, surrounded by others of his fellow countrymen.*

Frank Young was a man of few words, especially in the matter of his deepest feelings. What impressed everyone who knew him was his quality of simplicity and directness. He did not pretend to want to go to war – especially after seeing and enduring the real thing – but there was always the same willingness and cheerfulness about him. The war had to be fought and he – like other young men who made the ultimate sacrifice – was prepared and willing to do his part and do his best. Frank Young was recognised as a man who was able to act with promptness and decision, and very few people were surprised when they heard of his valiant and distinguished end on the battlefield. It is now incumbent on the future generations of Europeans to ensure that we keep faith with Frank Young VC, and millions like him, if we truly desire peace.

Frank Young, who died aged 23, was one of only two men from his regiment to be awarded a Victoria Cross during the First World War. Although he was originally buried in a battlefield grave on the edge of Havrincourt Wood, his body was later recovered by the Imperial War Graves Commission, and today Frank lies in the Hermies Hill British Cemetery, France.

It was an immense honour, as part of the centenary commemorations for members of the *Herts at War* Team, to guide members of the Young family to the precise location of Frank's death. The Young family have been an integral and highly supportive element of the project.

PRISONER OF WAR – ELPHINSTONE CHAMBERLAIN

Elphinstone Chamberlain was born in Birmingham in 1897, before moving to the emerging town of Letchworth. 'Elphy', as he was known, worked at Letchworth's Phoenix Motor Works in civilian life, after finishing school. Underage when war was declared, he enlisted in the British Army at the first opportunity in 1915. Within a year, albeit still officially underage for foreign service, he found himself 'doing his bit' on the Western Front, serving with the Essex Regiment, seeing considerable action both on the Somme in 1916 and during the Third Battle of Ypres in 1917.

Elphinstone Chamberlain.

Having come through two of the most formidable battles of the Great War unscathed, he was unfortunate to be wounded in action and taken prisoner on 21 September 1918. For 20-year-old Elphy's mother, receiving the news that her boy was 'Missing in Action' would have clearly been a terrible shock, especially considering the largely positive news coming from the Western Front. Available information suggests that Mrs Chamberlain was left completely unaware of whether her son was dead or alive until after the Armistice, when she received the incredibly welcome news that he was in fact alive.

> 26, General Hospital, B.E.F., France.
> Dec. 5th, 1918.
>
> Dear Mr. and Mrs. Chamberlain,—An American soldier, called Private M. Cosgrove, 2671449, 106th Infantry, G. Coy., A.E.F., has just been admitted into this hospital suffering from a fractured right arm. He was wounded Sept. 27; taken prisoner same day. About a fortnight after he was admitted into a Belgian hospital. A young soldier named Elphinston Chamberlain came in with a bullet wound of left arm, also a prisoner of war. Cosgrove had your address given to him, and he was asked to let you know that Elphinston Chamberlain (I have no number or rank or regiment) was in the Hospital Militaire, Rue de Fer, Namur, Belgium. The sister at the hospital said Elphinston Chamberlain was not dangerously ill, that he was recovering from his wounds, but that the poison of his wound was affecting his system. He (Cosgrove) said that they were very kind to them at this hospital since the Germans had left. Cosgrove, being unable to write himself, is anxious that I should send on this information to you. He does not know whether Chamberlain is your son or nephew. You probably ere this know all these particulars yourself.—I am, yours faithfully,
>
> (Lady) MAY BRADFORD,
> (Letter writer for the Ward).

Letter from Lady May Bradford published in the *Hertfordshire Express*.

Due to the nature of his wound and the limited treatment he was able to get in the nearby local hospital on an ad hoc basis, Elphy had stayed in Namur, where his wounds were bound and changed using old newspaper – such was the shortage of supply at that time. Clearly delighted that her son was alive, Mrs Chamberlain wrote a letter to Elphy, which reads as follows:

My Dear Elphy,

Still no letter from you & Dora has been home today & she tells me she has not heard from you. Oh, if you do get this letter do just send a card if you cannot a letter theirs a dear, as it will soon be your birthday & I shall want to send you a parcel & it won't be any good if I don't hear anything of you & you will be 21 it doesn't seem horrible does it now. Do let me have a line theirs a dear to relieve me all at home & send lots of love & hope you are well & safe, & most from your own lovely mother.

C Chamberlain

P.S write if you can

Elphinstone was in hospital at a time when there were significant changes and a certain amount of confusion relating to repatriation of prisoners, and it seems that tragically, this letter never reached Elphy in Namur. The next notice to be found in historic records is the letter opposite dated 3 December 1918.

This truly awful news was confirmed by a Madame Delaye, who contacted Elphy's mother to inform her of her son's tragic death. Clearly confused and devastated at her son's untimely death after the guns had fallen silent, Mrs Chamberlain and Madame Delaye began a dialogue of letters between Hertfordshire and Namur that would tell the powerful story of Elphy's final days. Mrs Delaye's letters – written in English – provided detail, and perhaps a measure of comfort to a grief-stricken Mrs Chamberlain.

> Namur, 3.12.18.
>
> Dear Madam,—I am afraid you will be greatly shocked by the terribly sad news I have to send you. Your dear loved son died on Monday night, about 10 o'clock. I stayed near him until 8 o'clock. He suffered much from time to time, but the end came rapidly, and I am thankful to say quite calmly and painlessly.
>
> I can find no words which will convey to you all the sorrow I feel for you in your terrible loss.
>
> We loved him so much; he was all the day in my house, but slept in the hospital. My husband, my children, and I loved him as a son, and he loved us very much. He was so kind and always so gay, and so happy to be with us.
>
> If it will be any consolation to you, Madam, let me tell you, that we shall take care of his grave.
>
> He seemed to have only one desire, that was to see yourself. He spoke much of you. He said to me more than once "I am dying to see my mother," or "Do you like me? You are my mother now."
>
> The funeral will take place at 3 o'clock on Wednesday, December 4th. A lady friend and I shall bring him some nice white flowers as a last adieu. We will never forget him in our prayers, and keep his souvenir amongst the dearest.—Believe me, dear Madam, very sincerely yours,
>
> M. DELAY.
>
> I gave your son a little box that one of his friends gave me back as he began to be worse. When the post will be in order I shall send it to you with a last photo which was taken on Saturday, 30th November.

Letter from Namur on 3 December 1918, published in the *Hertfordshire Express.*

Namur the 28.12.18

Dear Madam,

I hope dear Madam, you will pardon me for keeping you so long before I answer your letters. I got the first on the 16, the second on the 23 of December. I was in Paris for a fortnight, I am just come back. How sorry I am that your first letter is confirming so late. I wrote you every day a little card in the end of November when he became ill and never, I received an answer, it is so long to come. I saw your dear son about the 15 of November, perhaps the 20, the first time he was with a group of prisoners on the street, the day was very cold, he pleases me immediately and I ask my husband to take him. He answers me, he will, but it is impossible to take him alone and not the others when we were finished to talk, they were gone. Perhaps an hour later he entered in my shop to ask for a cheap watch, he was alone. I thank God who had send him to us. Directly we pleased each other; he tells me he was 21 years old on the next Sunday and I decide that we should have a little family feast for his birthday, he was first a little shy to accept, but it was only a moment.

I give him little clothes, he had so little and it was so very cold, when he went, we were friends. He continue to come every day to dinner and to stay with us until the evening, he slept in the hospital on account of his arm. He brought with him his friend Michael Cosgrove, who certainly will write to you, we passed very good hours together, your dear son was very gai, and very pleased with us, he spoke me from you, from his father, sister and his brother who is 14 years old. I know you all but I never saw a photo he had no photo and we never received one from you. I think the last letter he got from you was sended in September. When he becomes to be ill, the doctor defended that he came out, he had a fever who was stronger every day. He was feeded with eggs, cream, milk, wine all strong things, after 4 days, the fever was over, all was quite well, but he got always weaker. The doctors had hope until the last days. I was near him every afternoon or evening. He always ask me if his mother would soon come, if I had write to you. He speeks very much of you, I saw he must be a loved child and I was very sad I never could bring him a letter from you.

On the Friday, he suffered much on his head, he was sad, to condole him I give him a little handkerchief and I kissed him that do him great pleasure, he knows he was my spoiled child, as I told him. He every day asked me 'Can I go with you tomorrow', and I promised him every day surely to tomorrow, you come home and we shall do a walk all together. On the Saturday was taken this photo that I send you, it is not very well done. On the evening he was very bad, we thought it was all. The Sunday, we thought he was very quiet the Monday came, he was gay, he sang a little, we thought the worst was over on the evening he very often fall asleep and at ten o'clock he is gone quite painlessly. I never could go back to the hospital since I loose him.

He had lost his cap and ware a little black and white cap that a lady give him. I give him a little watch, I hope you received his clothes and things.

Believe dear Madame I am your sincerely

M. Delaye

Dear Madam,

I received your welcome letter and was very pleased you will come, of course you stay at my home, and I hope we will have a good time together.

My husband took the boat in Dover for Ostende and direct trains are coming from Ostend to Namur at 20.45 start from:

London Char Cross 8.45

- *Dover 11.30*
- *Ostende 16.46*
- *Namur 20.45*

I am very glad to see you and we will speak together from your dear lost. If you will send me a little word the day exact you come I will wate you. In hope I send you the best thoughts from all the family.

M. Delaye

Dear Madam,

Such a long time I had not given you some news from Belgium, but they are so rare, alle is quiet and not easy as it is everywhere.

We were twice at your son's grave and we will go on the 2 December again. For spring I hope I shall do paint the cross, because it ought to be painted, you know the rain has changed the colour and if you like it, we will do it in white instead of black. The name is well on little iron cards, it is very clean. I hope dear Madam you are all right, I was not well that last month, you know I am tired and have always much to work.

I saw by your last card you were in a nice country, I hope you had good holidays and you keep your health well.

With the best wishes for yourself and your family I am your sincerely
M. Delaye

Two mothers, clearly finding a bond by this shared tragedy, did eventually meet in the post-war years, when they attended Elphy's grave together, an act that must have been incredibly emotional but also a true example of humanity and compassion.

Today Private Elphinstone Chamberlain lies buried in Belgrade Cemetery, Namur, Belgium, the town where he found comfort and care in his final moments.

Over the years the Delaye and Chamberlain family lost touch; such is the passage of time. The information presented here was provided by the Chamberlain family – the letters and documents having passed down the generations. Upon reading the correspondence, the *Herts at War* project contacted a local Belgian

The grave of Elphinstone Chamberlain at Namur Cemetery, showing the original wooden cross which was later replaced with a CWGC Headstone.

Madame Delaye, who cared for Elphinstone Chamberlain.

newspaper in Namur with a request for information about the incredible Madame Delaye. Several months later there was a response from a descendant of Madame Delaye, who – completely unaware of the family story until now – was proud to hear of what her grandmother had done. She also provided a photograph, finally putting a face to the compassionate lady who comforted young Elphy in his final moments.

In September 2018, as part of a BBC Radio series, members of the *Herts at War* team travelled to Namur with Mrs Dawn Kite and Miss Sheryl Kite, great niece and great-great niece of Elphinstone Chamberlain, where they met the granddaughter of Madame Lucile Delaye at Elphy's grave, rekindling a powerful familial bond that had been lost for close to a century.

DEAD MAN'S PENNY – LIEUTENANT CUTHBERT FOSTER MiD – ROYAL AIR FORCE

Within the collection of archive materials at the Stevenage Museum, you will find several First Word War Memorial Plaques nicknamed 'Dead Man's Penny', because of the similarity in appearance to the penny coin. The Memorial Plaque was issued after the First World War to the next of kin of all British and Empire service personnel who were killed as a result of the war. Some 1,355,000 plaques were issued, each one uniquely named.

Lieutenant Cuthbert Foster.

One of these is named to Lieutenant Cuthbert Foster, who was born in Great Wymondley on 18 October 1898 as the son of John and Charlotte Foster. The family later lived at 39 Walkern Road, Stevenage, and after completing his education, Cuthbert began work as a bank clerk. By this time, the Great War had begun and he was carried along with the wave of patriotism like so many young men of his generation. Shortly after his 18th birthday he volunteered for military service and joined the army in February 1917. At this point in the war the exploits of the men of the Royal Flying Corps, particularly the fighter pilots, were the subject of intense media attention, and the romance of this new form of warfare cast a spell upon many young men, including Cuthbert.

In November 1917 Cuthbert was selected for a commission in the Royal Flying Corps and soon began his pilot training. During this period he suffered two crashes, both of which he managed to survive, which – with flying still in its infancy – was something of an achievement in itself. Despite these setbacks, he eventually graduated as a pilot on 27 February 1918 and after gaining his 'wings', he was swiftly posted to 'C' Flight of No. 88 Fighter Squadron, which had only recently been formed. The men of the squadron departed for France aboard the HMS *Australind* on 16 April 1918, arriving at Le Havre the following day. They operated from airfields at Berques-Capelle, Drionville and Serny.

Local newspaper reports state that during his time on the front, Cuthbert was credited with shooting down six enemy aircraft and was responsible for damaging a great many more. Squadron records, however, indicate only one entry which credits him with the destruction of an enemy aircraft. This was on 4 September 1918, when Cuthbert and his observer, Lieutenant Beltram Hutchinson Smyth, were in combat with a Fokker biplane over Seclin. The enemy aircraft was seen diving to the ground out of control to its destruction. Cuthbert was mentioned in despatches for this action.

On 27 September 1918 Cuthbert climbed aboard his Bristol F2b fighter, E2153, along with his observer, Sergeant Thomas Proctor (212137) a 31-year-old from Belfast. Together with four other aircraft, they were to perform an escort role for aircraft of No. 103 Squadron who were on a bombing mission. During the flight, they were attacked by a number of enemy aircraft and Cuthbert was seen to perform a double loop whilst outmanoeuvring a German aircraft that was on his tail. Having done this successfully, he was last seen in full control of his machine but flying low and heading for the British lines. It was assumed at the time that his aircraft was suffering from engine trouble and that he was attempting to make his way back to base. Sadly, neither Cuthbert and his observer, nor the aircraft were ever seen or heard of again, but recent further research has established that the aircraft is believed to have been shot down over Abancourt by Vizefeldwebel Fritz Classen of Jasta 26.

Their names are recorded on the Arras Flying Services Memorial, Pas-De-Calais, France.

THE SPANISH FLU

The influenza pandemic of 1918 was one of the greatest disasters of the twentieth century. A global contagion, it was an airborne virus which affected every continent and was nicknamed 'Spanish flu' as the first reported cases were in Spain, although there is no evidence to substantiate that this is where it actually had its beginnings.

Although not caused by the First World War, it is believed that in the UK the virus was spread by service personnel returning home from the Western Front. Soldiers were becoming ill with what was known as *la grippe*, the symptoms of which were sore throat, headache and loss of appetite. Although highly infectious in the cramped, primitive conditions of the trenches, recovery was usually swift and doctors at first called it 'three-day fever'.

The outbreak hit the UK in a series of waves, with its peak at the end of the Great War. Returning from northern France at the end of the war, many troops travelled home by train. As they arrived, so did the flu and it spread from the railway stations to the centres of cities, then to the suburbs, and out into the countryside. It was not restricted to any class; anyone could catch it. Prime Minister David Lloyd George contracted it but survived. Some other notable survivors included the cartoonist Walt Disney and Kaiser Wilhelm II of Germany.

Young adults between 20 and 30 years old were particularly affected, and the disease struck and progressed quickly in these cases. Onset was devastatingly quick. Those fine and healthy at breakfast could be dead by tea time. Within hours of feeling the first symptoms of fatigue, fever and headache, some victims would rapidly develop pneumonia and start turning blue, signalling a shortage of oxygen. They would then struggle for air until they suffocated to death. Hospitals were overwhelmed and even medical students were drafted in to help. Doctors and nurses worked to breaking point, although there was little they could do as there were no treatments for the flu and no antibiotics to treat the pneumonia.

The pandemic affected a quarter of the British population and by its conclusion, only one region in the entire world had not reported an outbreak; an isolated island called Marajo, located in Brazil's Amazon River Delta.

Many serving Hertfordshire soldiers returning from combat duties contracted the disease. Corporal William Canfield, one of four soldier sons of Philip Canfield of High Cross near Ware, served with the Hertfordshire Regiment during the Great War and had been wounded on three separate occasions; this being borne out by the fact that the left sleeve of his uniform tunic bore three wound stripes. William was not to fall on the battlefield but instead, his life was taken on 25 November 1918 as a consequence of influenza. He was aged 24, and was buried a few days later in St. Mary's Churchyard, Thunderidge; the only Great War soldier to be buried there. This, and a great many stories like it, were continually repeated across the county throughout the pandemic. The Great War claimed an estimated 16 million lives, whilst the influenza epidemic is estimated to have infected one fifth of the world's population and killed an estimated 50 million people.

A VERY DOUBTFUL CASE – GUNNER ERNEST LEWIS

Ernest Lewis was born in St. Albans, Hertfordshire in 1888 as the son of William and Ellen Lewis. He was baptised on 27 June 1888 in the parish of St. Michael's, St. Albans.

By 1901 the family were living at 142 Fishpool Street, St. Albans, and by 1911 his parents were living at 35 Bedford Road, St. Albans. By this time they had been married 36 years and had produced 15 children, 4 of whom had died.

A railway porter by trade, he had served with the 4th Battalion, Bedfordshire Regiment, part of the militia, from 1906 and joined the Royal Artillery at Bedford on 16 February 1907, when he was aged 18 years and 10 months. Standing at 5′ 7¼″ in height and weighing 125 lbs, he had brown hair, grey eyes and a fresh complexion, bore a brown birthmark above his right buttock, and had a scar on the middle finger of his left hand. Records show that his regimental number was 45981.

Ernest was posted to the Royal Field Artillery Depot on 16 February 1907, after which he was posted to the 33rd Battery at Preston, Lancashire on 16 April 1907. Whilst here, he was admitted to hospital on 1 February 1911, suffering with a sprained left knee. He spent 14 days in hospital before returning to his unit. On 7 October 1911 Ernest was posted to the 46th Battery, RFA. He was transferred to the Army Reserve on 15 July 1913 following the expiration of his army service, but was mobilised on 19 September 1914 as a consequence of the outbreak of war.

Grave marker of Gunner Ernest Lewis in the Regina Cemetery, Saskatchewan, Canada. with the incorrect regimental number etched upon it.

Following his re-enlistment, Ernest was posted to the 21st (Heavy) Battery, RFA on 30 November 1914. It was at this point that he was found to be suffering from the symptoms of a gastric ulcer. He was discharged from army service on 29 January 1915, under King's Regulations (Para 392 xvi) as being no longer physically fit for war service. At the time of his discharge his address was The Post Office, Regina, Saskatchewan, Canada, and his trade was farmer. Although he was granted a pension for his service, which expired on 29 October 1916, the cause of his discharge was determined not to have been as a consequence of war service.

Records show that Ernest wrote to the Imperial Pensions Board in Ottawa on both 14 and 21 September 1917 with regard to his pension. The Board examined his case and determined that his condition *'has and will improve'*. Thus, they offered Ernest 20 per cent of his pension for a period of 6 months after the expiration of his last award on the basis that his condition may have been aggravated by service after the declaration of war, but their offer was final on what they called *'a very doubtful case'*. This was on 2 January 1918.

Ernest died four weeks later. He is buried in the Regina Cemetery, Saskatchewan, Canada. His grave bears a marker but it is not a standard CWGC headstone.

The Commonwealth War Graves Commission have, for almost 100 years, incorrectly shown his regimental number as being 85981, instead of 45981. Although this is a somewhat minor error, it can have a considerable detrimental effect for researchers in the future. Therefore, the *Herts at War* project is working with the CWGC to rectify this error. Digital records have already been amended and in the fullness of time, the headstone marker will also be amended.

BRAVERY IN THE FIELD – WILLIAM JEFFERY SELL MM

As described earlier in this publication, 31 July 1917 was the opening day of the Third Battle of Ypres, more commonly known as the Battle of Passchendaele. It saw the brave lads of the Hertfordshire Regiment attack strongly-held German positions on the outskirts of the village of St. Julien in Belgium. This devastating action would see all of their officers and 75 per cent of the other ranks become casualties. Amongst their number that day was a young stretcher bearer, William Geoffrey Sell, an Old Contemptible who had served his regiment faithfully since their arrival on the Western Front in November 1914. This is the story of a simple soldier who served his King and Country well, and was to be awarded a gallantry medal for his bravery, and whose life was taken at an early age.

William was born in Royston, Hertfordshire in 1895 as the eldest son of Jeffrey and Emmaline Sell. His father worked as an engineer's driller for a boiler-making company based in Hitchin, and the family later moved to 68 Tilehouse Street, Hitchin. They eventually settled at 13–14 Chapmans Yard, off Queen Street.

After leaving school, William was initially employed on a local farm as a house boy. He later became a labourer for the Willmott building company in Hitchin, where he went on to learn the trade of carpenter. On 20 May 1913, at the age of 18 years and two months, William enlisted in the Hertfordshire Regiment at its headquarters in Hertford as a private soldier with the regimental number 2197, and was placed in 'G' Company. Described as blue-eyed, fair-haired and standing at 5′ 6½″ in height, he spent the twelve months before the outbreak of the Great War as a part-time soldier. He would have attended the Drill Hall on the Bedford Road at weekends, where he would have been trained in the art of soldiering, and would have attended an annual camp in order to ensure that he received his annual bounty payment.

Following the outbreak of war on 4 August 1914, William and the men of the 1st Battalion, Hertfordshire Regiment were mobilised and made ready for overseas service. This small contingent of less than 1,000 men was to be one of the first Territorial Army units to be posted overseas, arriving in France on 5 November 1914.

William was to see action up and down the Western Front, as the Hertfordshire Regiment moved with the various brigades and divisions to which it was attached. He saw action at Shrewsbury

Private William Jeffery Sell wearing his stretcher bearer armband.

Forest near Ypres, where the battalion was to see its first fatal casualties. He served with his chums during the Christmas truce of 1914, when Sergeant Tom Gregory and Private Percy Huggins were killed by snipers. He was present at the Battle of Festubert, and in the trenches at the Cuinchy brickworks.

During the Battle of Loos, William witnessed Corporal Alfred Burt gain the regiment's first Victoria Cross, and also saw Private Reg Evans be awarded the Distinguished Conduct Medal. He travelled with the battalion when they served on the Somme battlefields, and took part in the action at St Pierre Divion in November 1916, when the battalion again achieved a number of gallantry awards, and where numerous comrades – both old and new – were to become casualties. He found himself once again in the salient at Ypres in the winter of 1917, and trained hard throughout the spring of that year as the British army prepared for its summer offensive in the region.

Memorial to the men of the Hertfordshire Regiment who fought at St. Julien on 31 July 1917, including William Sell. The memorial was designed and unveiled by the *Herts at War* project.

Records show that throughout this entire period, William did not receive a single scratch. At least not one that was worth recording or required any significant medical attention. That was, of course, until 31 July 1917. On this day, William played the role of stretcher bearer. Little did he know what demands would be placed upon him that day, as comrade after comrade fell victim to the intense fire of German shot and shell.

The action at St. Julien saw 28 gallantry awards bestowed on members of the Hertfordshire Regiment and those attached to the unit. Amongst these were 265330 Private William Sell, who was wounded in the hand and face by shellfire. He was evacuated from the battlefield and never returned.

Document reporting the death of William Sell on 18 August 1918.

After being wounded at St. Julien, William was first evacuated to No. 132 Field Ambulance for initial treatment. He was quickly sent on to No. 64 Casualty Clearing Station at Mendighem, after which he found himself at No. 54 General Hospital at Wimereux. His wounds were bad enough for him to be evacuated by hospital ship back to the UK.

Once he recovered sufficiently from his injuries, it was established that he was no longer fit for war service. William was then attached to the 5th Bedfordshire Regiment and on 15 November 1917 was officially transferred to the war reserve. He then took up a civilian occupation as an Army Reserve munitions worker at Spencer & Co. in Hitchin.

William married Catherine Jane Baker early in 1918, and she soon fell pregnant. Sadly, William died at home on 18 August 1918 at the age of 23 as a consequence of a weak heart. He is buried in grave W. 171 at Hitchin Communal Cemetery, Hertfordshire. Although his headstone bears his name, rank, and regimental number, it does not show his award of the military medal. The *Herts at War* project is working with the Commonwealth War Graves Commission to address this.

He never saw his son, William Arthur Frederick Sell, who was born a few weeks later, on 31 October 1918. On 9 April 1919, the Ministry of Pensions wrote to William's widow and advised her that because his death was regarded as his own fault, a pension was not payable, leaving her penniless with a young child.

In the spring of 1919 Catherine married a bricklayer, Edward Thomas Cotton, and a year later their daughter, Catherine, was born. The couple eventually moved to Salisbury Road, Welwyn Garden City, Hertfordshire. Catherine Jane passed away in 1985 at the age of 88. William's son, William Arthur Frederick Sell married Wilhelmina J Keech in 1942 and the couple lived in Knella Road, Welwyn Garden City. William passed away in 1978, aged 60, and Wilhelmina passed away in 2003, aged 84.

The grave of Private William Sell MM in Hitchin Cemetery. The gravestone does not record his award and the *Herts at War* project is addressing the matter with the Commonwealth War Graves Commission.

Chapter Six

1919 – A New Enemy

For the majority of people the First World War came to a conclusion on 11 November 1918, thus bringing an end to the 'war to end all wars'. This, however, was most definitely not the case with a great many servicemen and women who lost their lives whilst still in the service of their country across the world throughout 1919 and into the early 1920s.

Within two days of the Armistice on the Western Front being signed, war broke out in Eastern Europe. On 13 November 1918 hostilities opened as a result of the Kingdom of Romania and the First Czechoslovak Republic laying claim to territory held by the First Hungarian Republic – later known as the Hungarian Soviet Republic – and did not cease until 3 August 1919. Meanwhile, in May 1919 the Greco-Turkish War broke out. The campaign was launched primarily because the Western Allies had promised Greece territorial gains at the expense of the Ottoman Empire, recently defeated in the Great War. British troops occupied many of the locations involved and it was not until the end of 1919 that they were relieved by French troops. The Greco-Turkish War eventually reached a ceasefire in 1922.

The collapse of the Russian empire in 1917, and the subsequent Bolshevik revolution, seriously compromised the Allied war effort. The situation was exacerbated by the signing of the Treaty of Brest-Litovsk in March 1918, an agreement that stripped Russia of the last vestiges of its European power and gave Germany a free hand to pursue its imperial ambitions in the east. German troops quickly occupied the former tsarist Baltic territories of Belorussia, Transcaucasia and the Ukraine. In the meantime, anti-Bolshevik agitators began to form a volunteer army that would form the basis of 'White' opposition to the newly installed Communist government.

Some 30,000 Allied troops, almost half of them British, were stationed at the Arctic ports of Murmansk and Archangel under General Edmund Ironside during the latter part of 1918. A similar number of men were under arms in the Caucasus and southern Russia, where General Denikin was recognised as the leading White general. In reality, the Allied commitment to their cause was muddled and half-hearted. The strapped war economies of Britain and France provided minimal levels of financial and military support. During the first few months of aid, for example, Denikin's forces in southern Russia received just a few hundred khaki uniforms and some tins of jam from its Western allies.

Allied troops in eastern Russia were of little help to the Whites. The British troops that arrived in the region in July 1918 consisted mostly of men declared unfit for battle, whose primary job was to guard Allied stores and keep the Trans-Siberian railway open. In Siberia and elsewhere, the Allied powers dispatched a sufficient number of troops to maintain a show of interest in Russia's fate, but not enough to give the Whites a real chance for victory. Soviet propaganda, nonetheless, portrayed Allied intervention as a conspiracy of international capitalism.

By the summer of 1919, it was evident that the Allied venture in Russia had run its course. The expedition was diverting precious resources from vital post-war reconstruction programmes. Public opinion was unwilling to sanction further loss of life in a distant conflict and despite the limited remit of the Allied forces in Russia, men were still being killed in action there, almost a year after the Great War was supposed to have finished. One of the last decisions made at the Paris peace conference was to withdraw all Allied forces from Russia and by the autumn of 1919, this operation was largely complete. The Russian civil war lasted until 1921 and cost 1.2 million lives, including a handful of British servicemen who came from the county of Hertfordshire.

Closer to home, the Irish War of Independence occurred between 21 January 1919 and 11 July 1921, but there had been a great deal of violent conflict between the British state and Irish Republican guerrillas before this date, and there was more to come after it, too. The violence was initiated by a small number of determined Irish Volunteers, known from August 1919 as the Irish Republican Army (IRA). They were convinced that a republic could only be gained by force. Some had been preparing for action since shortly after the Easter Rising in 1916. Out of necessity, they adopted a guerrilla campaign, since a conventional war with large-scale open conflict was not feasible given their lack of men, training and arms. They were initially organised into numerous small, fragmented, fiercely independent units, who – acting on their own initiative – launched frequent low-level surprise attacks, then melted back into the civilian population.

The Commonwealth War Graves Commission records for the First World War cover the period from 4 August 1914 to 31 August 1921. In the period between 11 November 1918 and 31 August 1921 at least 130 men and women from Hertfordshire perished as a consequence of accidents, sickness, and continuing military action. Although this number is stated within the CWGC records, the true total is in fact much higher. From Private John Philip Young, a Hoddesdon man who died a day after hostilities ceased whilst serving with the Labour Corps, to Private Frederick James Hiskitt, who took his own life on 4 September 1919, many of the official records demonstrate the continuing losses suffered by the county following the Armistice.

MISSING AT YEMETSKOE – GEORGE HARRY DRURY DCM

George Harry Drury was born in 1898 in the town of Hounslow in the county of Middlesex to a working-class family. George's father, Robert, was a bricklayer by trade and a father of six; five of his children survived to adulthood. At the time of the 1911 Census George was a 13-year-old scholar, but he simultaneously worked as a baker's boy, a mark of the family's working-class situation. Sometime between 1911 and 1914 the Drury family made a move northward to join the influx of Londoners to the emerging town of Letchworth, an entirely new concept town created to balance the positives of urban and rural life. Once here, George and his family moved into a small property at No. 20 Shott Lane. George picked up employment on the local horse-drawn bus route around Letchworth and the surrounding villages, acting as a conductor, doubtless becoming a familiar face with the local population. Within a year or so after the family move, George Harry Drury joined the local Territorial unit, the 1st Battalion Hertfordshire Regiment.

As a member of 'E' Company – made up primarily of men from Letchworth and Royston – George spent weekends and an annual summer camp training with his friends for the relatively unlikely possibility that they would be asked to defend their country in times of war.

Of course, we now know that war was on the horizon and as a Territorial soldier, it would not be long before George would serve his country. Having been born in 1898, he was only 16 when war was declared, although ever the keen recruit, he managed to volunteer and was duly accepted for overseas service with his friends in the Hertfordshire Regiment.

George was to become one of the 'Herts Originals', who first sailed on 5 November 1915 to France and saw action almost immediately. During three years of fighting, he was wounded twice, served at Loos, on the Somme and at Ypres, rising to the rank of Corporal in the process. George also spent his 18th birthday in the trenches of the Western Front, no doubt enjoying it with his comrades who by all accounts esteemed him as a very brave young soldier. However, by 1918, his time with the Herts Guards had come to an end.

George Harry Drury DCM.

Once recovered from the effects of his second wound, George was transferred to serve with the 1st Battalion of the Bedfordshire Regiment, a regular army unit who – like the Herts – had seen service on the Western Front since 1914 but at the time were in action on the lesser known Italian Front.

Sent to his new battalion on an entirely new battlefield to shore up the Allied positions after the disastrous battle at Caporetto, George spent the next three months in action, where the battalion acquitted itself well, but his posting to Italy was not to last.

In the spring of 1918, with the Russians finally knocked out of the war and a Soviet Government installed, the 1st Bedfordshires were taken back to France by train on 12 April 1918 to again shore up the British defences. These had been rocked backwards after the start of a huge attack on 21 March where the Germans put specially trained Stormtrooper units to use, who had previously been employed on the now redundant Eastern Front.

The Bedfordshires were brought into the Lys sector and were 'up the line' by the second week of April. They settled into defensive positions despite several gas and trench mortar attacks causing casualties. George, who was now a Corporal in 'B' Company (despite having been an acting Sergeant with the Herts just prior to his first wound) was in the line close to the Nieppe Forest throughout this time.

On the evening of 25 April 1918, 'A' Company and one platoon of 'B' Company (including Drury), 1st Bedfordshires, were selected to form part of an attack alongside the Gloucestershire Regiment on German positions near Bedford Farm. The attack was planned as a night operation with Zero Hour being 9.30 pm. The Operational Orders still exist and report the following:

> 'A' Coy. and one platoon of 'B' Coy. will advance its line from LES LAURIERS Road. The Gloucester Regt. will conform with a similar movement on our right as far as VERTBOIS.
>
> 2. ARTILLERY will form a creeping barrage, rate of advance will be 1 minutes for first 300 yards. The Barrage will stop on line of new enemy trench. One Newton will fire on certain targets. Four light Trench Mortars will give a hurricane bombardment from ZERO to ZERO plus 1 minutes playing on an area around BEDFORD FARM. They will then lift and play for half an hour round building and orchard on Road. They will then stand to for S.O.S.

Large-scale night attacks were notoriously hectic on the Western Front and often led to unforeseen issues, which made the role of George's 'B' Company platoon especially important, working as a reactive force to any unseen situations arising.

The following citation recounts Corporal Drury's role in the action:

For conspicuous gallantry and devotion to duty during operations in patrolling the enemy's line and bringing back valuable information. During the attack he led a patrol party through, and, on reaching the objective, pushed on to the enemy's main line and reported their position to his platoon commander. The success of the operation and the covering of the consolidation were greatly due to his courage and skill. He captured a machine gun and made the enemy personnel carry it back.

The leadership and skill George displayed on 25 April 1918 earned him the coveted Distinguished Conduct Medal, the citation appearing in *The London Gazette* in September 1918.

Little is known of the nature of his third wound, which was believed to have been sustained shortly after his DCM action, but records indicate that George was returned to the UK and spent two months in hospital in Chelsea before taking a short (and very well-deserved) period of leave, destined never to see the Western Front again.

Whilst in hospital recovering from his third wound in four years of frontline service in France and Belgium, young George met nurse Cissy Goodwin, a Birmingham native. George and

George Drury and Nurse Cissy Goodwin during his convalescence.

Cissy seem to have hit it off immediately and begun a relationship whilst he was still recovering. With the stalemate on the Western Front broken and the German Army in retreat, it seemed that the future for young George, a celebrated veteran of 1914, DCM recipient and still only 20 years old, was rosy indeed.

Sadly, the British Army was not yet done with Corporal Drury. Once recovered, he was reposted to the 3rd Battalion, Bedfordshire Regiment and instead of being sent to the Western Front as he might well have expected, he found himself heading for an altogether different location.

The Russian Campaign in 1918–19 is something of an enigma in the annals of twentieth century history, usually occupying no more than a cursory mention in articles and textbooks. Although for those men posted there in late 1918 it was certainly no small campaign, and the dangers were no less real.

Sent to Russia as an experienced and decorated NCO with real leadership qualities, George was attached to the NREF headquarters for deployment to White Army units who were fighting the Reds in hopes of displacing the new soviet government and installing a more traditional regime.

It was in a windswept northern Russia that Drury first heard of the defeat of the German Army and the end of hostilities in Europe. One can only imagine his feelings on hearing the news, particularly as his entire adult life had been spent in the conflict. Perhaps he thought about those comrades who had left Letchworth train station with him in 1914 never to return. Maybe he reflected on the fact that whilst others went home, he was still facing the prospect of combat in a part of the world that was entirely unfamiliar to him.

Thankfully we can reach back into the past and hear George's thoughts from late November 1918 onwards in a series of letters written by him in Russia and sent to his family home in Shott Lane, Letchworth.

On Saturday, 23 November 1918 he wrote:

My Dearest Mother,

Just a few more lines for you, trusting this will find you all at home keeping well. I am pleased to tell you that my knee is much better now after resting it for these last few days so now I think I shall be quite fit for duty by the time Monday rolls around once again. After all I shall not be sorry to start again as the time hangs so heavy on one's hands with nothing to do, and what makes it worse is that we have nothing much to read. Well mum we are still waiting for that ship to come from Blighty with the mails, so as usual our question each day is 'any mails in yet from home?' and the answer is still no. But so long as you at home are getting our letters and know that we are getting along alright we won't grumble because we can manage to look after ourselves. But mum you bet we shall be a happy crowd when a mail does arrive and lets us know how things are going at home. Mum it has just gone 3 o'clock by our time and I am having to finish this letter by candlelight and looking out on the streets all we can see is snow and sledges out on the streets instead of carts. Mum I don't intend to make you feel cold only when we go out now we need our large fur coats on to keep us warm, and my word you have not got to hang about once you are out or you soon know all about it and now both of the big rivers here are frozen over and it seems funny to look across the river and see the boats stationary in mid-stream with ice all over them. So, I expect very shortly they will start to employ the ice breakers to keep the river open for the boats coming from England. And perhaps you shall get a better idea of the class of weather we expect as they lay a railway track across the ice and run the trains across into town for about four months of the year! And now Mum I have to try to get some cards to send you for Christmas but I have not seen any suitable so you will have to take my very best wishes in writing. Well Mum this is all for this time, I will conclude now trusting you will all have an enjoyable time this coming Christmas.

I remain, your ever-loving son,
George xxxxxxx

It is believed that George was based in Archangel at the time of writing as part of the Elope Force occupying the peninsula. The river he wrote of was the Dvina. At the time of writing, it is clear he was well in the rear of the fighting area and awaiting an assignment. A week later, on Sunday, 1 December, he wrote:

My Dearest Mother,

I now have the pleasure of letting you have a few more lines just to let you know I am still getting along alright out here and sincerely hope that everyone is keeping quite well and fit at home. Say we have not been lucky enough to get any letters from England yet but of course we all hope to get a mail in the near future. As at present we are all about fed up with waiting for any news, but of course we won't mind so much after we get our first letter so we will then know at least you got our first one to say that we had arrived here safe. Well Mum Christmas is beginning to draw very near so I hope all of you at home will have a very enjoyable time and you need not worry about me because I think we shall manage to have a good time enough ourselves and up to now nothing whatever stands in our way as we can obtain nearly anything we wish from our own Canteens and now we have two YM's (YMCA Huts) to spend our evenings in besides pictures, theatres etc. so we can generally knock an evening's fun out of one or the other for instance Friday we had a good concert party at the Y.M here, and on Saturday evening I went to the Y.M in town where a party of Russian Ladies gave us a very enjoyable concert so you see we don't do too bad taking things all around. Well Mum I suppose you hear from Ciss now and then, at least I hope so because I think having a letter from each other helps to pass things off a bit and I expect you all miss having the regular letters from me, but of course you know it is not my fault and at present I know you all have a letter in the mail here waiting to come to England so with this one you will have two arrive at the same time cos I think a boat leaves here sometime this week. Well Mum our cold weather is still holding out but it is dry thank goodness and now I see the people here are just starting to lay the tram lines etc. across the ice so you can just guess what sort of frosts we have been getting. But in spite of this weather I have not really felt cold out here yet, of course the rain has that sharp nip in it but walking about you can always manage to keep warm. 2654188 Cpl G Drury 3rd Battn Bed Regt, Elope Infantry Instructors Att G Hqrs NREF Russia. Well Mum I think this is all for this time so I think I will conclude now, trusting this will find you all intending to have a good time this Christmas. And I hope you are still getting good news about Roy. Good-bye.

I remain, your loving son
George xxxxxxxx

George wrote to his mother again on 9 December, finally reporting the receipt of many letters and sending his best wishes home. Three days later he wrote to his father:

Dear Dad,

Here are a few more lines for you to read trusting this finds you all quite well as I am pleased to say this leaves me. I have been writing to mother and Ciss B'Ham this morning and quietly roaming about, not recovering the parcels they sent me. I had only just had my dinner when the post corporal came and brought me two parcels which had been roaming about the town for about a week. I had one from the Spirella Needle Guild as our Ciss is a member containing a shirt, two pairs of socks, a towel scarf and a tablet of soap, also a Christmas Card so all of these things will come in very useful for me out here, so I am writing tomorrow thanking them for their kindness in sending me it. The other came from my Fiancée and she sent me the articles I wrote from here and a few extra things. Her parcel contained a writing pad, soap, chocolate, cigs, three papers and the most important of all, a letter. Well Dad I think I am a lucky chap in getting such a good girl as Ciss for instance in today's letter she mentions that she has been buying lots of things for our home so it is up to me to buy the extra things to make us a good home and as you know we are both working together for that day when I return to England to make her my wife and I don't see what is going to stop us and I don't want to give you too much of a surprise but if the army pays up what it owes me I won't be bad off, for instance I have only drawn a sovereign since I have been out here and I still have enough money to last me for at least another two months without drawing out. When you are writing to mother you can just mention that to her, say that's the results of being steady and I don't think it's so bad when one considers how dear things are out in this country. Wish you were here to read the letter from her dated Oct 27th as it would do your heart good to read it if you were out in a forsaken country like this. Well Dad the wedding will come off as soon as I take my discharge and get a decent job. Well now I have been gassing to you about that subject I will ring off and tell you a little news about myself although it is not much. First off it is beginning to get very cold out here and we are getting very little of what you in England call daylight as it does not get light until 9.00 AM and you want to have the lights on again directly after dinner and what's more they tell us after Christmas they only have about three hours daylight so what a cheerful outlook for us. 265418 Cpl G Drury DCM 3rd Battn, Bedford Regt, Elope Infantry Instructors, Attd G Hqrs NREF Russia. Well Dad I think this is all for this time so I think I will ring off. Wishing you all the best of luck and buck up and get your discharge.

I remain, your loving son,
George xxxxxxx

Three days later George wrote to his father again, this time informing him of a pay rise of sixpence a day due to the weather conditions in the Arctic Circle. He mentions the temperature being 30 degrees below zero. The next letter written by George is dated Saturday, 8 February 1919 and is as follows:

My Dearest Mother,

At last we have run into luck's way again as we have had a mail in and I have had 6 letters and parcels from Ciss, one from Fred, two from our Ciss and three from Dad, three from you and four lots of papers which I thank you for. And Mum don't go sending me any more cigs in the letters as it smashes the letter up and they arrive out here to me all unsealed. Well you will see I am sending my letters to Dad to home as I am expecting by now he will have taken his discharge and as of now I will just carry on and write one letter for both of you. Well for now Mum I don't think we shall be coming home just yet so or now just let things take their course and don't worry about me as I am getting along out here alright and I have plenty of work to keep me amused. And now I am just sending you on a check of what money you ought to have of mine by now. I know you have got the first two lots all correct so the next lot should have been £7.00 £5.00 £5.00 so you should have £20 in cash for me, also in the last mail I sent you home 700 roubles to be changed amounting to £17.10.0 and you should have received from Warley £20.00 off my account so if Dad has been able to change the roubles you should have £57.10.0 for me. If you ever want any cash you always know where to go for it and tell Dad to deduct his money from that amount and also his expenses if he has to go to London to change that money for me. Well dear Mum I am very sorry to hear you have been unwell of late but I surely hope this will find you much better. And now Mum you know I intend to get married as soon as I return home, that is of course if I can get hold of a decent job to walk into. But that's going away from the point I want to tell you about so here goes, I want you to look on Ciss as a Daughter-in-Law as she has written to me saying that all is not going as well as she would like them to be in B'ham, you see now Fred's back home you can easily see the reason why the girls are not wanted and I expect it is hitting Ciss pretty hard poor kid. So, Mum will you do me favour and write to her as often as you can, but whatever you do don't mention this news to her as it is our own secret. By the way I have bought her a complete fur skin which I am sending with this mail and if I have enough money I will bring one home for you as they cost £6.5.0 each and I have not enough money in Roubles to send you one just yet and I don't want to part with my English cash. This is about all, trusting this will find you at home keeping well.

I remain, your loving son,

George xxxxx

On 24 February George wrote to both his parents at their home in Letchworth:

My dearest Mum & Dad,

*   At last I can settle down and let you have a little more news about myself as I don't suppose you have received many letters from me just lately and you know that is no fault of my own. First of all, I am very sorry to think I have caused you a lot of trouble and worry by being so abrupt and telling you I was going up the line, so now I will try and straighten things out*

Along with one of his letters home, this time George sent a photograph of himself and other NCOs of the Elope Infantry Instructors, complete with fur boots and hats. George can be seen here with three 'wound stripes' and a marksman's badge on his left sleeve (front row second from right).

and explain to you more fully. So, to start with we are bound for the front but I cannot tell you when we are likely to get there as the Bolsheviks are going back now so we are standing by to see what is going to happen. At present we have about another 200 miles to go before we come in contact with the enemy so I don't think you will need worry about me for at least another few weeks. And then Mum I shall be quite alright as I like my job and there is not much danger to worry about. So now we are staying in this village for at least another month for training and my company consists of all Russians and Chinese. I am in charge of this company as sergeant major and I am the only English Warrant Officer and I have Russian Sergeants and of course I have two English Officer's a Captain (Captain Card) and Lt and the Colonel back at Headquarters (Edwards) so I do just as I like. And I have my own two servants, one as a cook and the other as my orderly. And I have a topping Billet in a private house with two rooms for myself so I am quite comfortable. So now I will tell you about my journey here on the sleighs, it takes us 4 days to do 72 miles and the first day was very cold, 42 below zero and in spite of all my furs I was cold and the second day it was worse as we started off in a gale and what with the wind and snow we couldn't see a yard ahead of us. And of course, I have my own two sleighs, one for my kit and the other for riding in. I got in my fur sleeping bag and then my face and left hand got frost-bitten so I stopped the convoy and rubbed them with snow so now I am alright again and still laughing. I have three English chums of mine back at headquarters but I don't see them very often so tonight is my first night with not much to do so I have ordered my sleigh and I am going to pay them a visit. And now you have to be careful with what you send me and see that the letters are sealed etc. as they have a long way to come and tomorrow my orderly has got to take these letters 72 miles to get them posted and buy me some cigs so you can just see how I am fixed. Well Mum I hope you have Dad at home now and everything running smoothly and I hope Dad will be lucky enough to get a job as it seems to me that there is not much work at home just yet. I think this is about all for this time so I will close now with my fondest love to all at home.

I remain, your ever-loving son,
George xxxxxxx

The final letter in the recently discovered collection – and quite possibly the last he ever wrote – was sent to his parents on 11 March 1919 and reads:

My Dearest Mother and Dad,

Here is just a few more lines for you trusting this will find all at home in the best of health as I am pleased to say this leaves me. I have just returned from another five days patrol in the Forest and I feel just about knocked up as it is very hard work tracking in the snow. Well I have received no letters or papers for some time now so I really don't know at all how things are going at home or in England. As you know my time expires in three days from now and I don't see any hopes of returning to England just yet. Of course, I shall see my colonel again about returning home but I suppose that is just about as far as it will get as no troops will be leaving the country for at least another two months. And I am beginning to think that us poor devils are having the worst part of the deal now, and those that waited to be called up are having the last laugh. At times I start thinking about different things and I feel just about fed up with everything. Anyway, just wait until I do come home and then I will have the time of my life for a few weeks. Well Mum I think I have told you all about my troubles so I will tell you about my travels etc. Well I have been working very hard and I have managed to get 40 miles through the Forest and found what I was after so after I have had a few more days rest I am starting out again so if everything still goes on smoothly I shall be doing myself a good turn as the colonel is very pleased with my latest success. Say I am getting quite an expert on my snowshoes and I can travel fairly quickly, you see they are made more like a tennis racket so you can walk on any depth of snow without sinking in. But if you fall over then one starts to say some nasty things about them. Well Mum I am sending on a cable-gram to you today just to let you know how I am getting on and I will forward them on rather often as I am unable to write as often as I would like to.

I remain,
Your ever-loving son.
George xxxxxx

A final telegram dated 12 March 1919 written from Leonova, Russia and addressed to Mrs Drury of 20 Shott Lane, Letchworth stated simply *'Don't worry quite well. George'*. Little did she know at the time, but this was the last she would ever hear from her son.

About ten days later, on or around 22 March 1919, 21-year-old Company Sergeant Major George Harry Drury of Letchworth set off with his makeshift company of Russian soldiers, commanded by Captain John Victor Card MC, a man who had risen from a private in the Grenadier Guards to officer rank and who – like George – was a veteran of four years fighting on the Western Front. The company's objective was to attack and capture a Soviet-held village south of Archangel. After a march of an incredible 80 miles in very deep snow, the company arrived on the outskirts of the village late in the evening of 25 March. During the day George had met CSM Tovey, one of his few fellow British NCOs. The pair exchanged greetings and joked about being 'back in action again' but Tovey said he *'considered it little more than a scuffle'*. Wishing each other luck, the two men parted and prepared to lead their troops forward into the attack with several companies of men, George's company forming the left flank of the advance.

Now, 100 years on, little is known of the North Russian conflict, let alone this one small action, although the few surviving records shed some light on the events of 25 March 1919. The order to advance was given at about 11.45 pm and Captain Card's company of Detachment 'A', Elope Forces emerged from the tree line to see the enemy-held village illuminated only by the snow-covered ground in the middle distance. As was his style, Card led the company from the front and as they advanced towards the enemy village, the silence of the night was broken by a burst of machine gun fire from a concealed position 30 yards away from the company commander. Card fell in the snow – gravely wounded – as the surprised company took to ground and returned fire.

As Captain Card fell, command of the company devolved to CSM Drury. Quickly taking stock of the situation, George decided that his Captain must be brought in, and at around midnight he left his company back in the tree line on the approach to the enemy village, and ventured forward alone. He did not return.

Back home in Letchworth Garden City, Mr and Mrs Drury would have been unaware – for some time at least – that their son was 'Missing in Action'. Due to the sporadic nature of mail coming home from Russia, they may not have been unduly worried about the lack of contact from George. Sadly, the fears that Mrs Drury had expressed in a letter to George several months before were to come true.

Official news probably arrived in April 1919 that CSM Drury was reported as 'missing, believed killed' on or about 25–26 March 1919. It is hard to imagine the devastation felt by George's parents at the realisation that their son might never be coming home. After enduring daily worry for his safety for over four years, it must have been bitter indeed to see other sons and loved ones returning from Europe, only to find out four months after the end of the Great War that George was presumed dead.

As one might imagine, the Drury family embarked on a frantic search over the next few months, contacting government departments, fellow servicemen and anyone who may have been able to help, asking for news of their son.

The letters highlight the increasing desperation of Mr and Mrs Drury, who were left in what must have been an agonising state of uncertainty.

When news finally did arrive, it was in the form of a letter by George's commanding officer, Lieutenant Colonel Edwards, confirming the death of young George, aged only 21.

On 18 July 1919 the following letter was delivered to No. 20 Shott Lane, Letchworth.

Dear Mr Drury,

Owing to having been moved about, I have only just received your letter. Firstly, I want to let you know that I asked Sergeant Tovey to give me your address so that I could write you a letter sympathizing with you on your loss and giving you details. The Russian Company with English officers and English NCOs did a wonderful march for 80 miles through forest and then a very strong enemy village had to be taken, to do this there were Russian troops and English Companies also. The Russians attacked on the left, and their officer, Captain Card, got under machine gun fire and was wounded in thick snow, thirty yards from the village, then your son went to his assistance and was killed by the same machine gun fire.

This was about 12 o'clock at night, in morning a patrol was sent out and saw the dead bodies of your son and Capt Card, quite near together in the snow. He died giving his life for his beloved officer. Now I will answer your question, it was hard to lose your son, after his wounds in France, but we are fighting the cause of common humanity here, the atrocities of the Bolsheviks are almost uncreditable, and his tyranny far worse than the German, in the same Company as your son was an officer who had been wounded severely four times and who joined in 1914, and never had any leave, his spirit, like your son's was to serve his country, your son's letter was quite accurate and he was in the right groove for very high promotion. His unit was very much appreciated, always cheery under the most trying circumstances. His promotion came out properly in orders and War Office can look it up. The Russian Company, after its losses, got broken up, and he had his fur helmet and wristwatch with him. I gave orders for his personal belongings to be looked after by Sergeant Tovey, and I trust you have received them.

If there is any information I can give you, you must please let me know.

Once more allow me to offer my profound sympathy to you and your wife at the loss of your brave son.

Yours Sincerely,
Lt Col Edwards

George's body was sadly never recovered and today he is remembered on the Archangel War Memorial to the missing in Russia.

Ordinarily, George's story would now reach its end; a tragic tale of a young man who endured so much, only weeks away from finally coming home and marrying his young fiancée – a fairy-tale ending that sadly would never be. Now, 100 years on and for the first time, it may actually be possible to add something more to this episode. By tracing through records and combining available material with what we already know, we can perhaps further this story. We know that George was killed alongside an English officer, named by Colonel Edwards as Captain Card. A search of the Commonwealth War Graves Commission records revealed the following information: a Captain John Victor Card is recorded as having died in North Russia on the same day as George. Given the rarity of his name, and the number of troops in North Russia at the time, we can be sure that this is the same man.

Upon further research, we found more information in Captain Card's records. A 'Concentration Report' for the small churchyard named Yemetskoe (today Yemetsk) in Russia shows that in 1927 five bodies were moved from the town churchyard to the Allied Cemetery in Archangel. Among those buried in Yemetskoe prior to 1927 is Captain Card – the man who according to Colonel Edwards, George was attempting to save when he was hit by machine gun fire.

Looking back at the letter sent by Colonel Edwards, we know that the village Captain Card's company attacked was reached *'after a magnificent march of some 80 miles through thick rainforest'*. In attempting to identify the village mentioned, we can turn to modern mapping.

By measuring the distance between Archangel and Yemetsk, we find that the two are exactly 133 km (83 miles) apart, separated by a large forest. We can also tell from historical sources that the village of Yemetsk was in an area heavily fought over in the early months of 1919. Considering the various possibilities, and perhaps more importantly, the fact that Captain Card was buried there, we can at least speculate that it is probable that the village attacked on the evening of 25–26 March was that of Yemetskoe.

By locating the place of burial of Captain Card, we can once again return to a letter written by Colonel Edwards – this time to the parents of Captain Card. In it he writes that *'his sergeant major was killed trying to bring him in. A party was sent out the next morning to bring their bodies back but they had been removed during the night by the enemy.'* With this in mind, we can further explore the Commonwealth War Graves Report for Yemestkoe, which names the five graves in the Churchyard. Four of those

Document listing an Unknown British Soldier at Yemetskoe, which may actually be the body of George Drury DCM. (*CWGC*)

are named, the fifth is an 'Unknown British Soldier'. Could it be that this was actually a reference to George Drury?

In weighing the probability of evidence in favour of this assumption, we know:

- George served in the same company as Captain Card.
- Their company travelled south to take on a 'strongly held enemy village'.
- Card was wounded and George attempted to save him, himself being hit in the process.
- The two men were seen by a patrol on the morning of 26 March 'quite close together'.
- The bodies were recovered at the same time, by the enemy.
- They were the only two British soldiers in the company.
- Card is identified as having been buried at Yemetskoe.
- Yemetskoe is 83 miles from Archangel. Colonel Edwards reported that the march to the enemy village was '80 miles through thick forest'.

Given all this information, it is perhaps likely that the 'Unknown British Soldier' is George Drury, but truthfully, we will never know. The bodies of Captain Card and the 'Unknown British Soldier' were due to be reburied in Archangel Allied Cemetery, although deteriorating relationships between the Soviet Government and Britain made that task a particularly difficult one and reburial never took place. Sometime in the 1930s the churchyard in the village of Yemetskoe was bulldozed and the headstones removed. It is perhaps most likely that the body of Letchworth-born George Drury is still in an unmarked grave, thousands of miles from his home.

After their son's death, Mr and Mrs Drury lived in Hertfordshire for the rest of their lives, rarely speaking about George but proudly displaying his medals and memorial plaque in the family living room. George never saw his prized DCM; it was presented to his parents in 1920, a year after his death.

No record of George's fiancée, Cissy Goodwin, can be found, although it is believed she never married.

PHOENIX RISING – STOKER JACK FINNIS & THE LOSS OF SUBMARINE *L55*

Stoker Jack Finnis

For many people, there exists an opinion that the war on the Western Front was brought to a clean and successful conclusion at 11.00am on 11 November 1918. Admittedly, a great many men were killed that morning and there are instances whereby some were killed an hour or two after that time, but all in all, it is regarded as a fairly clean break by most.

For the Royal Navy, hostilities at sea had ended long before this date. So, it was surprising to find that a group of submariners lost their lives in the Baltic Sea in June 1919, not fighting the Germans, but in a conflict with the Bolshevik Navy. Amongst those lost was a young Hertfordshire man, and on researching

Stoker Jack Finnis. (Mike Churcher)

his story, not only was a tale of high seas venture to be unearthed, but also the story of the death and rebirth of a naval vessel.

Born on 8 March 1891, Jack Files Finnis was the son of Henry Joseph and Agnes Finnis, of 191 Lancaster Road, New Barnet, Hertfordshire.

There was a long history of seafaring in his family and therefore, it was not surprising to find that Jack joined the Royal Navy on 30 September 1912, prior to which he had worked as a road labourer. Records show that after undergoing his basic training, Jack became a stoker, an important but arduous role that involved providing steam and power for the ship. It was not necessarily a role that involved shovelling coal, as there were numerous mechanical jobs that were carried out by men of this rank. Like so many other stokers, Jack served for a while on HMS *Renown*, a ship that was specifically used for training stokers.

With his training complete, Jack joined the crew of HMS *Psyche* on 20 June 1913 and served with her

HMS *Renown*, a ship that was specifically used for training stokers.

as she sailed around the world until January 1915, after which he returned to the UK to begin training in a new and deadly aspect of the war at sea: being part of a submarine crew. It would be 18 months before Jack took part in a high seas operation, but when it began, it would have deadly consequences.

On 17 January 1917, Stoker Jack Finnis joined his first operational submarine at Harwich, the *E43*. The E-class submarines were an improvement to the D-class – Britain's first overseas submarine with a diesel engine and the ability to carry more torpedoes. In total, 58 E-Class submarines were built, all fitted with a 12-pounder gun and additional torpedo tubes. This type saw action in the Atlantic, Baltic, Dardanelles and the North Sea. Although the E-class went through several modifications as submarine technology improved, it was seen as the backbone of the submarine fleet, eventually being replaced by the L-class submarines.

At 7.30 am on 17 January 1917, two British submarines, the *E36* and the *E43*, left Harwich to patrol two areas off Terschelling, Holland, watching for German ships leaving the ports of Wilhelmshaven, Bremerhaven and Emden. A strong northeasterly wind was blowing and at 11.26 am, just before they left the coast behind, *E43* signalled to *E36* to proceed independently.

At 1.30 pm the *E36* was on the port beam but was out of sight by 3.00 pm. The sea was running fairly high and at 6.50 pm the *E43*, having lost her bridge screen, eased to 5 knots and turned 16 points to fit a new one. This delay allowed the *E36* to overtake her, and at 7.50 pm, just off the Haaks, the *E43* altered course to true north when she suddenly sighted a submarine, 3 points on the port bow, apparently steering east and only 50 yards off. The helm was put hard to starboard and engines full astern but the *E43* struck the *E36* aft from the stern, rode right over her and saw her vanish on the starboard quarter in the darkness. Although *E43* went astern, nothing could be seen in the darkness and heavy sea, and nothing more was seen or heard of the *E36*, or her crew. Within 24 hours of joining his 'boat', Jack Finnis had diced with death, and survived.

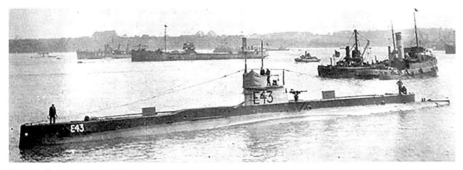

British Submarine – *E43*.

British Submarine – *L55*.

Jack remained part of the *E43* crew until 6 August 1918, when he was posted to HMS *Dolphin*, a submarine base and training facility located at Gosport near Portsmouth, where he remained until 11 February 1919. The following day he joined the crew of the submarine *L55*, which was launched in September 1918 and played a little part in the Great War.

As part of the Allied intervention in the Russian Civil War, the *L55* was based in Tallinn, Estonia, where she served with the Baltic Battle Squadron, supporting the Baltic states in their fight for independence. On 9 June 1919 in Caporsky Bay in the Gulf of Finland, the *L55* attacked two 1,260-ton Bolshevik Orfey-class minelayer-destroyers, *Gavril* and *Azard*. The *L55* missed her targets and was forced into a British-laid minefield. Soviet sources claim that the *Azard* sank her by gunfire but the area was riddled with British mines and it was the striking of one of these that caused her to sink with her whole crew, including Jack Finnis.

This was not the end of the *L55* though, and not the end of Jack's story, either. In 1926 a trawler came across the wreck of a submarine and by 1927 Russian minesweepers confirmed the find – it was the *L55*. The now established Bolshevik government was on the hunt for new submarine technology and in 1928 announced it had successfully lifted the *L55* out from a depth of over 100 feet of water. The British, aware that 42 of its souls were aboard at the time of the sinking, requested the return of the bodies. This was agreed by the Russian Government, but the return would be made by a merchant vessel, as the Russians refused to have any of Britain's destroyers in its waters.

The merchant ship *Truro* was used to collect the bodies and as the 34 coffins were transferred to HMS *Champion* in Reval, Estonia, the local

Memorial to the crew of HM Submarine *L55* in the Haslar Royal Naval Cemetery, Portsmouth.

brass band played 'Nearer, My God, to Thee' and the town's flags were lowered to half-mast.

The return of the bodies to England became caught up in the continuing grief of the time. The Unknown Warrior represented the servicemen from the Western Front, but now the population had 34 named sailors to grieve over as well. The coffins were returned with a great ceremony and were buried in a communal grave in the Haslar Royal Naval Cemetery in Gosport on 7 September 1928. The *Spectator* newspaper gave the following account:

> *The British submarine L55 was raised in Russian waters from the bed of the Baltic where she has lain for nine years. Naturally it has been desired to bring the remains of the crew to this country. It is not a matter on which wrangling is seemly, nor one in which a generous sympathy might not be hoped for. It has, however, been with some difficulty that arrangements have been made for a merchant vessel to approach the Russian coast to take the coffins on board and outside Russian waters to tranship them to a man-of-war. This is plainly the kind of vessel which should bear home the remains of sailors of His Majesty's Navy who died at their duty, whatever may be thought of the policy which sent them into those waters. The brotherhood of the sea generally arouses the best emotions. Its violation during the War probably shocked the world more than anything else in the policy or actions of our late enemies. It was pleasant to see it reassert itself in the Arctic regions where the ice-breaker, Krassin, proved that her crew could rise to the highest and most humane endeavour.*

Whilst the men were laid to rest, for the *L55* it was the chance to live a second life. After a refit of some one million roubles, the *L55* became a member of the Russian Navy, and having given up many of her technical secrets, spawned a new L-class of submarines for the Bolsheviks. Rebranded the *JI-55* and renamed the *Atheist*, the now-Russian submarine entered trials in 1931. After nineteen days, she sunk yet again and this time took 50 lives with her. She was still not to rest and was again recovered, this time off Kronstadt. The *Athiest* became a training craft until 1941, when she was again damaged, before being scrapped in 1953.

Panel of the New Barnet War Memorial on which the name of Jack Files Finnis is inscribed.

Stoker 1st Class Jack Files Finnis has his name inscribed on the screen wall dedicated to the crew of H.M. Submarine *L55* in the Haslar Royal Naval Cemetery, Portsmouth, Hampshire, and on the New Barnet War Memorial at the junction of Station Road and Lyonsdown Road.

THE LIFE AND DEATH OF CORPORAL HAMLET BLOXAM

Hamlet Bloxam, his name often being misspelled as 'Bloxham', was born in Chesham, Buckinghamshire in 1873 as the son of John Stanners Bloxam and Rebecca Bloxam (née Hawes). After his formal education ended, Hamlet gained employment in a local foundry, where he worked as an iron trimmer, a heavy and demanding role in the production process.

In October 1904 Hamlet married Emily Turvey Smith and the couple moved to Watford, Hertfordshire. They went on to have four daughters: Florence Emily (1905–1914), Ellen Elizabeth (Later Robbins: 1907–1977), Dorothy Annie (Later Plummer: 1909–1991), Rosa Irene (Later Mann: 1911–1990).

Men at the time could earn additional income by being a member of the Territorial Army, and Hamlet – like many others – enlisted when he had the opportunity around 1910, serving in 'D' Company of the Hertfordshire Regiment, whose drill station was at Chorley Wood, Hertfordshire. Attending annual camps and regular weekends brought the payment of a bounty, which would help support a young family, as well as provide him with the opportunity for some relaxation with a group of pals. Tragically, as Hamlet and his chums prepared for the certainty of war, he was to suffer one of the worst events a parent could face, the loss of a child. His eldest daughter, Florence Emily, died at home in the presence of her father on 5 February 1914 as a consequence of diphtheria. Following the outbreak of war with Germany on 4 August 1914, the Hertfordshire Regiment was mobilised and ordered to prepare to serve overseas. As part of the British Expeditionary Force, the battalion arrived in France on 6 November 1914 and, after moving to the Ypres Sector in Belgium, were soon in action. Hamlet was serving as a Lance Corporal and by the end of the year, he was to witness a tragic and significant event in the history of the regiment.

On Christmas Day 1914, by which time the regiment found itself back in France, a young Watford soldier,

Corporal Hamlet Bloxam.

Private Percy Huggins, was occupying a British sap poised precariously close to the German line. In the late morning, a solitary shot rang out across no man's land; an enemy sniper had shot and killed Percy with a single bullet to the head. Enraged by this action on such a holy day, Sergeant Tom Gregory, also from Watford, and a great friend of Hamlet Bloxam, demanded to take Huggins' position in the sap and 'return the favour'. Permission was granted and within minutes, Tom and Corporal Bloxam returned to the site of poor Percy's demise. Scanning the frozen ground along the German line, the old veteran Gregory spotted the sniper and with skill acquired by years of hard campaigning, killed him with a single shot.

The grave of Hamlet Bloxam in Watford Cemetery, along with the plaque to his daughter, Florence Emily, who died on 5 February 1914 aged 8. (*Source: The War Grave Photographic Project*)

Sadly, this was not the end of the exchange. Unbeknown to Gregory, a second sniper in the German line had spotted him and as he brought his own rifle up to the aim, he was shot, thus raising the death toll in this tragic Christmas exchange to three. Hamlet Bloxam witnessed the entire event and was to watch his comrades laid to rest, side by side, in Le Touret Military Cemetery, France.

As the war progressed, Hamlet Bloxam, now aged 42, found his health deteriorating as a consequence of his war service and by the end of 1915 he was invalided home. He was posted to No. 575 Employment Company, Labour Corps, part of Eastern Command, whose role was to guard German prisoners of war at one of the numerous PoW camps found in Hertfordshire at the time.

In May 1919 Hamlet Bloxam was taken ill at the Eastern Counties Command Centre in Watford and was admitted to the Middlesex War Hospital at Napsbury, where he passed away on 22 May as a consequence of a psoas muscle abscess (a collection of pus in the psoas muscle compartment). This is normally caused by various types of bacteria which may have infiltrated the surrounding organs. In Hamlet's case, it was caused by inflammation of the left adrenal body.

The 1914 Star, the British War Medal and the Victory Medal.

His grave is one of the 107 service burials to be found in Watford cemetery. It contains a poignant tribute to his daughter; a memorial plaque dedicated to Florence Emily can be found close to her father's headstone.

For his service with both the Hertfordshire Regiment and the Labour Corps, Hamlet Bloxam was awarded the 1914 Star, the British War Medal and the Victory medal. These were issued in 1920, so sadly, he did not live to receive them.

Chapter Seven

The 1920s – Cogadh na Saoirse

On Easter Sunday, 1916 a small group of Irish nationalists led by Padraic Henry Pearse seized the General Post Office in Dublin, Ireland. They stood on the steps leading to the entrance and read a statement that proclaimed an independent Republic of Ireland. Pearse and his supporters hoped that other Irish nationalist groups would join them and instigate a general uprising by the Irish population. Their hopes quickly went unrealised and the British Army responded with overwhelming force, crushing the rebellion and arresting Pearse's group. British firing squads shot several of the Irish nationalist leaders and the British government imprisoned many more. The Republic of Ireland existed for no more than a week and – from the British perspective – the rebellion was finished. However, for the Irish, it was just the beginning.

After the First World War, the powers in Europe sat down to redraw the boundaries of Europe. Sinn Féin attended these meetings and attempted to have Ireland included in this redrawing. They argued that Ireland should be granted independence through the treaty. However, the leaders of Europe largely ignored Sinn Féin and they returned home empty-handed. The Irish Volunteer Force (IVF) decided that they had waited long enough and that they would have to take action to increase the pace. They also hoped that by becoming a formidable military force, they could persuade the government to introduce complete independence rather than the proposed Home Rule solution. In 1919 they renamed themselves the Irish Republican Army (IRA), which signalled the start of a new phase in their history.

On 21 January 1919 the IRA shot dead two Irish policemen in County Tipperary, and this marked the beginning of what is now known as Cogadh na Saoirse, the War of Independence. However, the British clamped down hard in response, and soon a guerrilla war was underway in Cork and Tipperary counties. With the demobilisation of the British army, there was an opportunity to offer former soldiers a chance to serve as temporary constables with the Royal Irish Constabulary. The combination of black police uniforms and tan army outfits gave rise to the term 'Black and Tans' for these men. The Black and Tans were seen as undisciplined, and they often shot innocent civilians in reprisal for attacks on them. Unfortunately, these attacks only helped create and strengthen local support for the IRA.

In 1920 the IRA, led by a Corkman named Michael Collins, decided that the conflict was not having the desired effect and took steps to intensify the war. On 21 November 1920 the IRA shot dead eleven British agents, including Hertfordshire man Lieutenant David Alfred Rutherford MC & Bar. In reprisal, a group of Black and Tans fired randomly into a crowd of civilians at a Gaelic football match at Croke Park, Dublin. Twelve people were killed and the day became known as Bloody Sunday (not to be confused with another Bloody Sunday much later in the century). Ten days later the IRA shot dead seventeen British soldiers in Cork.

Meanwhile – despite the conflict – the government decided to press ahead with Home Rule and passed the Government of Ireland Act. This gave Ireland two Parliaments, each with its own Prime Minister. One for the Unionists and one for the Nationalists, but both Parliaments were still answerable to the British Parliament in London. Six counties, Londonderry, Tyrone, Fermanagh, Antrim, Down and Armagh, were to be under the Unionist Parliament, and the citizens there agreed to the creation of Northern Ireland by way of a referendum. The first elections for the Northern Irish parliament were held in May 1921 and the Unionists gained 40 of the 52 seats. It first met in Belfast in June 1921. The new prime minister of Northern Ireland was the Ulster Unionist leader, Sir James Craig.

The elections for the Nationalist Parliament in Dublin were held on 13 May 1921 with Sinn Féin, under Éamon de Valera, taking 124 seats of the 128 available. The remaining 4 were taken by Unionist candidates. However, Sinn Féin refused to recognise the Parliament and instead continued to meet in Dail Éireann. The IRA, under Michael Collins, continued to fight for more independence, and made regular attacks on Protestants. Finally, a stalemate was reached and a truce was signed between the IRA and the British on 11 July 1921. After four months of negotiations, a treaty was hammered out, which Michael Collins signed on behalf of the IRA. However, he did not fully consult his colleagues, many of whom were horrified that he had accepted partition. This is why he is now regarded by some as a traitor and this probably contributed to his assassination a short time later.

The Anglo–Irish Treaty, which was agreed between Collins and the British government, replaced the Dublin Home Rule Parliament that had been created by the Government of Ireland Act. The new act created an Ireland which was much more independent than it would have been under pure Home Rule, and certainly much more independent than the part of Ireland ruled by the Northern Irish government.

The new country was to be called the Irish Free State and would have its own army, although it would remain within the British Commonwealth. Britain would also have a representative in Ireland and would keep some naval bases in Irish waters. The Sinn Féin leader, Éamon de Valera, became the first Prime Minister of the Irish Free State.

A SECRET MISSION – LIEUTENANT DAVID ALFRED RUTHERFORD MC & BAR

Long after the armistice of 1918, the men of Hertfordshire continued to give their lives in the service of their country. There were, of course, a great many amongst them who succumbed to injuries and illnesses resulting from their service in the Armed Forces, as well as those still in service who lost their lives as a result of both sickness and accidents. There were also those who were to give up their lives in this new fight, the Irish War. Amongst these was Lieutenant David Alfred Rutherford of Bushey Heath; a distinguished officer who had seen significant service on the Western Front and then began to undertake dangerous work combating the IRA.

David was born in 1899 in Waltham Cross, Hertfordshire as the second of three sons born to David Carter Rutherford and his wife, Charlotte Ann. His father was an import and export merchant and in 1901, when David was two years old, the family lived at The Hollies in Cheshunt. By the time of the 1911 Census, they had moved to Ivy Lodge, Cheshunt, and David and his younger brother were pupils at Mostyn House School, Parkgate, in Cheshire.

On 10 May 1916 David Rutherford, now a gentleman cadet at the Royal Military Academy, gained a commission as a Second Lieutenant in the Royal Garrison Artillery. He served in France with the 115th Siege Battery, which was part of 'Y' Group, 65th Garrison Artillery Brigade. These batteries were equipped with heavy guns, sending large calibre high explosive shells in fairly flat trajectory. The usual armaments were 60-pounder (5-inch) guns, although some had obsolescent 5-inch howitzers. As British artillery tactics developed, heavy batteries were most often employed in destroying or neutralising the enemy artillery as well as putting destructive fire down on strongpoints, dumps, stores, roads and railways behind enemy lines.

On 15 June 1917 David was awarded the Military Cross for conspicuous gallantry and devotion to duty when acting as forward observation officer. The citation for the award reads:

> *He sent back most valuable reports on the situation, and eventually succeeded in establishing a telephone line in close proximity to the enemy.*

On 22 June 1918 a bar was added to the Military Cross, again for conspicuous gallantry and devotion to duty. On this occasion, the citation stated:

> *When in command of the forward section of the battery he kept all his guns in action under a heavy fire, until being ordered to withdraw late in the day he got*

his guns safely away across open country and over a railway embankment, the
roads having become unpassable from shell fire. His quick and determined action
saved the guns.

On 15 October 1918, as the Great War drew to a close, David was appointed acting
Captain but relinquished the rank on 8 April 1919. By this time, the Irish War
of Independence, which began on 21 January 1919, necessitated the diversion of
troops to Southern Ireland, and David Rutherford was deployed there with the
28th Siege Battery, Royal Garrison Artillery.

Rutherford became attached to the Royal Irish Constabulary's Auxiliary
Division. This force, raised in July 1920, was mostly recruited from former
commissioned officers in the British Army and was promoted as a highly trained
elite force by the British media. Generally known as the Auxiliaries or 'Auxies',
they were a paramilitary unit, whose role was to conduct counter-insurgency
operations against the Irish Republican Army. The Auxiliaries became infamous
for their reprisals on civilians and civilian property in revenge for IRA actions,
such as the burning of Cork city in December 1920. The Auxiliaries were distinct
from the so-called Black and Tans, former soldiers recruited into the RIC as
temporary constables. The Auxiliaries and the RIC were disbanded in early 1922,
following the Anglo–Irish Treaty.

On 29 October 1920 Lieutenant Rutherford and Lieutenant Bernard Loftus
Brown MC took a three-day leave on the pretence of 'travelling the counties'.
They departed from their base at Moore Park, Kilworth, Fermoy, at 3.00 pm,
each riding a motorcycle, dressed in mufti and carrying officers' haversacks and
bedding. A Sergeant on the base remarked, *'They don't look much like civilians.'*
They told the regiment that they intended to go to Killarney and they had
bedding and primus stoves with them in a sidecar, as well as sufficient food for
two to three days. They were last seen filling up on petrol at Kilworth village.

Charlie Browne of Macroom IRA, who are likely to be the ones who seized
the two officers, said that Brown and Rutherford were dressed in civilian clothes,
were armed, and that they were later executed as enemy spies. Their bodies were
never recovered. British Army records state that Brown and Rutherford had been
employed from time to time on intelligence work and that this may have been the
reason for their murder.

A Sergeant at the inquiry into their kidnapping stated: *'Mr Brown was occupied*
in operations against Sinn Feiners on patrols, or with one man or by himself. He has
told me of going out and pulling down Sinn Fein signs. I know of him being out more
than once at night in the battery trap.'

The date of their death was given as 1 November 1920. Just a few days after
the announcement of their death, the Kilmichael Ambush was carried out by the

Irish Republican Army in which thirty-six local IRA volunteers, commanded by Tom Barry, killed seventeen members of the Royal Irish Constabulary's Auxiliary Division. The Kilmichael Ambush was noted as being both of political and military significance and marked a profound escalation in the IRA campaign.

It was not until 20 November 1921 that the British finally got proof from the IRA that Lieutenant David Rutherford and Lieutenant Brown had been executed.

Mostyn House School, where David was a pupil, created a rare carillon of 37 bells on the roof over the entrance to the school chapel as a war memorial. The names of all former pupils who fell in the Great War are shown on a panel in the entrance to the chapel. David Rutherford's name appears there. In 2012, the carillon and the commemorative panel were transferred to Charterhouse School. After the war, David and Charlotte Rutherford, now Lord and Lady Rutherford, gave a peal of eight bells to St. Peter's Church, Bushey Heath, in memory of their son, which were dedicated by the Bishop of St. Albans on 29 October 1921.

David Rutherford is remembered with honour at Hollybrook Memorial in Southampton, which commemorates by name almost 1,900 servicemen and women of the Commonwealth land and air forces whose graves are not known. He was entitled to the Military Cross, British War Medal and Victory Medal.

BLACK WHITSUN – SINN FÉIN STRIKE IN DUBLIN AND ST. ALBANS

The darkest moments of the Irish War of Independence were between January and July 1921. During this period, more than 1,000 lives – both British and Irish – were lost, representing approximately 70 per cent of the total casualties suffered during the conflict. On 14 May 1921 the Whitsun holidays across the United Kingdom and Ireland commenced and were to become known as 'Black Whitsun'. Not only as a result of the parliamentary elections in Ireland, but as a consequence of a series of violent attacks by the IRA.

Early that morning, a Hertfordshire soldier serving in Dublin was to be caught up in a renowned IRA plot that would cost him his life, and the county of Hertfordshire – an unlikely battleground for the Irish War of Independence – was to witness the terrifying activities of the Irish Republican Army at the home of a former Great War soldier and his wife. These are their stories.

Albert George Saggers – The Mountjoy Prison Raid

As you pass the War Memorial in the village of Stanstead Abbots, you may not notice the name of Albert G. Saggers, oddly placed on the neatly-ordered panels which list those men who gave their lives in the Great War. In the local cemetery, his grave is marked by a private memorial, as opposed to the standard Commonwealth War Graves Commission headstone you find in many military cemeteries and it gives no indication of his service or the circumstances of his death.

The simple fact is that Albert joined the army after hostilities had ceased and his death occurred long after the Armistice, but within the period the Commonwealth War Graves Commission are responsible for (4 August 1914–31 August 1921).

Albert was born in 1900 as the son of William and Lizzie Saggers of Roydon Road, Stanstead Abbots. He attested for service in the army at Hertford on 21 June 1920, at which time the family lived in Vicarage Road, Stanstead Abbots. Him being a butcher by trade may explain why he did not enter the army earlier, as his skills may have been needed on the home front. Albert was attached to 'D' Supply Company, Army Service Corps, which at the time was stationed at Marlborough Barracks, Dublin, and was allocated the regimental number, S/11267.

At about 9.00 am on 14 May 1921, a party of British soldiers arrived at the Corporation Abattoir on Dublin's North Circular Road

Casualty list from May 1921 showing the men of the British Army who had been killed or wounded in Ireland. Albert Saggers is amongst them.

to collect meat for their barracks. This was a daily event, but as a result of the increased attacks on army personnel, the vehicles were now being escorted by an armoured car. Whilst most of the soldiers, including Albert, went inside to eat breakfast and prepare the supplies they were due to collect, they left their armoured car outside, guarded by a single soldier. As the meat was about to be

Vinny Byrne, the IRA assassin who was amongst the group of raiders who shot and mortally wounded Private Albert Saggers.

The grave of Private Albert Saggers in St James Churchyard, Stanstead Abbots. The headstone gives no indication that he was a serving soldier, or the cause of his death.

loaded onto the trucks, a group of armed men approached the guard and told him to surrender. He refused and attempted to bring the car's guns to bear on the raiders, but he was shot and seriously wounded.

The group, believed to be members of No. 3 Battalion, Dublin Brigade, were led by Paddy Daly and Emmet Dalton, and included IRA assassin Vinnie Byrne, one of Michael Collins' group known as the Twelve Apostles. They rushed inside, taking the soldiers and civilian operatives by surprise, and shouting, *'hands up'*. The soldiers were ordered to surrender their weapons but Albert Saggers either refused to obey or did not hear the order, and was shot in the head, falling to the floor, seriously wounded.

The panel of the Stanstead Abbots War Memorial, showing Albert Saggers' name having been added at a later date.

The death certificate for Private Albert Saggers, which shows he died from a bullet wound to the head.

The raiders then removed the soldiers' weapons and stole their armoured car, which was later used to gain entrance to Mountjoy Prison in an effort to free Seán Mac Eoin. However, the plot was discovered and the IRA volunteers in the car had to shoot their way out of the prison. The car was later abandoned near Clontarf railway station.

Albert Saggers was taken to the King George V Hospital in Dublin but he died of his wounds later that day. His body was brought home to Stanstead Abbots and laid to rest in the St. James Churchyard.

There are no British medals for service in this campaign, and precious little recognition for those British soldiers who took part. Whilst most of the 'Tans' and 'Auxies' were hardened veterans of the First World War, most British troops stationed in Dublin in 1920 and 1921, such as Albert Saggers, were raw recruits who had not served in the European war and had not been through years of brutalisation in the trenches.

Lancelot Ashby – A Knock at the Door

On the same day that Albert Saggers was killed in Dublin, the city of St. Albans would see the Irish War of Independence brought to its doorstep – literally.

Lancelot Ashby was born in St. Albans in 1896 as the son of Albert and Margaret Ashby. His mother, an Irish woman, described herself as 'a reservist's wife', and was to produce six sons: Herbert, Lancelot, Cecil, Victor, Bruce and Albert. Their father, a house painter by trade, had served in both the militia and the regular army, seeing service in South Africa during the Boer War with the Bedfordshire Regiment and the Hertfordshire Imperial Yeomanry. He would be awarded the Queen's South Africa Medal with 5 Bars. As if this wasn't enough, Albert went on to serve with the National Reserve and at the outbreak of the Great War, joined the cavalry, serving with the 9th Lancers. He was compulsorily transferred to the Royal Flying Corps in 1916 and was with the Royal Air Force at its formation. He was to achieve a total of 34 years and 30 days service for his country. This perhaps explains the manner in which his wife describes herself.

With regard to Lancelot, he enlisted in the Territorial Army on 6 December 1912, aged 16, serving as a gunner with the 4th East Anglia Brigade, Royal Field

Artillery. Attending regular training sessions and annual camps along with listening to his father's campaigning stories, it is not surprising that he signed an agreement to serve overseas following the outbreak of the Great War. A Service Record has not survived for Lancelot which may have provided a more detailed insight into his military career. However, there a number of historical documents that show he served in the Army Service Corps with the Regimental Number M2/032570, arrived in France on the 10 May 1915 and was awarded the 1915 Star, British War Medal and Victory Medal, and remained in uniform long after the cessation of hostilities. His older brother Herbert was serving in the Royal Air Force along with their father, and their younger brother Cecil was serving in France with the Highland Light Infantry.

After the war ended, Lancelot – like a great many other young men – was faced with prospect of returning home to mundane, and often poverty-stricken lives. They sought excitement and an opportunity to remain in the armed forces, but most of all they were looking for an income. For Lancelot, this came in the guise of Royal Irish Constabulary, a police force that had been suffering devastating casualties in their fight with the Irish Republican Army. As a consequence of the attacks on the RIC, they began to see a significant number of resignations, depleting their numbers even further. In late 1919 Winston Churchill created the Royal Irish Constabulary Special Reserve, a force of temporary constables recruited to assist the RIC with their fight against the IRA, and the pay was 10 shillings a day.

With their improvised uniforms, many of the recruits were British Army veterans of the Great War who answered the British government's call. Although most had received campaign medals for service in the Great War, there was to be no formal recognition for their time in Ireland.

Lancelot Ashby joined the Black and Tans in 1920 as a driver. He is described as 'being responsible for driving a raiding charabanc', a passenger-carrying vehicle that was used by the RIC during their missions to destroy the IRA and its supporters. The Black and Tans became renowned for their attacks on civilians and civilian property, and this may have been the reason that Lancelot became known to the IRA.

In early 1921 Lancelot married Harriett Ordoyne, a 27-year-old Nottinghamshire woman, and this may have been what prompted him to leave the Auxiliaries. On Friday, 13 May 1921 Lancelot, having resigned from the RIC earlier that week, arrived in St. Albans after travelling from Dublin. He went directly to the house in Catherine Street, where he and his wife had lodgings.

At 9.45 pm on Saturday, 14 May four men knocked at the door of the house and asked the landlady, 72-year-old Mrs Austin, if they could speak to Mr Ashby. When Lancelot came down, three of the men entered the property, each of them then produced a revolver. Lancelot was ordered to go upstairs, closely followed by the intruders, and into the room where he and his wife were eating supper.

Whilst one of the men stood by the door, another of the intruders said to Ashby, *'I know you, Ashby, you have been in the RIC.'* Then pointing to a box on the floor, he said, *'I want you to open that box.'* Just as Lancelot complied with the demand, a revolver was fired, and he fell to the floor, struck in the

Royal Irish Constabulary vehicles outside Limerick, similar to that driven by Lancelot Ashby.

head by a bullet. He was then hit on the side of the head with the butt end of a revolver.

Immediately, Harriett Ashby fell to the floor, also shot in the head, and was similarly treated. The landlady, who attempted to go upstairs to see what was wrong, was seized by the man at the door and was gagged. All three men then escaped, knocking Mrs Austin down the stairs in their hurry to escape and taking cover in the crowded streets where people were taking advantage of the start of a Bank Holiday weekend.

Lancelot, although badly wounded, managed to crawl to the front door where he was seen by a newsagent who lived across the street. He called the police, who were quickly on the scene, and the couple were taken to the St. Albans Hospital, where it was found that the bullets had pierced their scalps, but had not injured their skulls. Both victims were, however, suffering from shock and from the blows delivered by the butt end of the revolver. Lancelot said later that he recognised some of the intruders and had seen them near the boat when he was leaving Dublin.

The Ashbys both survived the ordeal and Lancelot went on to serve the City of St. Albans for many years as a bus driver. Eventually the couple moved to Harriett's native Nottinghamshire where they lived at 61 Standhill Road, Carlton. Harriett passed away on 4 October 1979, aged 86 and Lancelot passed away on 21 November 1982, also aged 86.

Despite the best efforts of both Scotland Yard and the St. Albans Constabulary, their assailants were never found.

Chapter Eight

The Home Front

Terror from The Skies – Air Raids Over Hertfordshire During the Great War

(With Grateful Thanks to Ian Castle – www.iancastlezeppelin.co.uk)

In the months following Britain's entry into the Great War there were concerns that Germany would mount airborne attacks on major cities across the country, especially London. German airships, in the form of the aluminium-framed Zeppelin and the wooden-framed Schütte-Lanz, had been in production since the early 1900s and their use for military purposes had been greatly explored independently by both the German Army and Navy.

Following the outbreak of war, Kaiser Wilhelm – due to his close ties to the British royalty – prevented the military from attacking Britain by air, believing that the war would soon be over. He did not want to be held responsible for destroying London's cultural heritage, but he soon came under pressure to attack the capital and finally approved the bombing of England in January 1915. However, he excluded London until May of that year. Initially, bombing attacks were only authorised on targets in East London but by July 1915, approval had been extended to the whole of the city.

Zeppelins quickly became known as the new menace of the Great War, placing British civilians directly in the firing line. Invariably, as the giant raiders made a course for London, their flight path from the North Sea crossed over the Hertfordshire borders, where the county towns, often within close proximity to the capital, came under attack.

The airships would drop both high explosive and incendiary devices during their flights, often doing little more damage than breaking windows and destroying crops. The

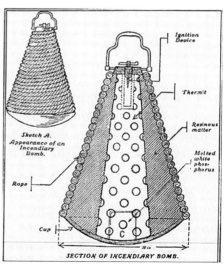

German incendiary bomb.

crews – desperate to escape the searchlights, anti-aircraft guns and fighters of the Home Defence force – struggled in the cloud-bound skies to navigate planned routes and identify targets, and as a consequence, attacks were often indiscriminate and their effectiveness limited. However, a great deal of structural damage was caused and there were numerous

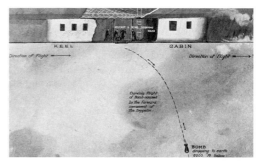

Diagram showing how German raiders dropped their payload.

casualties amongst both the civilian and military population, including children – instigating the media to quickly brand the Zeppelins as 'Baby Killers'.

In June 1917, the first air raid on Britain took place using the huge Gotha bomber aircraft. This was soon followed by raids using the German 'Giant' bombers. The threat from the air was met with new tactics in aerial combat as well as improved wireless communication and observation, enabling fighters to be dispatched to meet the attackers. Anti-aircraft fire and barrage balloons forced raiders to fly higher, thus compromising their bombing accuracy, and by August 1918, when the chief architect of the Zeppelin campaign, Peter Strasser, was killed aboard L.70, there would be no more air raids and the aerial threat to Britain was over.

There was significant damage caused across Hertfordshire throughout the Zeppelin campaign against Britain and at least 15 people are known to have died as a result of air raids. In addition, there were also 35 Zeppelin crew members who lost their lives over the county. The details of these incidents now follow.

7–8 September 1915

The town of Cheshunt was attacked twice by airships during the Great War. On the night of 7–8 September 1915 the Zeppelin LZ.74, commanded by Hauptmann Friedrich George, appeared in the night skies, seeking his objective of Leyton, East London. George believed that his ship was actually over the target area when he was engaged by ground fire from anti-aircraft guns at Waltham Abbey.

Wishing to lighten his load and escape the gunfire, he released 45 bombs while he was actually over Cheshunt. The bombs destroyed a row of greenhouses – which had probably been mistaken for a row of factory roofs – smashed numerous windows and damaged a section of railway track before making an escape by following the River Lea southwards towards London. Although there were a number of casualties as a consequence of the air raids that night, none occurred in Hertfordshire.

On 8 October 1915, the LZ.74 flew into a hillside in the Eifel region between Germany and Belgium. The crew survived but the airship was extensively damaged and was scrapped.

A 'P' Class Zeppelin, similar to that which dropped bombs on Cheshunt.

13–14 October 1915

On the afternoon of 13 October 1915 a group of five German Navy Zeppelin airships left their home base in what was to be the most daring and destructive raid up to that time, aimed at factories and military installations in the southern and eastern parts of London.

Four raiders, L.13, L.14, L.15 and L.16, flew in over the Norfolk coast in a close group, whilst L.11 flew in a little way behind. Oberleutnant zur See Horst Freiherr Treusch von Buttlar-Brandenfels, commanding L.11, dropped his bombs around the Norfolk area, causing little damage and no casualties. The L.14, however, commanded by Kapitänleutnant Alois Böcker, travelled south and attacked locations in Kent, including an Army camp near Lympne, killing 24 people and injuring 26. The remaining raiders headed further inland, crossing the home counties and seeking out their objectives.

In the picturesque county town of Hertford, people in the local community were going about their business and, although interrupted by the news from faraway battlefields of the death and injury of loved ones, life continued as normal.

For much of the civilian population of Great Britain, this was how wars had always been. The populous would read about events in newspapers and reports amongst townspeople, but the devastation of direct warfare had not been witnessed by the public first hand. The events of 1915 were to change the way many people at home thought of the war, as – quite literally – death and destruction rained down on their streets and doorsteps from the air.

Kapitänleutnant Heinrich Mathy, commanding L.13, arrived over Hertford just after 9.00 pm, but a 13-pound anti-aircraft gun situated at Birchwood Farm, near Hatfield, opened fire and drove the raider away. The ship dropped four high explosive bombs in response. One landed 70 yards from the gun but only damaged some windows of nearby cottages. As the airship continued on its course towards London, one wonders what Mathy's thoughts would have

Kapitänleutnant Heinrich Mathy.

been, had he known he would be killed in this very location just twelve months later. The L.13, however, survived the war and was decommissioned on 25 April 1917.

The L.15, commanded by Kapitänleutnant Joachim Breithaupt, crossed the county of Essex and arrived over Broxbourne at around 8.40 pm. Here, a 13-pound mobile anti-aircraft gun located in Church Fields opened fire with nine rounds. In response, the airship dropped four high explosive bombs; one failed to detonate but the other three landed in close proximity to the gun. The blast blew the gunners off their feet, and wrecked a wooden shed as well as a lorry and a car belonging to the detachment.

Kapitänleutnant Joachim Breithaupt.

This raider was deemed to have been the most successful of the night, as it was the only one to reach its objective: London. After leaving Hertfordshire, the airship was not observed again until it appeared over Westminster. Here, the L.15 was engaged by an anti-aircraft gun at Green Park. It then began to drop bombs in a number of significant parts of the West End and other locations across the city. As it rained terror down upon the city, it was eventually forced to climb higher to avoid the increasing anti-aircraft gunfire. It took a northerly course out of London and crossed the coast near Aldeburgh at around midnight, having taken the lives of 21 people and left a further 50 injured.

On 31 March 1916 the L.15, again commanded by Kapitänleutnant Joachim Breithaupt, was hit by anti-aircraft fire from Purfleet. With four of its gas cells destroyed, the Zeppelin gradually lost height and then crashed into the sea near Margate. All but one of the crew survived and were made prisoners of war.

The L.16, commanded by Oberleutnant-zur-See Werner Peterson, was the newest addition to the Imperial Navy's Zeppelin fleet, and had only been commissioned nineteen days earlier. The ship reportedly suffered engine trouble after leaving its base at Nordholtz, and eventually lost sight of its companions over the channel.

It crossed the Norfolk coast at Bacton around 6.40 pm, and then turned towards London. Ten minutes later L.16 dropped a high explosive bomb at Banningham, causing no damage. The ship then flew a somewhat erratic course towards the south, and came under ground fire

Oberleutnant-zur-See Werner Peterson.

near Kelvedon Hatch, forcing it to turn away from London. Now steering north, it appeared over Sawbridgeworth at about 9.45 pm, where Peterson saw lights about ten miles in the distance. These were reputedly from the hospital, and the factory of Garratt and Sons in Hertford. It seems that Captain Peterson was not the best at aerial identification, and was elated when one of the crew spotted a winding stretch of river in the darkness, surrounded by buildings. They believed this was their target. However, it was not London's East End or the River Thames that they had found but in fact, the River Lee and the town of Hertford.

The mighty Zeppelin arrived over the town at about 10.00 pm and, descending towards its target, began a 'bomb-run', using a mix of high explosive and incendiary bombs, on the unsuspecting townspeople below. In a sad twist of fate, hearing an unusual droning noise from above, and seeing a strange object in the night sky, a number of men and women took to the streets to observe the unusual spectacle.

Local resident Annie Swan later described the incident in her book, *My Life*:

I find it difficult to describe that appalling five minutes' interlude, while the monster ship with its death-dealing cargo passed slowly over our town, visiting us last and dropping eight bombs on our house and garden. The first of the bombs had destroyed the power station, so that the town was plunged in utter darkness. There were lights from the sky, however, as the incendiary bombs rapidly followed the explosive ones to complete the devilish work.

I had the feeling that it was the Day of Judgement, as we stood there, holding on to one another. Presently the great monster sailed over us, so low down that it brushed the topmost branches of the old cedar tree on the lawn.

Reports at the time state the first bombs dropped by L.16 were on the Folly and Bull Plain. Here, one high explosive bomb was dropped directly outside Lombard House – the local Conservative Club – killing four men who had emerged to watch the aerial spectacle.

The casualties there were: George Cartledge (aged 55), a draper who ran a shop at 28 Fore Street; John Henry Jevons (aged 57), the borough surveyor; James Lively Gregory (aged 54), professor of music, and an organist at All Saints' Church and Ernest T. Jolly (aged 29), a cashier at Barclays Bank in Fore Street. Now travelling in a northerly direction, the Zeppelin targeted Old Cross with incendiary devices, damaging homes in North Road and killing 21-year-old Bombardier Arthur John Cox of the Royal Field Artillery in the process. A single high explosive bomb also impacted on the ground outside the county hospital, killing another two spectators who had gathered in Garrett's Mill Yard to watch the unfolding events: Arthur Hart (aged 51), a local miller and Charles

Spicer (aged 32). Completing the tragic death toll that night were two young children: baby boy George Stephen Game (aged 3), who was killed by shrapnel, and Charles Waller (aged 13).

Then, just a few minutes after it started, Hertford was once more plunged into silence as the enormous airship disappeared into the night, leaving the townspeople in a state of complete and utter shock. The L.16 had dropped a total of fourteen high explosive bombs and thirty incendiaries, left ten buildings considerably damaged and 141 others with varying degrees of damage. Tragically, the raid on Hertford cost the lives of nine civilians and a soldier, and left fifteen others injured.

Peterson and L.16 returned safely across the channel to their base in Germany, reporting a 'successful raid on industrial and railway targets in East London'. The L.16 was damaged beyond repair during a training mission at Nordholz Naval Airbase on 19 October 1917.

It was reported that 71 people were killed across London and East Anglia that night, and a further 128 injured – the heaviest casualty list from air raids in the war – with 17 of the dead being military personnel. The names of the nine victims from Hertford are inscribed on the local war memorial.

However, a local report indicates that a lady died in her home from shock. Research has established who this lady was, and has also uncovered a tale of tragic family events that were to echo across the generations.

Francis George Percy lived with his wife, Sophia Charles Percy, and their six children at 9 Eleanor Road, Bengeo. In October 1911, their 5-year-old son, Stanley Charles, passed away, and just a few months later, in February 1912, their 2-year-old daughter, Alice Louisa, also lost her life, leaving their parents grieving and devastated. A small ray of hope for the couple occurred in 1913 with the birth of their daughter Mary, and again in 1914 with the birth of their son Arthur Francis.

Then in 1915 Sophia again became pregnant. On the night of 13 October 1915 the explosion of a bomb dropped by Werner Peterson from Zeppelin L.16 near their house was reported as being so loud that it caused Sophia to collapse and die from shock, also taking the life of her unborn child. Mother and child were buried in the St Leonard &

Hertford War Memorial. Perhaps the name of Sophia Charles Percy and her unborn child should also be inscribed along with the other civilians who died on the night of 13–14 October 1916?

Holy Trinity churchyard, Bengeo on 19 October 1915. Her devastated husband was now left with five children to raise, including a baby. With his life seemingly in tatters, the 40-year-old plumber opted to leave Bengeo, and moved to Chitty Street, North London.

In 1917, Francis married Elizabeth Keogh, who became a stepmother to the multitude of children. Tragedy, however, was not yet done with Francis. His young son Arthur Francis grew up and eventually joined the army, serving as a Private in the 1st Battalion, Royal Warwickshire Regiment. On 27 September 1936, in Poona, India, 22-year-old Arthur was shot through the head by another soldier from his regiment, Private Maurice Henry Durbin, a 26-year-old native of East Harptree, Somerset, whilst in a room at Wanowrie Barracks, Poona, India. Arthur was buried in the local cemetery the next day. Maurice Durbin was arrested for the murder of his comrade and brought before a civil court. He was

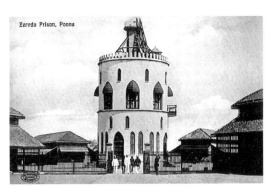

hanged for his crime at Yaravda Prison, Poona, on 6 March 1937 and is also buried in Poona Cemetery.

Francis Percy himself passed away in 1941 at the age of 66, and it would seem that his decision to move away from Hertford meant that Sophia's name was never added to the war memorial when it was created in 1919.

Yaravda Prison, Poona.

2–3 September 1916

On 2 September 1916 a fleet of fourteen airships made what was – at that point – the largest raid of the war so far. Over 500 bombs were dropped on unsuspecting civilians and military personnel between Kent and East Yorkshire.

Whilst eleven of the airships came under the operational command of the German Navy, the remaining three raiders belonged to the German Army, one of which was a Schütte-Lanz, SL.11, commanded by Hauptmann Wilhelm Schramm, a man who was born and raised in Charlton, London. His father worked at the local German-owned Siemens Factory and Wilhelm reportedly

Hauptmann Wilhelm Schramm.

spoke with a cockney accent. He knew London very well indeed, having grown up in the city, and would later use this knowledge to drop bombs on the capital. Schramm moved to Germany several years before the outbreak of war and joined the military, rising to command SL.11 by 1916.

The airship crossed the English coast at Foulness, Essex at about 10.40 pm and headed for London. It arrived in the St. Albans area at 1.10 am on 3 September, and began to drop some of its explosive load; three high explosives and three incendiary bombs landed in fields near Bell Lane, London Colney, and St. Alban's Road, South Mimms; and two more of each landed near a wood at North Mimms. Three bombs followed at Little Heath and a single bomb in the grounds of Northaw House. After dropping some more bombs and incendiaries in the Enfield area, Schramm turned and set a course for North London.

In the meantime, reports went out across England that a wave of enemy airships were incoming, after some of the raiders' communications had been intercepted. A total of ten Home Defence fighters of the Royal Flying Corps were dispatched to seek out and destroy the enemy invaders.

One of the pilots was Lieutenant William Leefe-Robinson, known as Billy, of No. 39 Squadron. He was the 21-year-old son of a coffee merchant, who took off from Sutton's Farm airfield in Essex in his Bristol BE2c aircraft (Serial No. 2963) at 11.08 pm as part of the 'search and find' operation.

Leefe-Robinson had, on several previous occasions, managed to meet enemy airships over London, but like his colleagues, had not achieved any success. In fact, not a single airship had been brought down by fighters to that date.

He spent the first two uneventful hours in the air, flying at around 10,000 feet, between the airfield and Joyce Green, near Dartford. At 1.10 am he spotted Zeppelin LZ.98 caught in two searchlight beams over Woolwich, South East London, and he set off in pursuit but quickly lost it in thick cloud when he attempted to engage the airship near Gravesend.

At 1.58 am Schramm approached North London, where the searchlights at Finsbury Park and Victoria Park caught him. With the giant airship trapped between the cones of light, the anti-aircraft guns opened a fearsome storm of fire, causing SL.11 to steer away to the northeast. Now over Edmonton, and in a desperate bid to escape the searchlights, it dropped bombs in the High Street at Ponders End, damaging the road and

Lieutenant William Leefe-Robinson.

seven houses, shattering windows in 56 houses and smashing water mains and some tram and telephone wires. It then dropped six on Enfield Highway, slightly damaging 15 houses and a number of commercial greenhouses. Now back over Hertfordshire, it dropped bombs in a field at Turkey Street, Bulls Cross, and Burnt Farm, Goff's Oak, but by this time, its fate was sealed.

Leefe-Robinson had seen the fires caused by SL.11's bombs and flew towards them to investigate. Having missed out on his first encounter, Billy was determined not to do so again, and as he continued his patrol in the incredibly cold and inhospitable open cockpit of his fighter, his fateful encounter with Wilhelm Schramm and SL.11 was set.

The aircraft was armed with a new type of ammunition known as 'Brock and Pomroy'. This new ammunition used both incendiary and explosive bullets to ignite the combustible gases within an airship and bring it down. Up until this point in the war, all that the RFC pilots were able to do was pierce airships without setting them alight. Billy recounted what happened next:

When I drew closer, I noticed that the anti-aircraft aim was too high or too low; also, a good many shells burst about 800 feet behind, and a few tracers went right over. I could hear the bursts when about 3,000 feet from the Zeppelin.

I flew about 800 feet below it from bow to stem and distributed one drum among it (using the new Brock and Pomeroy). It seemed to have no effect;

I therefore moved to one side and gave them another drum along the side – also without effect. I then got behind it and by this time I was very close – 500 feet or less below, and concentrated one drum on one part (underneath rear). I was then at a height of 11,500 feet when attacking the Zeppelin.

I had hardly finished the drum before I saw the part fired at, glow. In a few seconds the whole rear part was blazing. When the third drum was fired, there were no searchlights on the Zeppelin, and no anti-aircraft was firing.

I quickly got out of the way of the falling, blazing Zeppelin and, being very excited, fired off a few red Very lights and dropped a parachute flare.

Having little oil or petrol left, I returned to Sutton's Farm, landing at 2.45 am. On landing, I found the Zeppelin gunners had shot away the machine gun wire guard, the rear part of my centre section, and had pierced the main spar several times.

On the ground, schoolboy Patrick Blundstone, who had been staying with the Poolman family at East Ridgeway in Cuffley, wrote home of the events. The servant heard the sound of gunfire close by, and woke all those in the house. After making their way downstairs, Patrick heard 'bangs' and 'pops' when 'suddenly a bright yellow light appeared and died down again.'

The Poolmans' daughter exclaimed, *'Oh! Its alight!'* She paused and then reassured herself that the small fire they could see was *'only a star shell'*. Just as all in the house felt safe, a young woman staying with the Poolmans, Ms Blair, dashed to the windows with Patrick and *'looked up and... that right above us was the Zepp! It had broken in half and was in flames, roaring and crackling. It went slightly to the right and crashed into a field!!! It was about 100 yards away from the house and directly opposite us. It nearly burnt itself out when it was finished by the Cheshunt Fire Brigade.'*

ZEPPELIN BROUGHT DOWN IN FLAMES
AT CUFFLEY, NEAR ENFIELD, AT 2.30 A.M., SUNDAY SEPT 3ʳᵈ 1916.

This scene, witnessed by thousands of people across North London and Hertfordshire, caused a great stir at the time, with cheers and triumphant shouts echoing throughout the streets for many hours.

Even though they were enemy, if the spectators on the ground had known the fate of SL.11, perhaps their shouts of triumph would have been somewhat more sedate. The crew of SL.11, with no parachutes and no means of escape, suffered an awful death, being burned alive as the airship descended to the ground, finally coming to rest just behind the Plough Inn at Cuffley.

Patrick Blundstone joined the crowd of thousands that rushed to the crash site over the next few hours and later wrote: *'I would rather not describe the conditions of the crew, of course they were dead – burnt to death. They were roasted, there is simply no other word for it. They were brown like the outside of roast beef. One had his legs off at the knee and you could see the joints.'* Despite this macabre scene, much of the wreck was cut up and taken as souvenirs before the army was able to arrive in force and secure the site.

Over the next few months, William Leefe-Robinson gained considerable celebrity status and the downing of the 'Cuffley Zepp' was featured in postcards, paintings and newspaper articles for quite some time.

The burial of Schramm and the crew of SL.11 also occasioned quite   Wreckage of Schütte-Lanz SL-11.

a bit of controversy. It was decided that the crew were to be buried with full military honours in Potters Bar, much to the dislike of a number of locals who had termed 'Zepp' crews as 'Baby killers' and a staggering 300 special constables had to be on hand at the burial service to maintain control of hostile elements in the crowd.

Burial of Schütte-Lanz SL-11 at Cuffley. The bodies were later re-interned in the Cannock Chase German Military Cemetery, Staffordshire.

For his bravery in bringing down SL.11, the first airship to be brought down over Britain in the Great War, William Leefe-Robinson was awarded the Victoria Cross. Sadly, his story did not end so well. William later transferred to a fighter squadron in France and was shot down and captured by fighters of Jasta-11, led by Manfred von Richthofen, the famous Red Baron.

Once news of his earlier exploits reached his captors, and after making several failed escape attempts, Leefe-Robinson was treated horrendously, spending prolonged periods of time in solitary confinement. He died of illness, likely the Spanish flu, exacerbated by his poor treatment and malnutrition, on 31 December 1918, aged 23. There is some suggestion – although unconfirmed – that the commandant of William's PoW camp was actually the cousin of Wilhelm Schramm.

Today the spot where SL.11 came to ground in Cuffley is marked by an obelisk, erected after the war by subscription from readers of *The Daily Express*. The crew of SL.11 were moved to Cannock Chase German Military Cemetery in Staffordshire after the Second World War and were buried in a mass grave, where they remain to this day.

The Navy Zeppelin L.16, commanded by Kapitänleutnant Erich Sommerfeldt, crossed the Norfolk coast near Salthouse and headed Southwards. After dropping bombs and incendiaries near Norwich and Bury St. Edmunds, it followed a course to the northwest of London.

An obelisk marks the spot where the where SL-11 came to ground at Cuffley.

L-16 (P-Class).

At 1.30 am the airship flew over the Midland Railway line at Harpenden, and then dropped a high explosive bomb near Redbourn. It had reached South Mimms, heading towards Hatfield, when anti-aircraft guns opened up on it. The L.16 turned south to Potters Bar, where it arrived at 2.15 am just as SL.11, which was just six or seven miles away, struggled to free itself from the searchlights and anti-aircraft guns. At this point, Sommerfeldt chose to steer away, attracted by a searchlight at the village of Essendon. At 2.20 am he circled over the village, dropping sixteen high explosives and nine incendiary bombs. The bombs killed two sisters, Frances and Eleanor Bamford, aged 26 and 12, and injured a man and a child. Serious damage was caused to the church and rectory, three cottages were destroyed and others damaged. Moments after the bombs dropped, the crew saw SL.11 burst into flames and made off towards the northeast. Sommerfeldt then dropped an incendiary over Aston, near Stevenage, and a final bomb at about 3.30 am, an incendiary at West Stow near Bury St. Edmunds, before escaping out to sea near Great Yarmouth at about 4.20 am. The airship was damaged beyond repair during a training mission at Nordholz Naval Airbase on 19 October 1917.

The L.32 crossed the English coast at Sheringham, Norfolk at 10.00 pm. The airship was commanded by Oberleutnant-zur-See Werner Peterson (who had raided Hertford so successfully the previous year). He dropped bombs at several locations in rural Norfolk before flying a southwesterly course to Tring in Hertfordshire. When the airship arrived over the town, the crew could see the flames from the burning SL.11 blazing in the distance. This persuaded Peterson to turn back east, and after passing near Redbourn, they began dropping bombs near Hertford. Five high explosives and eleven incendiaries fell on Hertford Heath, killing two horses. This was followed by sixteen high explosives and eight incendiaries at Great Amwell, which killed a pony and broke windows in three houses. L.32's final two bombs landed near Ware, causing no damage as Peterson steered a northeast course and flew out to sea near Corton, north of Lowestoft, at about 4.15 am.

Flight Sub–Lieutenant Gerard William
Reginald Fane

Flight Sub–Lieutenant Edward Laston
Pulling (Left) & Flight Lieutenant Egbert
Cadbury (Right).

A few weeks after this raid, on 24 September 1916, the L.32 fell victim to No. 39 Squadron, crashing to earth at Great Burstead, Essex, and cost the lives of its entire crew.

The Naval Zeppelin L.21, commanded by Oberleutnant-zur-See Kurt Frankenburg, crossed the English coast at Mundesley, Norfolk at 10.20 pm. After flying an uncertain southwesterly course, the airship arrived over Hitchin, Hertfordshire at 2.25 am, just as Lieutenant Leefe-Robinson destroyed SL.11. Frankenburg, observing the fate of SL.11, turned away from London and headed northwards. He began to drop his bombs at Dunton, east of Biggleswade at about 2.40 am. Two incendiaries landed but failed to cause damage, followed by another at Hatley Park near Gamlingay. Twenty minutes later L.21 dropped a high explosive bomb at Sutton, west of Ely, on North Fen, followed by a high explosive and an incendiary at Horselode Fen at Chatteris, which damaged some wheat sheaves and mangelwurzels. It dropped a majority of its load in the Norfolk area before escaping out over the coast.

The L.21 was destroyed on 28 November 1916 when it was intercepted by three Home Defence aircraft flown by Flight Lieutenant Egbert Cadbury, Flight Sub-Lieutenant Gerard William Reginald Fane and Flight Sub-Lieutenant Edward Laston Pulling. Their Bristol B.E.2c aircraft fired phosphorous rounds into the airship, which caught fire and fell into the sea about eight miles east of Lowestoft. There were no survivors.

1–2 October 1916

The downing of SL.11 by William Leefe-Robinson at Cuffley marked a decisive change in the success of the Royal Flying Corps in bringing down airships. Within a fortnight, Second Lieutenant Frederick Sowrey had brought down L.32 near Great Burstead in Essex, using the same method that Leefe-Robinson had pioneered.

From this point on, the German Army lost considerable interest in Zeppelin raids over Britain, although the German Navy continued. Led by their most experienced commander, Oberleutnant Heinrich Mathy, raids on London continued.

On 1 October 1916 eleven Zeppelins left their bases in Germany to attack targets in the Midlands and London, again with veteran of 15 raids Heinrich Mathy taking the lead. In fact, it was Mathy alone, commanding Zeppelin L.31 who managed to reach London, crossing the channel at Lowestoft in difficult weather conditions and he made for the capital. At around 8.00 pm men of the Royal Engineers Barnet Searchlight Detachment, who had mounted their searchlight on a dark green painted tram, succeeded in illuminating L.31 in their beam and kept the raider in their sights with great skill.

With anti-aircraft batteries now firing at the illuminated Zeppelin, Mathy seems to have had a rare moment of indecision, in which he slowed down before deciding to release his bombload over Cheshunt, dropping 56 high explosives and incendiary bombs on the town, causing considerable damage, but only one – non-fatal – injury.

It seems that – under huge pressure and unable to shake the attentions of the Barnet Searchlight – Mathy decided to head for home. There is some question that Mathy may have had a sense of his impending fate, as he had written shortly before his flight, *'It is only a question of time before we join the rest. Everyone admits they feel it. Our nerves are ruined by mistreatment. If anyone should say he is not haunted by visions of burning airships, then he would be a braggart.'*

With the Zeppelin now turning for home and building both height and speed as rapidly as possible, it was down

Barnet Searchlight Crew – A detachment from the Royal Engineers.

Zeppelin L-31.

to Second Lieutenant Wulstan Tempest, a friend of William Leefe-Robinson, to give chase in his B.E.2c. At top speed, Tempest managed to catch up with L.31 and poured two long bursts of the new (and highly effective) Brock-Pomeroy ammunition combination into the Zeppelin as he dived down onto it. With no discernible effect, he lined up once more – this time beneath and to the rear of the airship – emptying an entire drum from his Lewis gun along its length. Almost immediately he saw a glow from inside the 'envelope' followed by intense flames as the Zeppelin took light and began to fall rapidly.

Second Lieutenant Wulstan Tempest.

With great skill and a good slice of luck, Tempest managed to avoid his aircraft being engulfed by the falling Zeppelin, and headed for home; his work was done.

Aboard L.31 itself, Mathy and his eighteen crew members must have been faced with an awful prospect. Falling from well over 10,000 feet, they had to decide whether to stay with the craft and almost certainly burn to death, or to jump – without parachutes – knowing that the end result would of course be the same. It seems that a number of crew members decided that their best option would be to jump, waiting until the last possible moment, in the hopes of losing sufficient height to give any chance of survival. A line of crewmen's bodies was later recovered along the path of the Zeppelin's descent as they jumped before the fire could reach them. The last to be found was Mathy himself. Having wrapped a thick scarf around his head, he had fallen several hundred feet and impacted the soft earth of Potters Bar, leaving an indentation in the ground, which was later photographed. There is some speculation that Mathy actually survived his fall and lived for a number of seconds, apparently witnessed by several locals. Certainly, even if he did survive, he did not live for long.

The Zeppelin itself, along with several crew members who chose not to jump, impacted the ground at Oakmere Park, a portion of the wreckage getting caught up in an old oak tree, which became known locally as the Zeppelin Oak. It stood for many years after the war, apparently with metal scraps still embedded in the tree from that night.

After the crash, much like SL.11, the scene became something of a fanfare, with spectators and souvenir hunters coming from far and wide to see the fallen airship. The army soon secured the area and came to an agreement with the local farmer that he could charge a shilling per person so that people could enter his

The Home Front   251

Like the crew of SL-11, the men of L-31 were moved in the 1960s and reinterred in a mass grave at Cannock Chase; fittingly, directly next to their ill-fated comrades from Cuffley.

An indentation in the ground believed to have been made by the body of Heinrich Mathy.

land and see the Zepp. One of those to attend and pay his shilling was Wulstan Tempest himself, who decided not to reveal his identity.

Once the dust settled, the bodies of Mathy and his crewmates were laid to rest in Potters Bar cemetery, ironically next to the graves of Wilhelm Schramm and his crew, who had been brought down just two miles away a little over a month earlier. It is known that in the years after the war, Heinrich Mathy's wife went to see his grave on at least one occasion, as did several senior Nazi officials in the 1930s, including Hermann Goering and Joachim von Ribbentrop, as part of the 'National Heroes' Day'.

Wulstan Tempest was awarded the Distinguished Service Order for his skill and courage that day. Incredibly, his fuel pump had also failed at the start of his flight, meaning he had to manually pump fuel for over three hours, whilst also undertaking all of his normal duties. He was so exhausted when he returned to his base at the end of the flight, that he very nearly crashed. Tempest went on to serve in France and commanded a bomber squadron. He survived the war and died in 1966.

The site of the crash has since been lost due to housing development on part of Oakmere Park, although two roads named Tempest Avenue and Wulstan Park cover part of the area where the Zepp came down, and where the Zeppelin Oak once stood.

Kapitänleutnant Robert Koch.

The L.24, commanded by Kapitänleutnant Robert Koch, crossed the Norfolk coast at 10.15 pm near Weybourne, west of Sherringham, and took a course towards Cambridge, with the apparent intent of attacking London.

After reaching Waterbeach, just north of Cambridge, he saw the flames of L.31 illuminating the sky, so he opted to change course, flying westwards for 25 minutes then resuming his original southwest course until he reached Shefford, Hertfordshire. By now it was 1.05 am and Koch could see lights to the southeast, so he steered towards them. These lights were, in fact, flares which were burning at a night landing airfield near the village of Willian, east of Hitchin. At 1.14 am the L.24 arrived over Willian and dropped ten high explosive bombs, of which nine detonated on the landing field and one fell in a boundary hedge. The bombs killed 48-year-old Private William Hawkes of No. 56 Company, Royal Defence Corps, who was in charge of the flares. Koch continued to drop bombs, both high explosive and incendiary, along a line in open country, ending near Tilekiln Farm, just south of the village of Weston. Koch reported that

he had dropped his bombs across Stoke Newington and Hackney in London. The L.24 turned for home, eventually crossing the coast at Kessingland, south of Lowestoft, at 2.35 am.

Kapitänleutnant Robert Koch was killed on 17 March 1917 whilst commanding Zeppelin L.39. The airship was shot down by French anti-aircraft fire near Compiegne, claiming the lives of all on board.

Kapitänleutnant Robert Koch at the controls of L-24.

19–20 October 1917

On 19 October 1917 a fleet of eleven airships set out to attack industrial targets in the north of England, in what was to be one of the last great Zeppelin raids of the war. Unbeknown to the small armada, there was a fierce storm blowing from the northwest at speeds of up to 50 mph. The raid proved to be a disaster for the German Naval Airship Division.

The L.52, commanded by Oberleutnant-zur-See Kurt Friemel, crossed the English coast near Mablethorpe, Lincolnshire, at about 7.30 pm. After encountering the high winds, and despite the best efforts of its crew, the airship was forced to head in a southwesterly direction. By 10.05 pm, and having descended below the wind, the L.52 passed south of Hertford, dropping eight bombs in fields just south of Bullock's Lane, which caused serious damage to five cottages, slight damage to five more, and injured a man. Friemel then released thirteen incendiary bombs as he approached Waltham Abbey but none caused any damage. Despite the best efforts of the crew, the wind continued to carry Zeppelin to the Southeast and after crossing Kent, it went out to sea near Dungeness at 11.15 pm. The airship was eventually destroyed by its crew on 23 June 1919.

Marine-Luftschiff L.55-Notlandung bei Tiefenort/Thür. am 20.Oktober.191

L-55 (V-Class).

The L.55, commanded by Kapitänleutnant Hans Kurt Flemming, crossed the Lincolnshire coast near Anderby at about 7.30 pm. After releasing some of his bombs near Huntingdon, Flemming, he followed the Great Northern Railway until he reached Hitchin, where he began to drop bombs. The first fell at Holwell Bury without causing any damage. Another bomb was dropped in a field in the parish of Snailswell, slightly damaging a pub, a cottage and breaking some telegraph wires. The next bomb landed close to the railway and 80 yards north of the Hitchin sewage works, breaking some telegraph wires, while another landed about 100 yards southeast of the junction between the main railway line and the Cambridge branch line, smashing some cottage windows. This was followed by two that fell in a field at Walsworth; they also broke some cottage windows. The L.55 then turned its attention to Stevenage, where it dropped two bombs in a field at Rook's Nest Farm and one in a field near Trott's Hill Farm. At Bedwell Farm, south of Stevenage, three bombs demolished a farm building, injured a man and damaged cottages. At Burleigh Farm, Langley, two bombs damaged buildings and, just north of Codicote, a high explosive and incendiary bomb landed harmlessly in fields east of a house known as The Node. The last of the L.55's bombs fell at Brocket Hall, about three miles northwest of Hatfield, but it caused no damage. The airship was then carried southeast by the wind, eventually going out to sea near Hastings at about 10.25 pm.

After his excursion over Hertfordshire and being struck by anti-aircraft fire on several occasions throughout the journey, Flemming brought the L.55 back over Germany but as he was running low on fuel, he could not get back to his base and made an emergency landing at the village of Tiefenort. Flemming and his crew survived and called for supplies so they could repair their damaged airship. It took four days for the equipment to arrive, as a consequence of German troop movements on the railways, by which time a storm had wrecked the airship on the ground. It was dismantled and the aluminium frame was recycled for military use. The covering was given to the local community and it is said that villagers wore black clothes made from airship hull for many months after its destruction.

Of the eleven Zeppelins that had taken part in the raid, only six returned to Germany able to fight another day. One complete crew was dead, as were four men from another crew, and three crews were now prisoners of war. The raid proved to be a disaster for the Naval Airship Division. The fate of L.55's crew has already been explained. The following provides a brief outline of what happened to the remaining raiders.

L.44 – Kapitänleutnant Franz Stabbert: The L.44 almost made it to German territory, but French anti-aircraft guns caught it just 10 miles from the frontline and it crashed in flames at Chenevières. There were no survivors.

L.45 – Kapitänleutnant Waldemar Kölle: The wind carried L.45 over France, and Kölle – unable to make headway to the east – eventually decided to make an emergency landing some 70 miles from the Mediterranean coast. The L.45 landed near Sisteron, where Kölle and his crew surrendered.

L.49 – Kapitänleutnant Hans-Karl Gayer: Struggling with engine problems and navigation, the L.49 crossed South East England with the wind carrying it across to France. Having seen L.44 shot down, with only two engines working and after being attacked by a squadron of French aircraft, Gayer decided to crash land to avoid being shot down. Once on the ground, the crew were prevented from burning the airship, leaving the Allies the intact prize of one the latest Zeppelin designs.

L.50 – Kapitänleutnant Roderich Schwonder: The fierce wind carried the L.50 southeast and Schwonder appears to have had serious navigation issues. The airship, with two engines out of action, wandered alarmingly over France and, having seen L.44 shot down and L.49 on the ground, Schwonder decided to crash land and at least deny his airship to the enemy. The massive dirigible struck a wood, which ripped off two of the gondolas, causing most of the crew to leap overboard and be taken prisoner. The L.50 then flew back up with four men still on board. The uncontrollable airship eventually disappeared over the Mediterranean. No trace of it or of the four men was ever found.

7–8 March 1918

On the night of 7 March 1918, RFA 501 despatched six 'Giants' to attack London but one turned back when an engine seized. Two of the raiders failed to reach London. One of these came inland near Foulness in Essex at 11.10

pm. Encountering anti-aircraft fire, its course deflected north of London into Bedfordshire, where at about midnight four bombs fell in Luton Hoo Park, just south of Luton, digging craters and damaging a small shed.

Now heading towards London, the 'Giant' ran into anti-aircraft fire from guns at Harpenden and Wheathampstead at about 12.10 am, which forced it to turn away to the northeast. More gunfire caused further changes of direction and at about 12.40 am, as the raider reached the village of Great Munden in Hertfordshire, a bomb dropped in a ploughed field on Mentley Farm. Moments later ten more bombs landed around the village of Much Hadham. The first exploded in a field on the Moor Park estate, not far from the mansion, eight fell in fields at Danebridge and one on a disused brick kiln nearby. The bombs damaged the kiln, the roof of a cattle shed, crops in a wheat field, and two cottages had their windows smashed and their ceilings damaged. After dodging more anti-aircraft fire, the 'Giant' eventually went out to sea near Harwich at about 1.55 am.

The civilian population of Hertfordshire would not see any further air raids, and by August 1918 the German bombing campaign over Britain had ceased.

A German 'Giant' leaves its home base to make a raid on Great Britain.

A MUNITIONS ACCIDENT – VIOLET ROSE EMILY CLARKE

The sacrifice of soldiers killed during the Great War is well documented, but the efforts of munitions workers is a story much less told. Working long hours in perilous conditions, the munition workers risked life and limb to supply ammunition to the frontline. This under-recognised workforce was made up of men who were either unfit or too old for military service, and a high proportion of women. They faced daily peril by handling explosive chemicals that carried the risk of them contracting potentially fatal diseases. For some, the effects of their work were immediately visible; a lurid shade of yellow that stained their skin and hair earned some women the nickname 'the Canary Girls', and denied them the ability to produce children later in life.

For others, such as Charles Sidney Phillips of Vicarage Road, Ware, the danger was far less visible and the consequences quick to impact upon his life. After just three days' service at the powder factory in Waltham Abbey, Charles was taken ill with what a doctor believed was a chill. He died a few days later and a post mortem established that the cause was handling TNT without gloves on.

Despite some improvements in workplace safety, accidents still occurred. One of these was to take the life of a Hitchin teenager, Violet Rose Emily Clarke.

Violet was born in Sandon, Hertfordshire as the daughter of Robert and Alice Rosetta Clarke (née Geaves). The family later moved to the market town of Hitchin, where they first lived in Portmill Lane, but later resided in The Lodge at Benslow Convalescent Home.

Her brother, Charles Frederick Clarke, was

Violet Rose Emily Clarke.

called up for service with the Bedfordshire Regiment on 12 October 1916, and was posted to France on New Year's Eve that year. Violet felt she had to be doing something to support the war effort and help her brother.

Following the outbreak of the Great War, the Phoenix Motor Company, a motor car manufacturer in Letchworth Garden City, founded by a Belgian, Joseph van Hooydonk, began to produce munitions for the British government. Violet was able to gain employment with the company as a machine operator. On 9 May 1918, she was working on the production of an 18-pounder shell when her overalls got caught in the machinery, and she was dragged against it. She was taken to Hitchin Hospital, and although apparently it was found that her injuries were not serious, she remained at the facility to aid her recovery. Over the next four weeks there was some improvement, and it was hoped that Violet would soon return home, but she suddenly collapsed on 1 June and died, as a result of a pulmonary embolism caused as a direct result of her injuries.

In this case, the amount of compensation payable was to be negotiated. An agreement for a one-off payment of £60, plus £8.8s.6d (£8.45p) in weekly payments in the form of a contribution towards funeral expenses was submitted to the registrar of the court, Wilberforce Onslow Times. He took the view, however, that the amount agreed was insufficient. The matter came before Judge Farrant for his decision as to whether the sum agreed was adequate. Birchham, the barrister appearing for Phoenix Motors Limited, claimed an agreement had been reached, inclusive of legal costs. The registrar first suggested that Violet earned an average of 36 shillings (£1.80) a week, and the sum agreed between solicitors represented just 9 shillings (45p) per week profit to the parents. After some discussion, Robert Clarke, the girl's father, went into the witness box and agreed to accept the amount arranged by the solicitors.

For Violet, there were no medals, no service record, no entry on a roll of honour or war memorial, and no entry into the records of the Commonwealth War Graves Commission, despite her death occurring as a consequence of her role as a munitions worker contributing to the war effort.

NO MEDALS FOR HOME SERVICE – PRIVATE GILBERT EDWIN ANGELL

In the burial ground of the Baptist Church at Breachwood Green – a small Hertfordshire village a stone's throw from the Hertfordshire–Bedfordshire border – lays the isolated military grave of Gilbert Edwin Angell. You would be forgiven for thinking that this may be the last resting place of a soldier who had succumbed to his wounds, or perhaps died in some form of training accident, given that the headstone carries the regimental badge of the Machine Gun Corps. But this is, in fact, the grave of a member of the Labour Corps; a man who never served overseas, and despite his initial training, never fired a machine gun in anger.

Gilbert Edwin Angell was born in April 1886 as the son of local carpenter, Edwin Angell, and his wife Martha. Prior to the Great War, Gilbert worked on local farms as a horse breaker (a person who trains horses to become accustomed to being saddled and ridden). He married a local girl, Matilda Butterfield, on 4 October 1906, just three weeks before their first child, Charles Edwin, was born. The couple went on to have five other children, Ivy Doris (1907), Mabel Irene (1910), Frederick (1912), George (1915) and Reginald (1917).

Gilbert attested for service in the army on 24 June 1916 and was called up on 7 December 1916. Initially, he served with 'A' Company of the 45th Reserve Training Battalion, based in Swanage, Dorset, where he would have completed his basic training. On 13 February 1917 he was transferred to the Machine Gun Corps in Grantham, Lincolnshire, to be trained as a machine gunner.

The grave of Private Gilbert Edwin Angell.

Casualty Card for Private Gilbert Edwin Angell.

After being classed as medical category C2, which means: *'Free from serious organic diseases, able to stand service in garrisons at home, and able to walk 5 miles, see and hear sufficiently for ordinary purposes.'*

Gilbert was transferred to the 432nd Agricultural Company, Labour Corps, based in Bedford, on 12 October 1917. He was deemed to be insufficiently fit for overseas service and possibly also demonstrated an inability to shoot straight.

The Labour Corps was formed in January 1917 and was manned by officers and other ranks who had been medically rated below the A1 category needed for frontline service. Agricultural companies were originally formed on a regimental basis, being filled by men who were not fit to serve overseas. These soldiers were hired out to local farmers, who had to pay 4 shillings (20p) a day for each soldier – half that if they provided lodgings – which was much less than agricultural labourers' rates. Some farmers complained that the soldiers were of little use, with some not understanding farm work at all. Most men were classed as B2 or B3 and, ironically, often found themselves working alongside much fitter German PoWs. In June 1917 the individual regimental companies operating in the UK were transferred to the Labour Corps, which employed around 175,000 men across the country by the time of the Armistice. They were always regarded as a second-class organisation. Men who died serving with the Labour Corps are often commemorated under their original regiment, as is the case with Gilbert Angell.

On 23 February 1918 Gilbert was posted to the 396th Agricultural Company, based in Oxford, where he remained until his death. He was to eventually lose his life as a consequence of the Spanish flu pandemic. He was admitted to the Central Military Hospital, Aylesbury, on 25 October 1918, suffering with pneumonia and passed away at 2.00 pm the following day. He was 32 years old.

His service record provides a list of very simple effects that were sent home to his wife, Matilda. These were: a purse with three coins, a wallet, a metal wristwatch, a letter and a belt. A rather cold note from the War Office states that his body was returned home to Breachwood Green. Today, he lays in the burial ground of the Baptist Church. Given that he never served overseas, Gilbert was not entitled to any of the Great War campaign medals, and with the exception of his grave marker, his service may have gone almost unnoticed.

In a sad postscript, Matilda Angell passed away in 1928 at the age of 42, leaving all six children as orphans. She is buried in the same plot as her husband, her grave unmarked.

SEVEN DAYS AT THE FRONT, FOUR YEARS IN CAPTIVITY – THE STORY OF HERTFORDSHIRE PRISONERS OF WAR

There were numerous occasions throughout the Great War when the men of Hertfordshire were taken prisoner by the enemy. The exact number is not known but many are recorded on the absent voters' list of 1918 and throughout the local newspapers of the period.

For many, their captivity was short lived, with a high proportion being seized during the German Spring Offensive of March 1918, such as Private Arthur Grebby of Pouchen End, who was serving with the 2/1st North Midlands Field Ambulance, and Private Joseph Stone of Apsley End, who had transferred from the Royal Flying Corps and was serving with the 12th Battalion, Suffolk Regiment; both of them were captured near Bullecourt on the first day of the German offensive.

Sapper William Drage of Reed, Hertfordshire was captured near Bac-St-Maur on 9 April 1918 whilst serving with the 229th Field Company, Royal Engineers. This was the opening day of the Battle of Lys and his unit, part of the 40th Division, was holding bridges across the Lys River. One of ten children, the former cabinet maker had joined the army in March 1916 and following his discharge in April 1919, claimed that he was suffering from rheumatism as a consequence of his service and his captivity. Despite suffering pains in both his upper and lower limbs, William was denied a pension by a medical board in

August 1919. He was awarded the British War Medal and Victory Medal for his service on the Western Front, but was denied any financial support. He passed away in 1959 at the age of 78.

Others of course were captured at an earlier stage in the war. Lance Corporal Walter Seabrooke Hoar of Queen Street, Hemel Hempstead, for instance, was serving with 'A' Company, 1st Battalion, Bedfordshire Regiment, when it was in frontline trenches at Fricourt, in the Somme region, on 23 September 1915. He had only been serving in France since 12 May 1915 and was part of a patrol which was sent out to observe enemy positions. Whilst in no man's land, he was shot in the left leg and was taken prisoner. The unit war diary simply records the loss of a Lance Corporal. Walter survived his ordeal and returned to Hemel Hempstead, being awarded the 1915 Star, British War Medal and Victory Medal. In later life he lived in Wiltshire, where he passed away in 1979 at the age of 93.

Private William Banfield of Bridge Street, Boxmoor, enlisted in the army on 1 November 1915. He was severely wounded in his right shoulder on 6 December 1917 whilst serving with 109th Company, Machine Gun Corps, and was taken prisoner. His injuries were so severe that on 6 June 1918 he was repatriated home and treated in the King George Hospital in Stamford Street, London. William was discharged from the army on 20 December 1918, being awarded the British War Medal and Victory Medal, as well as a Silver War Badge numbered 519557. It is at this point that most veterans' records – if they have survived at all – often cease and little is known about the difficulties they suffered later in life. William was one of eleven children, and after his discharge from the services, he lived with his brothers Tom and Harry, both veterans themselves, on Bridge Street. Before the Great War, William had worked in the paper industry, and he appears to have been able to maintain employment, working as a stock-keeper in a paper mill. He passed away in 1948, aged 62.

There are many such stories concerning the soldiers of Hertfordshire who were taken prisoner during the Great War, but it is the stories of those who were captured in the opening days of the conflict that perhaps prove the most poignant. For them, the years of captivity proved to be particularly harsh, their treatment often being well outside the boundaries of human decency.

One Hertfordshire soldier, Corporal Stanley Males of Knebworth, was serving with the 1st Battalion, Bedfordshire Regiment. He arrived in France with his battalion on 16 August 1914 and was taken prisoner, along with a number of comrades, a few days later, on 24 August.

Corporal Stanley Males.

Stanley Archie Males was the son of Samuel and Ellen Males, one of eight children. He was born on 22 November 1892 and was educated at the Knebworth Church of England School. He joined the Bedfordshire Regiment prior to the Great War, serving as a professional soldier in the regular army. On 23 August 1914 Stanley was amongst half of the battalion who were sent to Wasmes on the outskirts of Mons, Belgium, to select and dig trenches. With no immediate fighting expected, the men began to dig trenches but were unexpectedly shelled by German artillery, causing some casualties, including Stanley Males, who was taken prisoner. It was not until 22 November 1918, his 26th birthday, that Stanley would see the shores of Blighty again. He arrived in Hull aboard the SS *Porto*, along with a group of other prisoners from the Bedfordshire and Hertfordshire Regiments. In an interview with the *Hertfordshire Express* on 21 December 1918, Stanley gave a brief overview of his experiences during his three long years of captivity, and how relieved he had been for being amongst a batch of exchange prisoners at the end of December 1917, spending the rest of the war as an internee in Holland. The interview provides a shocking glimpse into the treatment of PoWs at the hands of their captors.

I will start from the time I was wounded. I was taken to a British field dressing station, but had not been there long when the Germans started shelling the place. I was then removed to a convent in the village of Paturages, near Mons. I was there with others for several days when the Germans found us out, and we were then told we were being sent to Brussels and on to England, and we were taken to the station at Mons.

There we were searched. We still had our Jack-knives in our pockets, and the Germans said we used them for pricking out the eyes of their wounded. The knives were taken from us, and we were shamefully knocked about by officers and men alike. One poor fellow was struck in the mouth with the butt of a German rifle, and had nearly all his teeth knocked out. This was more than British blood could stand, and he just let out and knocked the German down. At this there was a great uproar, the place being full of German soldiers passing through to the front.

The lot of us – 14 in all, and all wounded – were placed up against the station wall to be shot. We said goodbye to one another, and were waiting for the end when an officer appeared. He asked us what was the matter, and we explained the case to him, with the result that we were placed in a room and only the guards allowed to enter. There we were kept for about four hours, until a trainload of wounded Germans coming in appeared. We were told to proceed to Germany in it. As soon as we were outside the room where we had been confined, the Germans made a rush at us and started taking everything we possessed, hats, coats, puttees, jackets, shoes. In fact, we were nearly naked by the time the train started.

It was an old cattle truck we travelled in, the door and ventilation holes nailed up so that we could not get a breath of fresh air. The stench was awful, the truck not having been cleaned out since it was used for cattle, we travelled in the truck for two days with no bread or water.

We then had three days in cellars at Bonn before being taken to Cologne hospital. All this time our wounds had not been dressed, and they were in a frightful state owing to the heat and our lack of nourishment. We were placed in a room with the guard, and appeared to be kept as a sort of prize pets, being the first English prisoners they had had there. People used to pay to come and see 'the mad Englishman', and one Scotsman among us, wearing a kilt, was made to dress up every day, while visitors paid 10 pfennigs to see the 'Lady from hell' as he was called.

My wounds were nearly better by Christmas 1914, but they still kept discharging, so I was sent on 2 January 1915, to the camp of Wittenberg. We were the last party to arrive there, typhus fever having already broken out among the Russian prisoners through overcrowding, uncleanliness and the want of food. We had a very rough time on our way from the station of Wittenberg, the soldiers hitting us over the head and body with their rifles and bayonets, while civilians hit us with sticks and umbrellas and spat in our faces.

At the camp we were put into barracks with a lot of Russians who were alive with vermin of every description. It was a day or two after our arrival that the Germans closed the camp down on account of the fever, the inmates being simply left to die like rats in a sinking ship, with no medical assistance whatever. We did the best we could for one another, but we could not do much, and the men died in large numbers every day. Then six English doctors came from Halle to fight the fever. Arriving at night they at once went around the camp cheering us up to the best of their ability. We were in an awful state by this time, some of the doctors shedding tears when they saw the state of things had come to. One of the huts was turned into a hospital, and the worst cases were taken there. It was not half big enough, however, and six more places were opened. Soon they were all full. In one room of over 150 men, only two survived. It was a frequent occurrence to wake up in the morning and find the men each side of us gone on the long trial, and then we wondered if our time was coming next.

As if not content with the fever killing us off in hundreds, the Germans used to open fire around the camp and kill anybody unlucky enough to be out of barracks. This happened on three different occasions. We had nothing but the food supplied by the Germans, and this was served in such a filthy condition that we had to be starving before we could touch it. The soup we got was just plain water with a little bit of margarine thrown in to make it greasy. We soon lost three of the English doctors. They contracted the fever and were dead in a very few days. The fever kept on all through the winter until about May, when the surviving doctors got it under control. By this time everyone was alive with vermin of every description. The majority of the men had only one shirt, and some had none. Some of us went about with no shirt for two or three days to try and wash the one we had, but we had only sand to wash with, so we could not kill the vermin. In fact, many of the men went about with a bit of blanket wrapped round around them. At last the camp was declared free from fever, and the Germans erected a bath house and fumigator.

All this time we had not had a haircut nor a shave. I had my first shave with the lid of an old tin which the Russians had sharpened up to make a razor. I would never have another one with it! After the bath house was erected every man was shaved all over his body, and we all had a bath. We had to stand in the room naked while our clothes were being fumigated. The clothes came out really wet, and in some instances, dropped to pieces as the men were putting them on.

We had not been allowed to communicate with anyone all this time, but on 15 May we were given a card and told we might write home and receive letters and parcels of foodstuffs and clothing etcetera. In June we had our first lot of comforts from the American Comforts Society, consisting of shirts, socks, and cigarettes. There not being enough shirts or socks to go round, we drew for them, but I was lucky enough to get a shirt, and what a delight it was to wear a nice clean shirt again! One cannot describe the sensation of feeling clean once again after being alive with vermin for so long. We had about four packets of cigarettes each, and what a time we had with all those cigarettes! We sat up all night smoking. No one thought of going to sleep. We have been smoking the bark off the barbed wire fence around the camp. We also tried peat and dried grass, in fact, anything that would burn in a pipe or a piece of paper as a cigarette.

It was about this time that the Germans began to liven things up in the camp. Nearly all the under-officers used to carry a piece of India rubber tubing, about 18 inches long, but solid, and every time they got near anyone they used to lash out with it.

If a man was caught smoking in the barracks he was tied to a post. But first of all he was made to stand on a brick, and then the Germans, after tying him up securely, kicked the brick away, leaving the man hanging for about two hours. By the time he was cut down he was nearly always in a fainting condition.

It was about this time Gerard, the American ambassador, came, and then the camp began to get a little better. But there were still plenty of cases of ill-treatment. Sentries used to bring dogs into the barracks and let them loose. It was every man for himself, and God help the man the dogs caught! We began getting parcels from England, so we managed to do without the stuff the Germans used to serve up as 'food' – we would not give it to pigs to eat in England.

The Germans started to send us out to work. Gerard had told us that NCOs need not work unless they liked, as the English government had made an agreement with Germany on the matter. Eighteen of us refused to work. The Germans tried every means in their power to make us work. They stopped our parcels, and would not let us mix with the other English. We tried to get a letter through to Gerard, but the Germans found that out, and we were all put in prison on bread and water for five days, and allowed to come out on the sixth day to have a basin of soup and then go back to prison again for another five days. On 16 November 1916, we were sent to another punishment camp at Alten, Grabow. Here they tried to force us to work in the fields around the camp, and said it was all camp food that was grown there. If we refused to go, we were sent to prison without trial, and just got bread and water.

About July 1917, we heard a rumour that we were being exchanged, and great excitement prevailed throughout camp. For months no more news turned up, so we thought everything had fallen through, and we gave it up as a bad job. Then came the great day in my life. It was Christmas Day 1917, when an under officer came in and called out seven names, my own being among them. He told us to get ready at once, as we were for Holland. You can guess we were not long getting ready, and we said farewell to all the boys left behind, and with the band playing we marched out of camp.

We were taken to Aix-le-Chapelle, and here about 150 NCOs and officers joined us, on the morning of 29 December 1917, we started on our way to neutral Holland. Very shortly we were on the border, and what a relief! The men could hold themselves in no longer.

We gave a terrific cheer and started singing 'Britons never shall be slaves'. So, we entered once again into a life of freedom, having had more than enough of Prussian slavery. And now, after four years and three months, we are home again in England. It is just god's own country to us who have been away from it for so long, and in such circumstances.

Like so many other soldiers who served in Belgium at the outset of the war, Stanley would be awarded the 1914 Star, British War Medal and Victory Medal. His Medal Index Card simply being marked 'P of W'. After being demobilised from the army, Stanley returned to Knebworth where he married Jessie Clark in 1919. The couple lived quietly in Woolmer Green until his death in the summer of 1960 at the age of 67.

In stark contrast to the Nuremberg war crime trials following the Second World War, the dealing with German atrocities against Allied prisoners during

A list of repatriated soldiers from the Bedfordshire and Hertfordshire Regiments who arrived in Hull aboard the SS *Porto* on 22 November 1918. Stanley Males, who was 26 years old that day, is amongst those listed.

the Great War was nothing short of farcical. Originally, the Allied powers had planned for as many as 900 alleged German war criminals to be extradited and face trial in Allied courts. The German government, however, succeeded in averting their extradition and instead stated that it was willing to prosecute all Germans accused of committing crimes against nationals of enemy states or against enemy property, highlighting this promise with changes in German laws.

The Allies agreed to the German proposal and on 7 May 1920 presented a much shorter list with the names of just forty-five suspects and the details of their alleged crimes. The list was accompanied by an official note stating that the intention of this first compilation was to ascertain the seriousness of the self-commitment the Germans had promised, and that this new list was nothing more than a 'test'.

The trials of those named on the 'test list' finally commenced in May 1921. The first four cases were brought to trial at the insistence of the United Kingdom, of which three involved abuse of British prisoners of war. The Reich Supreme Court handed down a ten-month sentence against the commander of a smaller camp, a former non-commissioned officer. Another camp commander, a former Captain, was to serve six months, as was a soldier who had been a camp guard. Hardly justice for the deprivations they imposed upon their captives.

The Allies, and in particular the French, referred to what was happening at the trials as a 'farce' and a 'comedy'. In contrast to their original announcement, however, the Allies did not insist that the accused be extradited. Instead, they discontinued any form of cooperation with the Reich Supreme Court in Leipzig. This outcome was welcomed in Germany, where the court subsequently lacked sufficient evidence to conduct any further trials. Thus, by 1927, the proceedings were ended in more than 1,700 cases, either by court decisions or as a result of decisions made by the attorney general. For the Allies during the Second World

War, the conclusions were clear: it was not to be left to German courts to try and punish German war criminals. Nuremberg can be considered as the response to the Leipzig war crime trials.

CONSCIENTIOUS OBJECTORS

Refusing to fight in the war often took as much bravery as serving in the trenches. In March 1916, with the numbers of volunteers for the army dwindling, the Military Service Act introduced conscription for all men in England, Scotland and Wales between the ages of 18 and 41.

A small minority refused to obey the command to serve on the basis of religious and moral grounds. The outcome of these actions was forced labour or imprisonment. Conscientious objectors came from across Hertfordshire, the often socialist and independent thinking residents of the Garden Cities in particular. Others maintained their objection even when sent to fight. Many of these were repeatedly court-martialled, imprisoned and then sent back to fight when they were freed, only to go through the same process again.

Some fared even worse. In 1916, a group of thirty-five men who refused to fight on conscientious grounds were condemned to death by firing-squad – eventually their sentences were commuted to ten years' imprisonment with hard labour.

There were a multitude of reasons for conscientious objection: religious grounds, morality issues, personal circumstances and family life – all of which were heard by county-based tribunals and judged on a regular basis within the British legal system. These tribunals tended to be hard to convince, reflecting public hostility to conscientious objectors, who were widely viewed as shirkers and cowards, despite many undertaking work on the front, such as stretcher-bearing – which if anything was more dangerous than being a soldier.

Whatever the case or reason, it cannot be said that 'conchies' had it easy. Many were ridiculed in the streets, handed white feathers as a sign of cowardice, shunned by neighbours who they had known for years and ostracised from local communities.

Hertfordshire, with a strong Quaker tradition in certain areas, had a number of conscientious objection cases coming before its tribunal. The official tribunal records were destroyed after the war, but hearings were reported by the local press.

It is likely that a few individuals did use conscientious objection as an excuse for avoiding military service, as public perception believed. However, most of these men were willing to suffer abuse, brutal treatment and imprisonment, and even the possibility of death for their beliefs, and many undertook extremely dangerous work as an alternative. Whether or not you agree with their stance, they were heroes of their own consciences, and should not be forgotten.

In Remembrance

The war memorials of Hertfordshire contain the names of more than 23,000 individuals whose lives were lost during the Great War whilst in the service of their country. This, however, represents just a small percentage of the total figure of men and women who served in the armed forces or were employed in a civilian role in support of the war effort. The memorials, obelisks, plaques and headstones that are scattered around the county commemorate those who took an active part in the war. Some individuals, for a variety of reasons, have their names inscribed in more than one location.

The Commonwealth War Graves Commission records the names of just 3,896 men and 4 women whose details gave their place of birth, residence, or that of their next of kin as being in Hertfordshire. This figure belies the sacrifice made by the county and does not even begin to provide the reader with an indication of how many people across Hertfordshire participated – in one form or another – in the defence of their nation.

As a consequence of the continuing work carried out by the volunteers of the *Herts at War* project, many stories have been unearthed and hidden artefacts discovered around the county that may never have been seen or heard. Within the confines of this publication, we hope to have provided you with a very brief glimpse of some of the accounts brought to the fore by the project that portray the gallant efforts made by the people of Hertfordshire during the Great War. It is hoped that by revealing these stories of loss and sacrifice, we can create a platform that will ensure the act of remembrance is continued indefinitely throughout Hertfordshire, remembering the single most devastating conflict in British history.

Remember them.
Paul Johnson & Dan Hill

Sources & Bibliography

Ahigh proportion of the information found in this publication is taken from the individual profiles that can be found in the Herts at War Roll of Honour. These are produced by the project volunteers. Whilst every effort has been made to ensure that all sources have been identified and permissions sought, the authors are not responsible for any inaccuracies or misuse of web based data that may occur.

BIBLIOGRAPHY

Theirs Is the Glory – A Roll of Honour for Stevenage – Paul Johnson – RBL Publications (1999)

Our Boys – Ware Men in The First World War – Derek Armes – The Rockingham Press (1998)

The Royston War Memorial – Douglas Plowman – Royston & District LHS (2012)

The Valiant Men of Hertfordshire – Ted Sparrow – Tollesbury (2012)

The Street Memorials of St. Albans Parish – Alice Goodman – St. Albans A&A Society (1987)

Bedfordshire & Hertfordshire Regiment – The Royal Anglian Regiment History Society

16th Foot. The Bedfordshire & Hertfordshire Regimental History – Major General F Maurice

Reg Evans DCM: A Hero's War in His Own Words – Pamela Armitage Campbell – Wearewhitefox (2014)

SOURCES

Archives

The National Archives

WO 76/110/3	Horace Lockwood Smith-Dorrien
AIR 79/630/68219	Second Lieutenant Peter Francis Kent
WO 98/8/74	Surgeon Arthur Martin-Leake
WO 339/6869	Lieutenant Julian Missenden Smeathman. Royal Engineers.
WO 339/8202	2/Lieutenant Joseph Frederick Mead. The Royal Fusiliers.
WO 339/11825	2/Lieutenant Robert John Mead. The Royal Fusiliers.
WO 339/49248	Lieutenant Alec Joscelyne Bamford. General List.
WO 339/60040	Lieutenant David Alfred Rutherford MC & Bar
WO 339/80258	Second Lieutenant Peter Francis Kent
WO 374/63044	Captain Lovel Francis Smeathman. The Hertfordshire Regiment.

Hertfordshire Archives and Local Studies (HALS)
Absent Voters' List – 1918

Museums
Stevenage Museum (Jo Ward)
Royal Observer Corps Association (Peter Kent Story)
Evans Family Collection (Reg Evans DCM)
David Good Collection (Peter Francis Kent)
The Herts at War Archive
Hitchin Museum
The Garden City Collection
The Imperial War Museum
The British Newspaper Archive
The Ware Museum

Websites
Herts at War (www.hertsatwar.co.uk)
The Bedfordshire Regiment (www.bedfordregiment.org.uk)
The Long, Long, Trail (www.longlongtrail.co.uk)
Commonwealth War Graves Commission (www.cwgc.org)
The National Archives (www.nationalarchives.gov.uk)
The War Graves Photographic Project (www.twgpp.org)
Colourise History (www.colourisehistory.com)
Ian Castle – Zeppelin Raids, Gothas & Giants (www.iancastlezeppelin.co.uk)
The British Newspaper Archives (www.britishnewspaperarchive.co.uk)
Ancestry.com (www.ancestry.co.uk)
Findmypast (www.findmypast.co.uk)
Forces War Records (www.forces-war-records.co.uk)
Scotlandspeople (www.scotlandspeople.gov.uk)
General Register Office (www.gro.gov.uk)
The Roll of Honour (www.roll-of-honour.com)
Prisoners Of The First World War ICRC Historical Archives (www.grandeguerre.icrc.org)
The Gazette (www.thegazette.co.uk)
Royal Logistic Corps (www.rlcarchive.org)
Scarletfinders (www.scarletfinders.co.uk)
British Soldiers died in Ireland 1919–21 (www.cairogang.com)
McMaster University Library (www.digitalarchive.mcmaster.ca)
Library and Archives Canada (www.bac-lac.gc.ca)
Naval & Military Press (www.naval-military-press.com)
Uboat.net (www.uboat.net)

Individuals
Our most sincere thanks are offered to the following people, without whose help and support, this publication could not have been achieved.

The Ambrose Family
The Bullard Family
Mike Churcher
Maria Coates
David Good
Gareth Hughes
Nancy Jack
The Kite Family
Mark Khan
Eve Martin
Rebecca Mileham
Stuart Osborne
The Satterthwaite Family
Jonty Wild
Roger Yapp
Richard Young
Richard H. Young
Terry Young (Deceased)

Index

Military Units